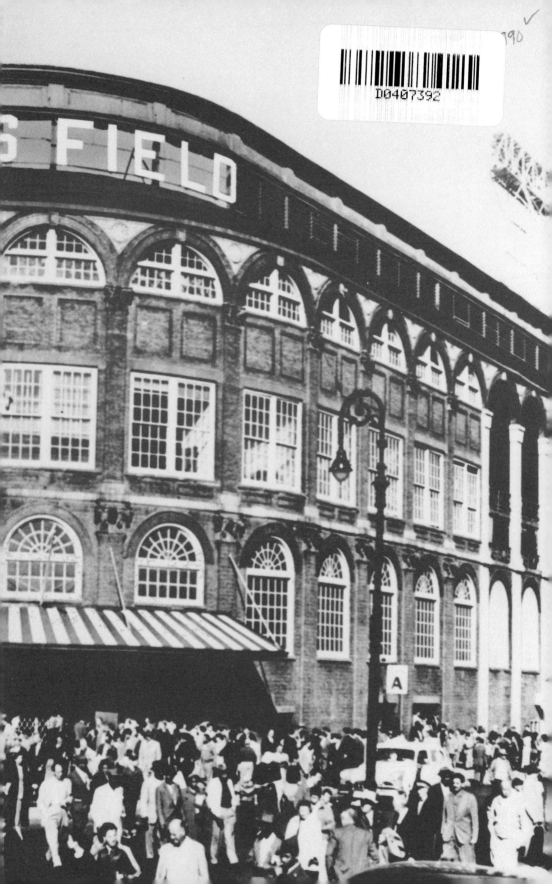

Once a Bum,
Always a Dodger

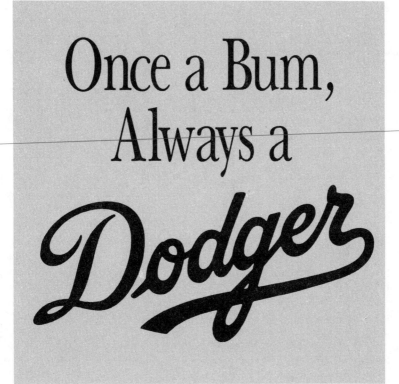

Once a Bum, Always a Dodger

Don Drysdale

with
Bob Verdi

St. Martin's Press/New York

Front endpaper photograph courtesy of the Brooklyn Public Library, Brooklyn Collection

Dodgers logo on the title page courtesy of the Los Angeles Dodgers.

Design by Amelia R. Mayone

Library of Congress Cataloging-in-Publication Data

Drysdale, Don.
    Once a bum, always a Dodger / Don Drysdale with Bob Verdi.
      p. cm.
    ISBN 0-312-03902-6
    1. Drysdale, Don. 2. Baseball players—United States—Biography.
    3. Los Angeles Dodgers (Baseball team)—History. I. Verdi, Bob.
    II. Title.
    GV865.D7A3 1990
    796.357'092—dc20   89-27080
    [B]   CIP

First Edition

10 9 8 7 6 5 4 3 2 1

Contents

Once a Bum,
Always a Dodger

1

Back to Brooklyn

I'll never forget July 11, 1987. That's the day I went back to Brooklyn. I won't forget it because of all the memories it called up.

It was a hot summer Saturday afternoon in New York. I was in town with the Chicago White Sox, as a member of their television broadcast team, but because it was a Saturday and the National Broadcasting Company had exclusive "Game of the Week" rights, the White Sox game at Yankee Stadium was being sent back to Chicago on radio only. So, I had the day off to do whatever I wanted to do in the Big Apple, and for thirty years, I had wanted to return to Brooklyn.

Believe me, it tugged at my heart strings when I drove toward the Brooklyn Bridge. I had all sorts of flashbacks to when I'd first set eyes on Brooklyn, as a naive and wide-eyed kid pitcher trying to make a go of it in the big leagues with the Brooklyn Dodgers. I'd spent virtually my entire life up until then in California, so I had no idea what to expect, just as I had no idea what to expect when I showed up again, three decades later.

I still had some vague idea of what direction I was headed, though I had to roll down the car window to ask a couple times.

Montague Street.

That was the key. Where was Montague Street? That was the main street, as I remembered. The old Brooklyn Dodger offices were at 215 Montague Street. And down the street, a couple blocks away, was the first place I'd stayed, the Bossert Hotel. In between,

1

there was the laundry where I took my clothes to get cleaned, and the barber where I got my haircuts, and the restaurant where I had my first meal as a Dodger, and many meals thereafter. It was a nice place, clean and friendly, with good food, reasonably priced. A place where I'd often gone by myself, or with a teammate, for dinner. Veal, they had great veal parmigiana.

If they knew you were with the Dodgers—and everybody in Brooklyn seemed to know everything about the Dodgers—they would knock a little bit off the price on the menu. Maybe ten percent off a full meal, which couldn't have been more than four bucks, anyway, or four-fifty tops.

I drove around a bit that Saturday, finally found a parking space, and started to walk around Montague Street, thinking to myself, What the heck was the name of that restaurant I'd been to so often?

"Hey, Drysdale!" somebody yelled.

I looked up.

Armando's, at 143 Montague Street. That was it. Here it was about noontime on a lazy summer day, I hadn't been there since 1957, and it was as though I'd never left. Jim McLinden, he said his name was. He was out in front of Armando's, where the folks who worked there were cleaning up and getting the place ready for business.

"I used to be a regular at Ebbets Field," McLinden said. "I've been in Brooklyn for forty-five years, and I was an usher at the ballpark when you first came up. I remember you. I remember all the guys. It's never been the same since you left, never been the same."

It was as though Brooklyn still hadn't recovered from the shock of the Dodgers leaving for Los Angeles in 1958.

"What's at Two-fifteen Montague Street now?" I asked.

"A bank," I was told by my new friend.

"And the Bossert?" I asked. "Is it still there?"

"Building's still standing," McLinden said. "But it's been taken over by some group—a church group, I think. It's not the Bossert anymore."

But Armando's was still there, like it always was, specializing in "Italian Continental Cuisine" and informing potential customers with a small sign on the wall that it accepted reservations for luncheon and dinner parties. I don't think Armando's was quite open for business that day, but I guess it was pretty obvious to all the guys on the early shift that I was itching to go inside and have a peek. No problem, they said. Come on in.

Well, Armando's hadn't changed all that much, I was happy to see. There were tables on the left as you walked in and the bar over on the right and pictures on the wall. Pictures of movie stars like James Cagney, W. C. Fields, John Wayne, and Humphrey Bogart, and pictures of athletes—especially pictures of Dodgers. Old Dodgers. Brooklyn Dodgers and Ebbets Field. I had been a little nervous maybe, driving out to Brooklyn that day, because I didn't know what to expect. When I got inside Armando's, though, I felt relaxed all over again. It seemed like I was back home, even though my job at the time was in Chicago during the summer and my winter home was in California, 3,000 miles away. But that's the way I always felt about Brooklyn, from the first day I set foot in this unique borough. It was always like home to me, a second home, a home away from home.

Growing up in Van Nuys, California, I had no real images of Brooklyn as a kid. We didn't have major league baseball in our area at the time, of course, so anything you knew about Brooklyn or the Dodgers was pretty much a hunch or an impression you got from reading the sports section of the newspaper every day or listening to major league baseball on the radio. I had been pretty sheltered in my youth, really, and one of the first things that struck me when I got to Brooklyn was how close everything was. In California, if you wanted to go from here to there, it seemed as though you always had to drive an hour. That's just the way it was. You took it for granted. That's the way it is today.

But, heck, if you drove an hour from Brooklyn, you were in another state. In Brooklyn, it was as though you were in your own little bubble, and that's what made it so unique. You were all part of one big but very close family, and the Dodgers were the main topic of everybody's conversations. When you brought your laundry to the cleaner's, and they knew you were a member of the Dodgers, you could sense the affection the people had for you. I don't know that such a thing exists anymore.

I remember that feeling when I went in to eat at Armando's, too. If you were a ballplayer for the Dodgers, you were special. You were family. You were like a god. And yet, the people around you would always let you eat in peace, whether you were alone or with

3

somebody. They respected you and your right to a certain degree of privacy, and you respected them for that. It was all very comfortable, being a Dodger in Brooklyn or a Dodger in Armando's.

But while you had your dinner—and it was mostly dinner, because we used to play all those day games and then go eat—you could pick up on how much these people knew about baseball and how much they cared. They might be talking about a hit-and-run play that didn't work that day, or about the next team that was coming to town. If a batter from the Philadelphia Phillies had 10 hits in his last 15 at-bats, if he was hot coming into Brooklyn, well, you darn well knew you would hear about it, from another table or from the bar. Those people knew their baseball and, oh, how they loved it. And, oh, how it hurt when the Dodgers left. Thirty years later, I could still sense the psychological scars.

"I think I'll walk around a little bit," I said to the folks at Armando's that Saturday afternoon. "Then, I'll head over to where the ballpark was."

I didn't get much of a response, but I was on my way. As I'd been told, there was no Bossert Hotel anymore. Not as I recalled it, anyway. That's where I settled in when I first came to Brooklyn for my rookie season in 1956, a season when the Dodgers were locked in a tremendous pennant race with the Cincinnati Reds and Milwaukee Braves. The Dodgers were coming off a great year—they'd finally beaten the Yankees in the 1955 World Series—and the 1956 club was another good one and I was lucky enough to be a part of it. A young pup out of Southern California, involved in a pennant race clear across the country.

There wasn't much to that hotel room at the Bossert. A double bed, a black-and-white TV, a radio, and a telephone—the kind you had to get the switchboard to make a call. There were no dials on the phone. I paid something like fourteen dollars a night for that room, which was fine. Even though my dad worked for the Pacific Telephone & Telegraph Company in its Van Nuys office, he didn't get any privileges like free calls, so we wrote a lot of letters back and forth. For sure, I was a little homesick that first year in Brooklyn, but if you were going to be homesick anywhere, Brooklyn was a good place. You felt like you were always part of a family there, because that's exactly what the Dodgers and their fans were. Plus, in many respects, my first minor league season before that—1955, at Montreal—had helped me deal with being away. The only time

I'd ever stayed in a hotel before I became a professional baseball player was when I stayed at the Padre Hotel in Bakersfield, California. So, being on the Dodger farm team in Canada prepared me somewhat for being away from my parents and friends. I've always been like a horse—get me home and I'll be okay—nothing too complicated. And the Bossert was comfortable and convenient. I could walk to dinner and walk to the Dodger offices, which was fine and dandy. Another landmark for me was the Bedford Hotel, where you could get just about the best steak in the world. And then there was Lucille Kelly, whom my fellow pitcher, Roger Craig, introduced me to. She had done some baby-sitting for the Craigs, and before long she became like a second mother to me. I stayed in her basement apartment for a while, at a very reasonable price. All sorts of perks were available to me. When we didn't have a day game, I plopped down on Lucille's patio and pretended I was back home in California, working on my tan. Besides the East Coast humidity, which I never have gotten used to, the weather in Brooklyn was a complete mystery to me. Where I grew up, if it was a clear day, it was a clear day. But on the East Coast, you might have a bright and clear morning followed by thunderstorms in an hour. It was very strange.

Every so often, Lucille would cook up some food to make sure I was eating right. Then I might hang around for one of the neighborhood parties, with all the Greeks and Italians and the rest of the people who made up this special world that was Brooklyn. Everything you needed was right there, which was just perfect for a young fellow like me who didn't think it was quite right to be out and about a lot. I liked to get my rest. I'm happy to tell you that I still talk to Lucille. She's living in Florida, seems to be in good health, and definitely is in good voice. Lucille finds me, wherever I am. There's no such thing as an unlisted phone number with Lucille, which is great. Talking with her brings back a lot of memories.

I wasn't too much for adventure or sightseeing in my rookie season, although I did head off to New York City on occasion. The first time I drove over the Brooklyn Bridge, I got lost, and there was another time I tried to take the subway out of Brooklyn and wound up somewhere on Long Island. To this day, I have no idea how far out on the Island I was, or how I got there, or how I got back. The East River Drive, which is now the FDR, was a little difficult for me to figure. If it weren't for the streets going one way in New York, and avenues going the other, I might still be trying to poke my way around. And we're not even talking about the times when I'd have to drive over to Jersey City, where the Dodgers played eight home games a year.

Eventually, though, I began making the trip into Manhattan every so often to have dinner at Toots Shor's, a very popular watering hole. You might see anybody in the world over there. There were show business types like Frank Sinatra, Joe E. Lewis, George Jessel, Jackie Gleason. Or you might see players from the Yankees, Giants, or whichever visiting team was in New York.

Toots took a liking to me, and I enjoyed going to his establishment, wearing one of the three sport jackets I owned or, if necessary, my one overcoat. I'd listen to Toots tell stories for hours. Even a kid from California with a lot of homebody in him eventually learned how to get over to this spot on Fifty-first Street without taking too many wrong turns. More importantly, with all those day games, I'd get back to Brooklyn in time to get my rest. I've always been that way. If I don't get my sleep, I'm not worth a damn, and I managed my eight hours a night, even in this new world I was experiencing—Brooklyn and New York City, or when I would drive uptown to the polo grounds, for a game against the Giants. In the distance, you could see Yankee Stadium, which was another world altogether. You didn't play over there unless you were in the World Series against the Yankees, and I was taking it one step at a time in 1956.

It was all big and impressive and, I admit, I was in total awe. I never did make it to the top of the Empire State Building, and still haven't, but as a kid playing for the Brooklyn Dodgers, I did a fair share of gawking at those skyscrapers in New York City. I gave myself away in a minute as a tourist from the West Coast. I'd be walking down those short city blocks with my head tilted up in the air, banging into people. I might have started walking with my head up at Fiftieth Street and by the time I looked down, it was Fifty-second. That's how flabbergasted I was by it all. I took a couple trips around Wall Street, and I saw the Statue of Liberty, and I was forever wondering, What do all these people do? I mean, that was one of the first things that struck me about New York—all the people.

In California, I had worked part-time as a box boy in the grocery store, and that's another thing that astounded me about walking around Manhattan. Where were all the supermarkets? Where did all these people in the middle of this huge city buy their food? It was enough to overwhelm you, all those sights and all those distractions and all that night life. But I had my priorities in order. Also, I never forgot what Buzzie Bavasi, the Dodgers' general manager, told me when I signed my first contract at 215 Montague Street.

"It's one thing to get to the major leagues, son," he said. "But it's tougher to stay here. That's the real test."

I always kept that thought in mind, because I thoroughly loved this great new environment and wanted to make it my home. Of course, the Dodgers and Ebbets Field were a major part of that. Unless you experienced the feeling, it's really impossible to describe. The people of Brooklyn didn't really care about the other boroughs. "You keep to yourselves, and we'll take care of ourselves over here." That's pretty much the way it was and you accepted it. You did more than accept it. You lived it, you enjoyed it. There'll never be another situation quite the same. Never. Impossible. And there'll never be another ballpark quite like Ebbets Field, home of the Brooklyn Dodgers, "Dem Bums."

The thing I remember most about Ebbets Field was the huge rotunda, right behind home plate. It was like a big lobby where fans could stand around before or after a game, just talking baseball. It was right at McKeever and Sullivan Places and that was the main entrance. For the players, there was another door down the street you could enter to get to the clubhouse, after you parked your car at the gas station. But most of the time, particularly if you took a cab to the ballpark, you would be dropped off there, right by the rotunda. It was pretty impressive. Then you'd walk into the clubhouse by first base . . . two or three pillars, as I recall, in the locker room . . . then the manager's office and the coaches to the right . . . the trainer's room to the far right . . . and directly across from you, as you walked in the door, the locker with the number 1 over it, the locker belonging to "The Captain," Pee Wee Reese. The showers were off to the left, toward the back. It wasn't elaborate by today's standards, I suppose, but it was unique. I felt something special when I walked into Ebbets Field because Brooklyn was a magic name and still is. You ask people in Saudi Arabia who the Brooklyn Dodgers were, and there's a heck of a chance they'll know.

No doubt about it, the ballpark contributed to the mystique and the atmosphere. There was the "Dodger Symphoney," our very own band featuring fans who would stroll around the stands during a game, playing songs or something that sounded like songs. Every once in a while, after a close call, the band would strike up a rendition of "Three Blind Mice" for the umpires. And there was Hilda Chester, who sat on the third-base side every game, ringing those two cowbells and holding up that sign that said, "Hilda Is Here." And Gladys Gooding, the organist, who always had the right song for the moment—a joyous tune for a rally, a dirge for a tense situation. And Tex Rickard, the public address announcer with that deep, gravelly voice (*"Attention, ladies and gentlemen . . . the boy who was lost has been found"*). And the hand-operated Schaefer scoreboard in the outfield, Schaefer Beer being one of the Dodgers' main sponsors, just like Lucky Strike cigarettes, which honored the "Player-of-the-Week" with a sign over the bullpen. And then there was Abe Stark, he had a pretty good deal. He was Brooklyn borough president and he also operated a clothing store there. His sign in right field promised that if a batter hit that sign on the fly, the prize would be a free suit: "HIT SIGN, WIN SUIT." But with Carl Furillo playing out there for us—and Dixie Walker before him—how was any guy on the other team ever going to hit that sign? Furillo caught everything that came near him, or so it seemed. And on top of that right-field area was a forty-foot screen that Duke Snider cleared so many times with those big home runs of his.

There was an intimacy about Ebbets Field that you don't forget. If you are a starting pitcher, you warmed up in front of the dugout before the game, not in the bullpen. You felt as though the fans were right on top of you, because they almost were. It was a carnival atmosphere, small and always jumping. It was so small, by today's standards, that if I'd have thought about it more than I did as a kid pitcher trying to get people out, it might have driven me crazy. But I was too thrilled to think. Believe me, when you walked through that rotunda, and into the clubhouse, and then out onto the field with all that beautiful green grass, you knew you were in the big leagues. You knew you were a lucky guy.

I still remember one time when Clem Labine and I were dropped off in front of Ebbets Field. I was in my Eisenberg & Eisenberg overcoat that my dad had helped me buy back in California. Labine and I got out by the rotunda and were immediately engulfed by a bunch of kids who wanted autographs. I signed for one youngster, and then, not a minute later, he was back again.

"I already gave you one," I said.

"I want another," he answered.

I was tempted to keep walking, except that in those days, kids were using fountain pens. You pulled a little latch on the side, and liquid ink came squirting out. Being in my one and only Eisenberg & Eisenberg, I wasn't about to take any chances on getting anybody angry. But they were great fans, those people in Brooklyn. They were the best. I might be wrong, but I've seen a lot of fans in a lot of cities throughout the years, and those Brooklynites are right on top of the pedestal.

After we clinched the pennant in that close race with Cincinnati and Milwaukee in 1956, there was a tremendous celebration in Brooklyn. The Dodgers had come off their greatest accomplishment yet—beating the Yankees in the 1955 World Series—and now here it was the Dodgers and Yankees all over again. But first the fans had to throw a party to mark the pennant, and they went crazy. The day we clinched, we stayed in the clubhouse for a long time, waiting for the crowds outside to clear. You could stand on a stool in the clubhouse, and look out the window at the street. The people were thoroughly enjoying themselves, but not in the way some fans "enjoy" themselves when teams win these days. Those people in Brooklyn didn't overturn any cars or light any fires or partake in any violence. They had fun, but they didn't become nuisances. They knew how to savor a moment without destroying it. The fans felt that they were lucky to have the Dodgers, and, believe me, the Dodgers knew that we were lucky to have those fans.

I still feel that way today, probably more so than ever. I'm forever running into people who bring up the Brooklyn Dodgers and Ebbets Field, whether it's a bellhop at some hotel or a cab driver at an airport. It's amazing how you go through baseball now, and someone or something will trigger a thought about the Dodgers of Brooklyn, just when you least expect it. There's something magical about the Brooklyn Dodgers, and being part of them was

9

the greatest experience of my life. Just making the big leagues was great, but making it in Brooklyn with the Dodgers was the icing on the cake. I feel very privileged. I sometimes wish I could have played there longer than I did, perhaps my entire career. Maybe it would have been even better if I'd have played there later in my career, so I could have appreciated it even more.

I mean, you look at the players who made it to the big leagues just after I did and they missed out on so much. They never saw Forbes Field in Pittsburgh or Crosley Field in Cincinnati. Most of all, they never got to see Ebbets Field. Ignorance is bliss, I guess, but I was the last active Brooklyn Dodger to retire and I'm thankful for it. A lot of changes have taken place in baseball, not enough of them for the better. But one thing you know never will happen again, and that's major league baseball in Brooklyn. Every once in a while, you read some story in the newspaper about some committee being formed to bring another team there, but that's not going to happen. And there's never going to be another Ebbets Field, not with all the multipurpose stadiums they're building around the country now. Fenway Park in Boston, Chicago's Wrigley Field Park, Yankee Stadium in New York, and Tiger Stadium in Detroit are just about all that's left. I suppose that's progress.

I suppose.

But I do know that going back to Brooklyn in 1987 was a bittersweet experience for me. Since I'd left, I'd run into a lot of people who had returned and whenever we got to talking about Ebbets Field, they'd just shake their heads and change the subject. I couldn't quite figure out why, until I went to see for myself, many years later.

I drove out on this warm Saturday in July, and kept expecting to see the light towers towering over the tops of buildings in the neighborhood. But the closer I got, and the more I looked for that intersection of McKeever and Sullivan Places where I had known the old ballpark to be, the more I realized the old ballpark wasn't to be seen anymore, not unless I dusted off the pictures in my scrapbooks. I got a little choked up when I finally pulled the car up to where the rotunda used to be, looked up and saw Ebbets Field Apartments. I can still visualize the ballpark and the light towers, but now all you can see is that damn guard tower.

Where the Brooklyn Dodgers had played from 1913 through the 1957 season, there was a twenty-five-storey apartment complex, containing something like 1,317 units. Overlooking the project was a watchman's perch, the kind you see in a prison, only this booth was where you might have seen the third baseman veering over to catch a foul ball near the railing in the old days. There was no gas station where I remembered it used to be; instead there was one of those fast-food chicken joints. No "Luckies Taste Better," no Schaefer sign, no Abe Stark, no nothing. There was just a big huge structure made out of tan bricks, the Ebbets Field Apartments.

I'm told it's a public housing project, but I had no desire to look around. I didn't even want to get out of the car. And you couldn't have dragged me into the apartment project with a lasso. Ebbets Field was history, and you don't replace history. You can tear it down and put up a bunch of ugly apartments, but you don't ever replace history.

When I got back to Manhattan that evening, I called my wife Annie in Chicago, and she was all excited that I'd finally returned to Brooklyn. Then I called my mom and dad, Verna and Scotty, back in California. They had some lasting memories of Brooklyn, too, because when the Dodgers made it to the World Series my rookie year in 1956, they flew across the United States to watch. The trip must have taken them eight hours on a DC-7, and I know Dad still remembers the night I took him and Mom to dinner in Bay Ridge, at the Hollenden House. I wanted to treat them right, and so we ordered shrimp cocktails.

Dad at first tried to steer me away from that, because it was too expensive, probably three-fifty. But we went ahead and ordered them anyhow, and instead of shrimps, they gave us prawns. They were that huge, and to this day, whenever I have dinner with my folks, we talk about the night we had those giant shrimp cocktails in Brooklyn before the 1956 World Series. Obviously, you're not talking about world travelers when you're talking about the Drysdale family.

I know that while I was glad I'd finally cleared some time to return to Brooklyn, I was genuinely choked up and sorry about seeing what was left of Ebbets Field. I can't say I wasn't warned. A few of the guys I had played with on the Dodgers had been back and whenever the subject came up, their expressions just went blank. In other words, you don't want to see it with your own eyes. But I did, and it tugged at me a little bit. I have some tangible

11

objects to remind me of Ebbets Field, like clippings in scrapbooks and a few of those terrific cartoons drawn by Willard Mullin, whose works were featured in the New York *World-Telegram & Sun.* I'm sure you recall the Emmet Kelly caricature, the scruffy clown figure, the bum who stood for the Dodgers, through thick and thin. Those cartoons are priceless, and so is a Dodger ring I have from our 1956 National League pennant-winning season. It features the rotunda, and it's beautiful, one of my prized possessions. What I have to get is a nice panorama picture of Ebbets Field. Peter O'Malley, the Dodgers' president, presented me with a nice picture—almost a mural, really—of Dodger Stadium in Los Angeles. I treasure that. But I'd surely like to find one of Ebbets Field in Brooklyn.

Until then, I'll have to rely on all my fond memories—the sights, the sounds, the smells. There'll never be another, I can be sure of that, and again, I'm so thankful that I was a part of it, even for a short while. It was something you don't forget, ever. People won't let you. Wherever you go, especially around baseball circles, you run into somebody who reminds you of Brooklyn or somebody who will bring up something about the Dodgers. And before you know it, you're sitting around exchanging stories. There's not too much in baseball even today that you can't somehow relate back to Brooklyn and the Dodgers. It's like apple pie and Chevrolet. You'll be sitting around a press room in spring training and you'll see a scout like Eddie Lopat or Hank Bauer come in and before long, you'll be talking Brooklyn Dodgers.

It was odd, how we on the Dodgers developed the image as munchkins. The Yankees were the Yankees, of course: pinstripes, "The House That Ruth Built," all that stuff. The Giants also were looked upon with great awe, maybe in part because of their name, the Giants: big, powerful, strong, the whole bit. We, on the other hand, were the tag-alongs, the guys with black pants and brown shoes and holes in our socks. You know, the third thumbs. The Yankees and Giants were the city slickers and we were the guys tucked away in our own little borough, on our own island of Brooklyn with a moat around it. The Dodgers had a great tradition with a history of great ballplayers, but that was the deal. We were the outcasts.

The people of Brooklyn dwelled on that pecking order and so did we. The fans simmered about it, and we enjoyed it. We were our own little bunch, and we reveled in the closeness. If Pee Wee and Duke and Gil and Campy were "bums," then great. You wanted to be a bum just like them. We hung with our own buddies and were content to do so. We cut our own grass. That was part of our strength, the unified feeling we had among ourselves and with our fans. Of course, it was a completely different story when we went on the road. We couldn't pull off that "poor soul" routine when we went to Cincinnati or St. Louis or Pittsburgh. The fans there looked at us cross-eyed, but that's because we were a hell of a baseball team, not because we were the unshaven outcasts. We were the big, bad Dodgers on the road. That's where we got swelled heads. Then we returned to Ebbets Field, and we were those adorable munchkins again, playing in the shadow of the Yankees and Giants.

In his cartoons, Willard Mullin captured that perfectly. The Yankees and Giants always looked like they just came out of a limo from the country club or dinner at the Waldorf. We were the hitchhikers. We were the oafs. The Yankees and Giants were sleek and streamlined, we were the guys with soup stains on our shirts. Perfect. The people of Brooklyn took that handle and ran with it, and so did we players.

I can't think of any other franchise in sports with that flavor, that kind of enduring grip on people. It's been so long since we played there, and yet every year you look up and somebody seems to be writing a book about Brooklyn and the Dodgers. And here's another one, right here. I can't help it. I loved the place. And by going back there thirty years later, I picked up another souvenir. A match book from Armando's. Some things in life, you just can't buy. Like memories. Great memories.

2

And Now . . . Pitching

*A*s far back as I can remember, I always had a bat and a ball in my hand. That's not surprising, I suppose, considering my family background. My father, Scott—"Scotty"—played some professional baseball when he was young. He was a pitcher with the Los Angeles Angels' chain in the old Pacific Coast League, but he eventually had to give it up at the age of twenty-four when he developed back problems at Ponca City, Oklahoma, in 1935.

So his minor league career amounted to a cup of coffee, although I seem to remember reading a letter he had from the Cincinnati Reds, indicating some interest in him. To this day, Dad says that old injury affects his golf game. He swings hard, but the ball doesn't go as far, not that a lot of us don't have the same problem.

Dad continued to play with some semipro teams around Southern California. I was born in Van Nuys. We call it "the Valley," which is short for the San Fernando Valley, and some of those ballclubs were not too shabby. You'd see a lot of players coming down from the major leagues to play during the winter, and a lot of Triple A players, too. He played for the Rosabell Plumbers and the Skylane Cafe, Signal Oil and others all around Southern California. Dad was working for the telephone company at the time, and we moved from Van Nuys down to Santa Ana for a few years, then back to Sherman Oaks, a town right next to Van Nuys in the Valley. Like clockwork every Sunday, we'd drive off to some ball-

15

game—maybe over to Pasadena, where the Plumbers were based, in the Arroyo Seco by the Pasadena Freeway. Then when the game was over, we'd all pile into our cars and stop at somebody's house for something to eat and then we'd come home. Not a bad way to spend the weekend, I thought. Not a bad way at all.

One of the other teams Dad played with was Signal Oil, and I kind of hung around in my free time, as did another youngster whom I never really got to know—a fellow named Merv Adelson, who was a good athlete and became one of the owners of the very successful La Costa Resort and Lorimar Productions. Anyway, several years ago, I was on his boat in Jamaica and we started talking about our childhood. He happened to mention that his uncle used to run a ballclub, Signal Oil.

"You mean Art Schwartz?" I asked.

"Yeah," he said. "How'd you know that?"

"Well," I said, "I was a batboy for that team."

"You were?" he said. "So was I."

Sure enough, I got ahold of Dad, who brought out an old eight-by-ten picture from his archives, and there we were—Merv and myself, batboys. One of my earliest adventures in following Dad around happened at Birmingham Hospital. I walked around the screen at batting practice and down toward the right-field line and I got hit square in the right eye with a line drive. That's kind of a rude awakening, getting dinged in the head with your first baseball as a kid. Everything turned out fine. We didn't have to go very far to have a doctor look at me. We were right at the hospital.

It wasn't until I was nine years old that I participated in my first organized program. A fellow named Harold Marks started the Valley Junior Baseball League. He got kids from North Hollywood and Studio City and Van Nuys and divided them up according to age groups, like nine-to-twelve in one category and thirteen-to-fifteen in another. Don't forget, we didn't have Little League then. I was a little bit of everything in those days. I was a third baseman, a first baseman, a catcher. Obviously, I was too young at the time to be thinking ahead, but I enjoyed the lifestyle. I was impressed with how my dad would take me around to all these different places, a ballplayer introducing me to other ballplayers. I couldn't wait for weekends when he was playing and when I started playing, I really looked forward to my games. When my parents couldn't find me around the house, it was a pretty safe bet where I'd be—at some playground somewhere, playing baseball.

I was a pretty good student, too. I went to Dickens Street School in Sherman Oaks, then to Van Nuys Junior High School and Van Nuys High School, where my folks had gone. One of my classmates there was a fellow named Robert Redford. We were in the same grade, though I can't lie to you and say that he and I were bosom buddies. I don't remember him ever expressing an interest in being a movie star any more than I was focused on being a baseball player. In those days, you were either into cars or sports or a little of both and you never gave too much thought to what you might do once you had to deal with real life. At least, that's the way I was. I never was a candidate for hypertension.

I was a B-plus student most of the way in high school. I still have all my report cards, in fact. But I can't honestly say that I was more into studies than I was into sports, and of course, when I got my first uniform, that was it. I mean, I felt like I was king of the world, and I'll never forget my first game over in North Hollywood, when I was playing third base and went 4-for-5. I wasn't real big then. Or, I should say, I wasn't real tall. Dad is six-foot-one, maybe six-two, and my mom, Verna, is five-foot-six. I didn't do most of my growing until right after I got out of high school, when I shot up four-and-a-half inches in a hurry. When I was nine, though, I was a little large in other areas, a little chubby, which I guess is why they called me "Porky." I don't think it was my sweet tooth. We didn't have any of that stuff in those days. There was just basic meat and potatoes on the table. Mom didn't do a lot of baking and I wasn't into eating much candy.

When Dad stopped playing, he started managing in the senior division of the Valley Junior League, the division I wasn't in. But then I entered American Legion ball, and he managed the same team I was on, and that's how it all really began for me, as a pitcher and as a Dodger. Goldie Holt of the Brooklyn Dodgers' scouting staff happened to be in the stands watching the game one day, the same day that our pitcher, Roger Grabenstein, didn't show up. I was between my junior and senior years in high school at the time. I had made the varsity as a freshman and had earned my letter as a second baseman. That day I was still a second baseman who had played some third and also carried around an old first baseman's glove. In a pinch, I could catch. I didn't play shortstop or the outfield.

And I hadn't ever pitched, at least until Roger Grabenstein failed to show. I had never even given pitching a thought. I'd thrown some batting practice, but that was about it. My dad, the manager, must have seen something in me. I remember him telling me that I wasn't fast enough to play any position in the field other than catcher, and I don't think he was too excited about me playing there. He'd played enough baseball to see what happened to a catcher's fingers game after game. It's like the old joke. Two retired catchers meet on the street one day and shake hands and they need an operation to separate them because their fingers get so intertwined.

If another father had been coaching the team, he might have picked *his* son. That's entirely possible. But Dad had seen me throw casually—during batting practice, or while playing catch with him—so he gave me the ball. All he told me was, "Don't get cute and throw strikes." Van Nuys and North Hollywood had a big rivalry in everything—in high school, we were the Wolves and they were the Huskies—and that rivalry extended to our American Legion games, where our team was Van Nuys Post 193. He was waiting and waiting and waiting for our regular pitcher to show up, so by the time Dad told me I was going to pitch, I only had time to warm up and get going. I didn't have time to get nervous, which was probably a good thing.

I don't remember too many of the details, like how many batters I struck out or how many hits I allowed. But I do remember that we won and I went all the way—pitched a complete ballgame. And after the game was over, Dad introduced me to Goldie, who just happened to be in the stands that day. They had a lot more scouts in major league baseball then, and more teams affiliated with the major league franchises, and Goldie probably had no reason in particular for being there, other than to see a ballgame and maybe find a prospect.

"You ever thought about pitching?" he asked me.

"No, not really," I answered.

"Well, why don't you come back over here in a couple of days and I'll watch you work out," Holt said.

Dad and I returned a couple days later, and there was just a catcher and me there. Goldie told me just to stand out on the mound and see how many strikes I could throw. I don't recall any instructions on how hard to throw or whatever. Just throw strikes, and it was one of those days when I had good control. If I threw 100 pitches, there must have been 85 strikes. Everything clicked. I wasn't really nervous, because I wasn't making a big deal about it. I had no idea what was going on. As I soon learned, the Brooklyn Dodgers, like a lot of other big league teams, had clubs throughout California for just the purpose of developing kids, giving them a chance to play some baseball.

You know, you always hear people say that they had this dream to become something when they were such-and-such age. But being a ballplayer never occurred to me. I had a bunch of odd jobs when I was a kid, just like most kids. I had a newspaper route when I was nine, delivering the *Valley Times*—which was then a free newspaper, a shopper that you just passed out. Since then, it's become the *Los Angeles Daily News.* I worked for a spell in the advertising department of the *Los Angeles Times,* where my aunt, Florence Ley, had been a long-time employee. I also worked at the Piggly-Wiggly in West Van Nuys as a grocery boy. I washed dishes at a place across from that market. I also worked with some of the farmers out there, loading squash and stacking hay and sacking onions. Real glamorous stuff. I was going along on a day-to-day basis, never really planning ahead, never thinking about someday being paid to play baseball. If you thought about anything, you thought about going to college and getting your diploma and getting a job, just like you're supposed to do. So, all this stuff was like a bolt out of the blue.

After that first game on the mound, Dad did say that if I ever had any idea of playing professional baseball, I'd have to pitch. That pretty much was his review of my debut as a pitcher. I don't think he was waiting to lay that on me. I don't think he was figuring on me becoming a ballplayer. That afternoon in the American Legion, I might have surprised him as much as I surprised myself. I liked the idea of pitching. I liked the idea of playing baseball, period. So, in time, my dad wound up catching me in his free time, teaching me pitching mechanics. Even my mom would catch me whenever she had a chance or when Dad was late coming home from work.

So, the pitching seed was planted in my mind, and it grew when Goldie Holt saw me throw all those strikes and said later,

"Maybe we'll try to work you in a bit with the Brooklyn Dodger Juniors." At the time, Larry Sherry was there and so was his brother, Norm. Also, George Anderson, whom most of you know as "Sparky." He went on to become a great manager in the major leagues with Cincinnati and now with the Detroit Tigers. I might be the last guy on the planet who still calls Sparky by his proper first name, George. He was living in Southern California, just like the Sherry brothers, and they would play during the winter on the Brooklyn Dodger Juniors, a team run by the Dodgers' two area scouts, Holt and Lefty Phillips. They didn't have a home field, but they did play a lot over in Glendale. There were games against the St. Louis Cardinals Juniors, New York Giants Juniors, and so forth.

I don't recall being too emotional about this giant step in my life, but I do remember putting on that Dodger uniform for the first time. Even if it was only a "Junior" uniform, and even if I did play just a few games for them, it was pretty heady stuff. Little did I know how much that Dodger uniform would mean to me for the rest of my life.

Unfortunately, I was having some health problems at the time. I hurt both my legs. How, I have no idea to this day. For all I know, I could have torn both Achilles tendons. They hurt that badly. Whenever I tried to run, I had to run flat-footed. But that wasn't the worst of my problems because as I headed into my senior year of high school, I found that I literally could not lift my right arm high enough to get a T-shirt over it. My arm was killing me. I don't know if it was because I had started pitching, but it might have been a blessing in disguise that I started throwing more and harder in my new position. The new strain might have forced the pain. I went to an orthopedic surgeon, who took X-rays and found that at the tip of my elbow, where it's supposed to hook onto the two bones coming down either side of the arm, there was a jagged edge, like a sawtooth line. If I bent my elbow, this edge—maybe a sixteenth of an inch wide—could be seen all the way across. It was very noticeable when you looked at the X-ray. I didn't understand the medical implications of all this, but I didn't have to. The doctor set me straight.

One, I was not going to be able to play football that autumn. I had been a backup quarterback for the Van Nuys High School team, but that was out. Two, he said that unless I promised him that I would not do any throwing whatsoever, he was going to put my arm in a cast. He wanted the thing in a sling, to keep it completely immobile. So here it was, my senior year, 1953, with one American Legion pitching performance under my belt and a few other games with the Brooklyn Dodger Juniors, and I couldn't throw a baseball! I couldn't even take a physical education class in school. I had to work in the gym office, shuffling papers.

Luckily, it wasn't a serious ailment. I was starting to grow very fast, and my bones weren't catching up with the rest of my body. They didn't have a chance to catch up. My senior football year was wiped out, but in time, the arm healed. We went back to the X-rays in a couple months, and you could see the progress. By the time baseball season came around in February, I was ready to play and by this time, the coach knew I was a pitcher. We had a number-one pitcher on the team, Jim Heffer, who had been around for quite a while. But we needed another one, and I was it, the number-two pitcher. My senior year, he pitched one game and I pitched the other. In April 1954, pitching for Van Nuys High against Hollywood, I threw a no-hitter and struck out 12 in winning 7–0. I was one base on balls away from pitching a perfect game. When people ask me now whether I pitched a no-hitter, I always say yes. Then they ask what year, and I tell them, 1954 against Hollywood High School. And I still have the baseball to prove it. I made All-City that year, and began to attract a little bit of attention. Babe Herman was right in our living room one day, discussing the possibility of me signing with the New York Yankees. Johnny Moore was there from the Braves, and so was Hollis Thurston from the Chicago White Sox. Plus, of course, Goldie Holt and the Dodgers. It was amazing, all these scouts wanting to talk to me.

All of a sudden, I had a decision to make. I could have gone to Stanford on a baseball scholarship, because I had pretty good grades. I had a scholarship opportunity with Southern Cal, too. But I wanted to play baseball. My thinking then was that I'd give baseball a try, and if it didn't work out, I could always start college. I didn't get any pressure from my parents, even though Dad was then working for the Dodgers' organization, doing some scouting. He knew baseball and he knew so many people in Southern California that the Dodgers decided they'd put Dad to good use as a part-time scout.

One day after my senior baseball season ended, Branch Rickey, who was then with the Pittsburgh Pirates, invited me to come to a tryout. It was very enlightening. He had that old Panama hat on and he was chomping on that cigar of his. Mr. Rickey never lit it; he just chewed on it. He had Eddie Malone catching me and Mr. Rickey grabbed a baseball. He drew a circle on the baseball and said to me, "Son, I want you to throw this baseball so we don't see the circle." And then I'd throw a few. And then he'd grab the baseball and draw another circle and say, "Son, now I want you to throw this baseball so we *do* see the circle." Basically, what Mr. Rickey was doing was testing your aptitude. He was seeing how you might grip the baseball to make it do what he wanted you to do with it. Smart. And then Mr. Rickey asked the catcher about the results, too.

After this little workout, the next morning we went to have breakfast with Mr. Rickey at the Beverly Wilshire Hotel. It was Mr. Rickey and his male secretary, Dad and Mom and me. We talked about my possibly signing with the Pirates. I'll never forget that meeting. It's been burned into my mind ever since, what a magnetic person Mr. Rickey was. He had to be in his fifties then, having left the Dodger organization a few years earlier, and what a mind he had. I'll also never forget the look on his secretary's face, every time Mr. Rickey took one of those scouting reports in his hand. He'd look over the plusses and minuses of a prospect on this sheet, all neatly typed on a piece of onion-skin paper. Then Mr. Rickey would fold it up and stick it in his pocket and his secretary would just cringe, knowing he'd have to write a whole new report up on another sheet of onion skin.

At the time, there was a rule in major league baseball about signing a kid like me. If you signed for more than $4,000, you were a "bonus baby" and you had to stay in the major leagues for two years. (That's what Sandy Koufax did with the Dodgers.)

Rickey offered me a $6,000 deal, which sounded pretty good, but it was for the Pirates' Hollywood team in the Triple A Pacific Coast League. How was he going to get around that "bonus baby" rule? He said there were ways, but we never did find out. Mr. Rickey's idea was that I would start with Hollywood, then have to pitch myself "off" the team—in other words, down to a lower level. Dad and I figured there was a pretty good chance of that happening. There were some pretty good players in that league, and on that team. Dale Long, for instance, who went on to have a fine major league career. I didn't think I was ready to start that high, and neither did Dad. We listened to other offers—from the White Sox, Yankees, Braves, Dodgers—but they were all just about equal. Except for the Pirates, who were dangling this extra $2,000 out there somewhere.

"Look," Dad said to me in the car one night, "if you're going to get a lot of money—like Billy Consolo, a $60,000 bonus baby— then it makes sense to take it and go to the major leagues and take your chances. But if you're not going to get a lot of money—and $2,000 isn't a lot of money—then why not go where you have the best chance to learn?"

Dad made a lot of sense, and the more I thought about it, the more I leaned to the Dodgers. They had sixteen farm clubs in their system, so I'd have a chance to play. If I was any good, I would move up. Plus, the Dodgers had gotten me started in this, with the Brooklyn Dodger Juniors. They were the ones who'd offered me the first opportunity to play, and I guess I had developed some sense of loyalty. Also, their farm clubs were all winning, and so was the big club in Brooklyn. From 3,000 miles away in California, I was impressed by what the organization stood for. Dad never pressured me to hook on with the Dodgers, any more than he ever pushed me toward baseball instead of college. The decisions were mine, and I wanted to give it a go with the Dodgers.

So we set up a dinner meeting in Sherman Oaks at a place the folks loved to go to—Otto's Pink Pig, on Van Nuys Boulevard. Lefty Phillips joined us and we made the deal that night, the first week in June 1954, just prior to my graduation from high school. I signed a contract and was sent to their Class C Bakersfield club in the California State League right away, the day after graduation. Fresco Thompson, who was in charge of the Dodgers' minor league system, was out from New York when I reported. Larry Sherry was there, too. He was about the only one I knew on the ballclub. I stayed at the Padre Hotel in Bakersfield and finished out the rest of the season there.

It was a painless transition. Bakersfield was about 100 miles from home, and my parents would come to see me pitch. Nothing was too far, whether you were playing in Salinas or Fresno or Modesto or San Jose or Stockton. That was the California State League. And here I was, still never having left the state of California. On Dad's advice, I took $2,200 of my $4,000 windfall in the form of a bonus, and took the rest as a $600 salary per month.

Some kids in my situation went for a bigger lump sum right at the start—maybe $3,000 of the $4,000. But Dad's reasoning was to set up a better base salary, in case I did something good. What the heck, he figured. If I did produce, they weren't going to cut me.

Sure enough, the next year, when I went to Montreal, the Dodgers upped me from $600 a month to $700. If I'd have started at $300 a month in Bakersfield, they would have bumped me up $100 to only $400 in Montreal. I'm sure glad I had Dad around to advise me on all these matters of high finance.

I had an 8–5 record for Bakersfield—nothing spectacular, but at least I won more than I lost in only my second year of pitching, ever. Actually, it was only a half-year. I was throwing a lot of fast balls at the time, but I also had a knuckle curve ball that helped me get by. I was throwing then a lot differently than the way I would finish my career. I was delivering the ball in more of a three-quarter motion without a whole lot of velocity. But I survived. Things went pretty well.

Getting paid for playing baseball was a nice new experience, but I don't recall ever thinking that I had it made. I knew I'd have to perform or be gone, so I didn't get too wild. I did buy a car, the first one I'd ever owned, right after I came home from Bakersfield following the season. Dad found me this 1951 Ford that was just perfect for my needs. He had it in the garage when I came home, just waiting for me, but I did pay him for it, something like $550. I got a job with the telephone company, where my dad was still working. During the winter, Lefty Phillips had me working out at Dorsey Playground with George Anderson and the Sherrys and a few other guys who lived in the area, most of them part of the Dodger organization.

By the time February rolled around, it was time for me to go to my first spring training. Naturally, this also meant my first trip ever outside the state of California. The all-day–all-night excursion took me on a plane from Los Angeles to St. Louis to Atlanta to Jacksonville, Florida, to Melbourne over to Vero Beach, where the Dodgers were based. It took forever, but before I even left California, my mom made sure I was in good hands. Mom and Dad drove me to the airport in Los Angeles.

"Please take good care of Don," she said to Norm Sherry.

He did, and before I knew it, I was clear across the country, at the winter home of the Brooklyn Dodgers, pinching myself.

24

I took with me some basic knowledge of what it was to be a professional baseball player, even though I had done it on a very low level for a very short time. I'd learned what it was like to be on my own for the first time, how to do my laundry and make it through all those greasy spoon restaurants without having indigestion. I also remembered some sound advice Dad had given to me one night on the telephone.

"How is everything?" he asked.

"Okay, except for one problem," I said.

"What's that?"

"Those bus trips," I said. "I can't find anyplace to get comfortable in those seats. They'll kill you."

"Well," said Dad, "there's one sure way to cure that problem."

"What's that?"

"Get out of the bus leagues," Dad told me. "And get into the big leagues."

3

Dodgertown, at Last

*B*etween our old TWA Constellation and Eastern's twin engine, they finally dropped us off in Florida that winter of 1955—Norm and Larry Sherry, George Anderson, and myself. Somewhere along the line, St. Louis I think, we picked up Jim Gentile connecting from San Francisco. That was a five-hour layover, all part of a twenty-four-hour excursion that delivered us to Vero Beach at eight o'clock the next morning. By this time, we were traveling in a twin-engine plane and I was working on a pretty good cold.

There was a school bus waiting for us—one of those square-looking jobs with "Dodgers" on the side. It took us over to Dodgertown, where one of my first expenses since leaving California for the first time in my life was to pay a buck for the key to my room. Everybody in camp had one. If you lost the key, you lost your dollar, and you had to pay another dollar for another key.

I was in awe of the surroundings. I felt at ease with the Sherrys and George, because I knew them from California. Plus, Norm and George had been to training camp there a couple years in a row and Larry one year before. They knew the ropes, so I just followed them around. Whatever they did, I did. We roomed together for what was a two-week early camp, beginning around the middle of February. It couldn't have been more than an hour-and-a-half between the time we landed and when we started our first workout. Before I knew it, I was in this big huge clubhouse, surrounded by wire lockers.

I knew we weren't in the main clubhouse, the one for the major leaguers. That was at the end of a sand parking lot, behind the mess hall. You didn't go in there if you were a young pup like me. There was no need to. Besides, you felt as though it was out of bounds. I was happy enough just to be issued a Dodger uniform—no number or anything, just a uniform. I couldn't get it on fast enough. If I wasn't in total awe before, I was then.

That sand parking lot was a place I'll never forget. A couple weeks after I showed up for the early camp, the veterans started arriving. I was walking across the lot one day and I ran into Herbie Sharfman, one of the Dodgers' official team photographers. They always had two or three of them around, taking publicity shots, and Herbie was one of the best.

"Don," he yelled at me this particular day. "Come over here. I want you to meet somebody—Gil Hodges."

Well, I about fell over in my tracks. Gil stuck out this huge hand, and he shook mine, and we said a few words. He was terrific, very friendly, very impressive. Now, I was really in the clouds. I'd met Gil Hodges.

After a couple weeks, with things going pretty well, I moved over to the major league clubhouse. It was an old wooden building. Right in the middle of it were all the steamer trunks with the gear packed in them, and as you looked around the room, you could see that the lockers were arranged numerically. Over on one side, there was number 1 for Pee Wee Reese. Over on the other, way over, I looked and saw "DRYSDALE 53." The lettering was very neat, the work of John Griffin, the clubhouse man who was referred to as "The Senator." He had great penmanship. To this day, I always maintain that it's not only general managers and managers who determine which players will stay with the big club after spring training. The clubhouse man has a voice, too, because he's in charge of the uniforms and the higher the number he gives you, the less chance he figures you've got of sticking with the major league roster. I had the highest number of the group. Herbie Olsen, a catcher, came in with number 55 a year later, but I was high man in 1955 with number 53—a number, by the way, I wound up keeping throughout my career. Thank you, Senator Griffin.

I took my stuff and emptied this grubby little gym bag I'd been carrying around. I looked up and there was my Dodger uniform—the real thing—and my Brooklyn Dodger cap sitting on top of the wire mesh. There was a jacket and sanitary socks, the whole bit, and while I was taking all this in, I was also keeping an eye peeled on the guys starting to trickle into the clubhouse. Carl Erskine came in. And then Duke Snider, who I knew a little bit. Duke was from California, too, and I'd met him at one of those hot stove banquets out there during the winter. He glanced over in my direction and waved.

"Hi, Don, how are you?" said Duke. It was like we were the best of friends.

Then Pee Wee Reese came over and introduced himself, and probably a few more players. I don't remember exactly who. I was in too much of a daze, I guess, but I'll never forget how they all made me feel welcome. I didn't know what to expect—I probably didn't expect that—but I've always felt that this was one reason why the Dodgers were unique in those days. No matter who you were, if you had a Dodger uniform on, they made you feel like you were one of them—like part of the family, the Dodger family.

"Hi, Don . . . I'm Clem Labine."

"Hello, Don . . . Jackie Robinson."

And on and on it went. Amazing.

Walt Alston, the manager, had a meeting that first day. It was short and to the point and then we all went out for the opening workout on diamond number 2. Joe Becker, the pitching coach, headed up the exercises and it didn't take long before I realized why they called him a "mule trainer." First of all, back in St. Louis he really *was* a mule trainer. Secondly, that's how he treated us. Did he ever work you hard! But he made it one of his favorite sayings: "You'll hate me in spring training, but you'll love me in October."

The first day of camp, I threw some batting practice. I had been there for a couple weeks, so I was in reasonably good shape. Most of the guys, the veterans, were still getting the kinks out, and a few of them were a little uneasy about stepping in against me. I was throwing pretty well, not only because I was loose but because something had happened to my body during the winter. I'd grown taller and stronger and for some reason, I'd acquired a lot more velocity on my fastball. Lefty Phillips, if he were still alive, would tell you that there was a big difference in me from the time he saw me in high school and when I reported to Vero Beach.

Jackie Robinson was one of the veterans who saw me out there on the mound and had second thoughts about taking a few cuts in the cage.

"Hey, I'm not gettin' in there against that kid!" Jackie yelled, smiling.

Alston just laughed. He was terrific to me, too.

"Just take it easy, son," he said. "Just throw it nice and easy. You're not trying to get anybody out."

I had a real good spring. I was getting people out when it counted during intrasquad games. We played a lot of those back then, more than teams do now—they can make more money selling tickets to games against other teams. I was throwing hard. I was throwing strikes. Everything was going well.

One day, early in the Grapefruit League season when we played other major league teams training in Florida, we faced the Yankees. Russ Meyer was pitching for us and he couldn't get the ball over the plate. Walt got irritated. If there was one thing that annoyed Alston, it was when his pitchers had control problems. Walt took Meyer out and replaced him with Pete Wojey and he couldn't throw strikes either. Now, Alston was really irritated. He jumped up in the dugout.

"Jesus Christ!" he yelled. "Can't anybody around here throw strikes?"

Just as he said that, I looked up from the bench. I was an extra pitcher, and we just happened to make eye contact.

"Can *you* throw strikes?" he asked.

"Yes, sir, I can," I answered.

"Well, get warm," Alston said. "You're going in there next inning."

So, there I was. My first exhibition game against another major league team and I was pitching against the New York Yankees, our usual October rivals. They had started the game with Ewell Blackwell and relieved him with Eddie Lopat. I came in to pitch the fifth inning. I don't remember the first batter I ever faced, but I do remember that Elston Howard was the first guy to get a hit off me—a hard grounder back up the middle, right through my legs. But I pitched a couple innings and got 'em out and felt pretty good about what I'd done. It went that way for a couple weeks, though I didn't know whether I'd made an impression on anybody.

Then one day, toward the end of spring training, I was standing in right field with Carl Furillo and Roy Campanella. Campy had caught me a few times in camp, so he knew how I pitched.

"Roy," I said, "what more do I have to do to pitch in the major leagues? What more do I have to learn?"

"Son," he said, "you don't have to do anything different to pitch in the major leagues. You could pitch in the major leagues right now. If we didn't have the staff we have, you could pitch in the major leagues today."

Then Campanella called over Furillo.

"Skoonj," said Campanella. "What more does this kid have to do to pitch in the big leagues?"

"Nuthin'," said Furillo, in his typically gruff way. "Just keep on doing what you're doing. Throw the ball. Throw strikes."

I'll never forget that exchange. Here I was a kid who'd never pitched above Class C ball, a kid who hadn't been out of the state of California until I'd arrived in Florida a month or so earlier, and now two of the Brooklyn Dodgers' greatest veterans were telling me that I had what it took to make it to the major leagues. Again, that was an example of what the Dodgers were all about. Campanella and Furillo didn't have to talk to me the way they did that day. As regulars on a great ballclub, they didn't have to talk to a pup like me at all. But the Dodgers were family. That's what they were all about. I can't say that enough.

I'll give you another example. Though we used to have our workouts and play our games at Vero Beach in 1955, we were actually based in Miami, at the MacAlister Hotel, an old pink building at the corner of Biscayne and Flagler. I was all by myself one hot afternoon following the day's work, so I strolled over to this little bar called The Sportsman's, where they had fifteen-cent draft beers. I figured I'd sit down and have a few cold ones while I decided where to go to dinner and what to eat. No sooner had I downed my first beer when I looked up and who came walking through the door but Snider and Hodges and Reese and Rube Walker. Well, my eyes got bigger than horseturds when I saw them stroll in. I got up and started to leave. I figured I didn't belong there.

"Where do you think you're going?" Hodges asked.

"Well . . . I was just heading out," I said.

"You're not going anywhere," they told me.

31

That was that. I went over and sat at a table with them and just listened. If I said something, it was quick and to the point, and then I went back to listening. They had a lot more to say than I did, anyway, with their stories and I was like a pig in slop just being able to be a part of all this. I remember buying a round or two, but not as many as the veterans bought. They were looking after the kid, I guess, but that was the Dodger way. The players on that team had such camaraderie. They had seen me getting up to leave and could have let me go right through the door, but they didn't.

Before long, spring training camp broke. It was time to get ready for the regular season. Alston called me in, as he did all the kids who weren't going north with the big club, and said he appreciated what I'd done during the spring. He said I'd worked hard and told me to keep working hard because they would be following whatever I did in the minor leagues. And just like that, the big club was gone. I stayed around in Vero Beach to find out where I was headed. Everything was pretty much the same except that the veterans weren't around anymore. Neither was my Dodger uniform or jacket or cap. That was the way The Senator worked. You still had your personal belongings, but the Dodger gear had been shipped up to Brooklyn. Now, what I had hanging in my locker was a Montreal Royals' uniform, number 25. Montreal and St. Paul were the Dodgers' top two farm clubs, and it appeared that I was headed to Montreal. I didn't know that I was even really with them yet, because that was a hell of a jump for me—from Class C of the California State League to Class Triple A, the International League.

Greg Mulleavy was the manager of the Montreal team, and I found out that he wanted me to play for him. Dick Walsh, who was vice-president of the Dodgers' minor league department, wasn't too sure about that. Nor was Tommy Holmes, who was the manager of another Dodger Double A farm club in Fort Worth. Meanwhile, my contract was still with Mobile, also a Double A club. That's where I was designated to go in the beginning, when I first signed, but I went to Bakersfield instead. I had talked a little bit with Holmes during spring training and he could see that I could swing the bat, so maybe that's why he wanted me in Forth Worth. But Mulleavy pushed and pushed and finally they all got together—Fresco Thompson, Lefty Phillips, Walsh, Mulleavy, and Holmes. They must have decided, What the heck's the difference?

If he goes to Montreal and can't cut it, he'll wind up in Fort Worth, anyway. So I went in and signed a Montreal contract for that $100 raise, all the way up to $700 a month, and I was in high cotton. I knew there was no chance that I'd make the big club at that age, especially with my lack of experience. They had Erskine, Johnny Podres, Billy Loes, Eddie Roebuck, Karl Spooner, and Jim Hughes, plus Sandy Koufax was there, and had to stay by contract. I had no expectations of making the Brooklyn Dodgers at the start of camp, although toward the end, thanks partly to what Campanella and Furillo had told me, I was thinking to myself that I maybe could pitch as well as some of the pitchers who were going to stay.

The Montreal club broke camp in Florida in early April, and took a train to Richmond from Vero Beach. That was another first for me—my first train ride. Then after our first series in Richmond, we went to Havana, which also had a ballclub in the International League. We stayed there a week to play games. Because of the travel, each team in the league only went there twice a season. After that, we flew to LaGuardia Airport in New York City on our way to Montreal for the opening of our home season. We spent our first night in New York sleeping on LaGuardia's benches and couches. By the time we landed in New York, it was too late to catch another flight for Montreal.

We'd been on the road for a long time, playing all over creation, and there we were, with no money. Nobody among us had any money and we were looking at this line of pay toilets in La-Guardia the morning of our flight to Montreal. Meal money then was something like five-fifty a day and mine was all gone and I know I wasn't alone. We took a poll of four or five of us, and all we had was forty-eight cents total. That wasn't going to go too far in the pay toilets at LaGuardia. It was ten cents a crack. Naive as I was, I was just about to slip a dime in the slot when Billy Harris, a teammate, caught me. "Don't do that," he said. "I've got a better idea." Sure enough, he crawled underneath the door and opened it to all the rest of us.

When we got to Montreal, we stayed in a hotel for one night and then scattered. Bob Addis, Gino Cimoli, and I rented a three-room house in the old French section of town. So, there I was, a kid from California who'd just been in three different countries within a couple of weeks and was now preparing to play for the

33

Royals in D'Lormier Stadium. I can sympathize with all those Latin players who come to the United States now to play baseball and have trouble with the English language. It was much the same for us playing in Montreal in those days. If you didn't speak French, you wound up ordering the same thing every morning for breakfast. I never ate more ham and eggs than I did playing for the Royals that one season.

The Montreal experience was a great one for me—I couldn't have asked for better. In those days, you not only had a lot of kids trying to make it to the big leagues, but you also had some veterans who were on their way down. You don't see that much in the minor leagues anymore, because there are so few minor league teams now compared to then. There's not as much room for the guys who aren't quite able to stick with the major league teams, but who can still play. And who can still teach. I was lucky enough to play minor league baseball when I could pick the brains of a guy like Johnny Bucha, our catcher in Montreal. He had played with the St. Louis Cardinals and Detroit Tigers and was as tough as nails. Having him around was great. You couldn't ask for a better scenario.

We had a pretty good pitching staff, too. Roger Craig was there, Kenny Lehman, Glenn Cox, Glenn Mickens, Pete Wojey, and Tommy Lasorda. Tommy never made it big in the major leagues as a pitcher, but I don't have to tell you how well he's done as a manager. Tommy's claim to fame was that the Dodgers cut him to make room for Sandy Koufax. They needed a lefthander and it was either him or Sandy. The fact is that Koufax was a bonus baby, and the Dodgers had to keep him. When you look back at the records, it was a pretty smart decision.

Lasorda had a rough start with us during the 1955 season. He had been cut by the Dodgers, and when he came to Montreal, the first words out of his mouth were, "Don't worry, fellas, the Warren Spahn of the International League has just returned." But Tommy got off to an 0–7 start, and he was looking for anything to turn it around. One day, four of us were walking down the street in Buffalo when a pigeon flew over Lasorda's head and let fly with a little deposit.

"Why me?" Tommy said. "I can't win a game, and now some pigeon shits on my head! Well, who knows? Maybe it'll change my luck."

Sure enough. Tommy won his next start and from then on, whenever he took a walk, he looked up at the sky for a pigeon.

We had a pretty strong lineup in Montreal. We had Rocky Nelson at first, Charlie Neal at second, Chico Fernandez at shortstop—all of whom went on to the major leagues. We had Jimmy Williams in left field, Bobby Wilson in right, and Gino Cimoli in center. We wound up finishing in first place by a half-game over the Toronto club, owned then by Jack Kent Cooke, who currently owns the Washington Redskins of the National Football League. Cooke is a native Canadian, and baseball was one of his first sporting interests. I hear that he's still trying to bring a major league team back to Washington, where he lives now.

Montreal was a nice place to play, and the stadium wasn't all that different from Ebbets Field, except that the left-field fence was a lot farther away from home plate than it was in Brooklyn. It had a short porch in right field with a scoreboard. We traveled by train a bit and did some flying, too. It was a terrific league, and I even got to save some money. At that time Canadian currency was worth more than American money. We got paid half in their currency and half in ours, and whenever I got my check, I'd send some money back home to my folks in California. They put it away for me, same as they did when I finally made it to Brooklyn.

I had an 11–11 record with Montreal in 1955. I started off well, going 9–2, but I didn't finish particularly strong. I broke my hand on a Coke machine in Buffalo around midseason and that affected me. I don't recall all the details, but I got knocked out of a game and took my frustrations out on the first thing I came into contact with. No sense keeping things inside. I never said anything to anybody, but I broke a bone in my right (pitching) hand—the metacarpal—and it was sticking out a bit, though not quite through the skin. I tried to keep pitching by freezing my hand with ethyl-chloride, but the injury took its toll.

At this point, though, I knew I could pitch in the major leagues. Don't ask me why. Maybe I was living in a dream world, or maybe I was just too naive to realize what the heck was going on. Maybe I didn't understand how difficult it was to get to the big leagues. But I was still uplifted by my brief time around the major league club in spring training, and when Roger Craig was called up to Brooklyn midway during the 1955 season, that just confirmed my notion because I thought that I was doing everything that Craig was. If he could go up and have success, I thought I could, too. I don't think I was being cocky. Maybe I was being stupid. All I needed was the chance.

I was about six-foot-five by the time I reached Montreal, and not setting any weight records. I was taking some type of formula to put on pounds, but it couldn't have worked all that well, because even when I made it to Brooklyn the next spring, I weighed only 174. Skinny as I was in Montreal, though, I was having fun. I had no reason not to have fun. Everything was new to me. Every day was a new and different experience, and the fact that I was throwing better and better, improving at my craft, well, I was feeling pretty good about life.

I was playing in a terrific city, Montreal, where the people were super. And the road trips were enjoyable, some more than others. In Syracuse, for instance, Bucha, Lasorda, and Wally Fiala had a friend who owned a sporting goods store and also had a house on Lake Onondaga. He invited us out to go water-skiing one day. We had permission from Mulleavy to stay out at this fellow's cabin. The rest of these guys didn't have a clue about how to water-ski, not that I did. But at least I was from California and I had watched some water-skiers in my young life, and it didn't seem right to me to leave all the slack rope on the ground by the shore and then take the speedboat and head like hell toward the middle of the lake while you're standing there waiting for all that slack to catch up with you. You didn't need to be an Einstein to figure that out.

Anyway, there was Lasorda from Pennsylvania, standing at the end of the dock, telling us, "Fellas, I got to tell you one thing . . . I'm not a real good swimmer." We say, "Fine, Tommy," and we toss him a fire-engine-red life jacket. So, Lasorda put that on, and he had the tow-bar in one hand and he tied the other piece of loose rope around his wrist. If it sounds like trouble, it was.

"Okay, take off," Lasorda yelled to Bucha, who was driving the boat.

Well, Lasorda stayed up on the water for a couple of seconds and then, boom, he fell right off. Bucha didn't see Lasorda right off the bat, but then, out of the corner of his eye, he did see Tommy struggling. Bucha knew that Lasorda had a life preserver on, though, so now it was fun to John. He wasn't about to stop that boat right then and there. And for the next few minutes, all you saw was this fire-engine-red life jacket bobbing up and down in Lake Onondaga, dragging with it Tommy Lasorda, who, it turned out, not only couldn't swim very well—he couldn't swim at all! He had let go of the wooden tow-bar, but he had wrapped that rope around his left arm—his pitching arm—and he was trapped. When he came back to dry land, we were all roaring with laughter and he looked like a drowned sewer rat.

Tommy was particularly good to be with when we went to Havana, because he could speak Spanish. When we traveled there, we always had black beans and rice for dinner. You had to get used to the meat, because you never knew whether they'd just butchered the cow a half-hour earlier. We had another adventure down there, involving Chico Fernandez, who was Cuban. He had a chance as a baserunner to take out Havana's shortstop one day, but he didn't and I got beat 1–0 in a ballgame. I came in and was so damn mad that I picked up a chair and wanted to throw it through the clubhouse wall. Mulleavy saw me and told me not to. "What will it prove?" he said. "The ballgame's over. Nothing you can do about it."

"If he wants to throw the chair, let him throw the chair," said Lasorda, who was observing all this from nearby.

I was so livid that I took his advice. I hurled that chair through the plasterboard wall and left a big hole in it. Well, in the second game of the doubleheader, Tommy was the starting pitcher and darned if he didn't also lose, 1–0. So what did he do? He came into the clubhouse, grabbed the same stool that I had used, and threw it at the same wall, making another hole, right near the one I'd left. Baseball in Havana would do that to you. Once, we played a Sunday afternoon doubleheader and it was so hot that not a single pitcher came to bat in either game. They just couldn't make it. Both teams went through their entire pitching staffs. That's pretty tough to do, but it was that oppressively hot.

Then we would go back to the hotel, and there was Rocky Nelson, sitting in the lobby, sucking on a big Havana cigar on one side of his mouth and chewing tobacco on the other. I couldn't comprehend that. I had tried chewing tobacco once in high school and had forgot to spit it out. Was I ever sick!

We won the pennant that year by that half-game over Toronto, but we didn't win the Little World Series. At the end of the season, I was really tired. My arm was sore. It had really caught up with me, all this throwing. Don't forget, this business of pitching was still relatively new to me. My arm wasn't used to throwing that much. So, I came home to Van Nuys after the season and didn't do anything. Didn't throw a ball for a couple months. Finally, around the first of the year, I knew I'd have to give it a try and that was a time of great anxiety for me. I realized I'd have to go and air it out sooner or later to find out if I could still throw without pain.

"If it's there, it's there," said Dad. "You have to see if you can still throw."

I got loose one afternoon over at Dorsey Playground, where I met up with George Anderson and Larry and Norm Sherry again, plus Lefty Phillips. My arm felt fine. Then I went to the mound and threw a little harder, and thank God, everything was okay. I could still throw hard. I could still throw strikes. I was ready for spring training again.

4

I'm a Bum in 1956

I was feeling fine entering spring training, 1956. No more soreness in the right arm. Whether I was ready to make the Brooklyn Dodgers, I didn't know. I was thinking to myself, What is "ready"? What do you look for? What are the standards? I had a pretty good minor league season at Montreal behind me. I also still had that conversation in the back of my mind, that pivotal talk I'd had with Campanella and Furillo the year before. Their "don't-change-a-thing" was advice I'd keep with me.

But I still wasn't sure what a major league pitcher was. I hadn't even seen a major league game yet, at least during the regular season. My impressions of what it took to get to the big club, and stay with it, were primarily taken from what I saw of myself and how that related to others around me. For instance, Roger Craig and I were pretty much side-by-side on the Montreal staff in 1955, when he got called up and I didn't. I later learned that the primary reason he'd gotten the nod and I hadn't was experience. Roger simply had more experience, and that was a valuable commodity to the Dodgers.

The Dodgers had gotten off to a tremendous start that season, something like 22–3. It would have been tough to blow that kind of a lead, but, what the heck, it had been done before and it's been done since. The Dodgers were too good, though. They were never caught. They even got that huge monkey off their backs in the 1955

World Series, when they finally beat the New York Yankees. That was the first world championship ever for Brooklyn.

So, the 1956 ballclub reported to Vero Beach on a big high. And yet, things were happening to affect the pitching staff. Johnny Podres, a talented lefthander who had defeated the Yankees 2–0 in the seventh game of the 1955 World Series, was drafted. The most valuable player of the "fall classic" went into the Navy. Then Karl Spooner came up with a bad arm. And then Billy Loes's arm went bad. And then Don Bessent hurt his arm throwing a golf club at a snake over at Vero Beach Country Club, of all things. Bessent had been called up from St. Paul, along with Craig, when the Dodgers had some injuries on their staff the year before. Both of them had pitched in a doubleheader against Cincinnati, and the Dodgers had won both games to help maintain their lead in the National League. Bessent was a pretty good pitcher. So were Spooner and Loes. To lose those three guys with arm problems, plus Podres to the armed services, well, I could see it happening all before me. There were some openings on this staff of the World Champion Brooklyn Dodgers.

We didn't know how long any of the missing pitchers would be gone. As it turned out, Spooner's injury proved pretty serious. He was 8–6 for the Dodgers in 1955 and never won another game.

At the time, I had a Montreal contract for $700 a month. Nobody knew where I was headed, least of all me, but I had another good spring. I was throwing strikes and getting people out. I stayed with the Dodgers and broke camp with the big club. We headed up north on the train, barnstorming with the Milwaukee Braves. That was another eye-opener for me. As we went through cities like Knoxville and Nashville and Chattanooga and Mobile, the black players on the traveling squad weren't allowed to stay at hotels with the rest of us. So, in a lot of instances, we'd just have our own pullman car pulled off in trainyards along the way and we'd sleep right there. When we got up the next morning, it was time to move on to another game.

In those days, when the Dodgers and Yankees reached New York from Florida, they would play exhibition games at Yankee Stadium and Ebbets Field to conclude the Grapefruit League season. In fact, I was supposed to start our final exhibition game at Yankee Stadium in April 1956, but we got rained out, so we just hung around and worked out, waiting for the regular season to begin. Even at that late date, I still didn't know where my regular season would be. I was staying at the Bossert Hotel, a day before opening day, when I got a call to see Buzzie Bavasi over at the Dodger executive offices down the street. This is it, I figured. Here it goes. Back to Montreal or wherever.

I walked into his office expecting the worst, and instead received the best news possible.

"Congratulations," he said. "You've made the ballclub."

It was then that Buzzie cautioned me about how much easier it was to get to the big leagues than it was to stay there.

"If you never remember anything else, remember that," Buzzie went on. "There's always going to be somebody else wanting to take your job. There will always be some new kid in the wings. So, don't ever take anything for granted."

That really sunk in. I remember thinking about that as I walked back to the Bossert Hotel, not that my feet were touching the sidewalk at that point. I might have been two feet off the ground the whole trip. I called the folks back in California and announced, "I'm a Dodger." I told them about my new contract for $6,500 a year, which was the major league minimum salary in those days. For a guy like me, getting an increase from $700 a month, it was as though somebody had just handed me a million-dollar bill. I was elated.

Alston, who had some serious pitching problems to solve, was asked about my youth and inexperience.

"I don't care if he's fifteen years old," Walt told reporters. "If Don Drysdale can win some games for us, he'll stay here and pitch."

I guess John Griffin, The Senator, wasn't too sure how long I'd be around because when I went into the clubhouse for opening day, I had number 53—the same uniform I'd had in spring training, the highest number on the roster. The Senator didn't want to screw up the numbering system, but I didn't care. Just being around long enough to be measured for the uniform was exciting. I was number 39 in high school, but even though I was a big leaguer now, I wasn't about to request it. I didn't want to mess with that. Number 39, after all, belonged to Roy Campanella. I was there, that's all that mattered at the time. I walked into Ebbets Field, went into the clubhouse, took a left, and there was my very own locker.

Opening Day against the Philadelphia Phillies! Don New-combe was the starting pitcher for us and Robin Roberts for the Phillies and we lost. It was a high-scoring game, and I wound up pitching the last two innings. That was my major league debut. Was I scared? Nervous? No, not really. I saw the ballpark full with all those fans for the first time, but I was able to block out the jitters. I don't know what it is with me, maybe an overabundance of tunnel vision. I've always been like that. I can be talking to you about something, and then my mind will drift off to something else, and I'll sit there for the next ten minutes thinking about my topic while you're talking about yours. I won't hear a word you're saying. I hear nothing. I don't know that this is a particularly good habit, or very polite, especially when you're in mixed company. I've excused myself many a time when people are talking to me and then ask me something about what they've just said.

I guess that trait worked well on the pitching mound, though, because I was able to block out all distractions. That day in Brook-lyn, Campy was catching me and I knew we were down by some-thing like 4 runs and I knew what I had to do. Throw strikes. If I didn't do that, Alston wouldn't be too happy. In fact, he'd be furious, because that was his pet peeve. And I still had this other bridge to cross. Just because you were on the final roster of twenty-eight, that didn't mean you'd make the final, *final* roster of twenty-five, after they cut three players a few weeks following the start of the season. I got my feet wet that day, and as time went on, I was used every which way. I was used in long relief, and as a spot starter, and I beat the hated New York Giants four times that season, which was a good way to endear yourselves to the fans of Brooklyn in a hurry. Why I was able to beat the Giants so often, I don't know. I only won five games all year. I was 5–5 but four of those five wins were against our crosstown rivals.

If you were a Dodger fan, that was the ultimate. I even hit my first home run that year, against Max Surkont of the Giants. I was a hero right away. You didn't have to be a rocket scientist to realize that the Dodgers vs. Giants was an extraordinary rivalry. We played each other often—twenty-two times, eleven in each ball-park. When we went to the Polo Grounds, it was full. When the Giants came to Brooklyn, Ebbets Field was rocking. I think Dodger fans hated the Giants more than the Yankees, because they were able to hate the Giants all season. The Giants were like the main course; if we got to play the Yankees in the World Series, that was dessert. The Giants were in our town and in our league, and even though they were down when I got to the big leagues in 1956, there was no lack of emotion. God help you if you ever got knocked out of a game in the Polo Grounds. A visiting pitcher had to walk from the mound all the way to center field, where the clubhouses were located. That's a hell of a road trip under any circumstances, but if you'd just gotten your ears pinned back by the Giants, the last thing you needed to hear was all the abuse from the fans in the Polo Grounds bleachers. It was damn near a 500-foot walk by the time you climbed the stairs and got to the visiting locker room, and the Giants' fans called you every name in the book. It was brutal, yet it was great. If you didn't get up for that, you weren't awake, and it's been three decades since I experienced the Dodgers–Giants rivalry in New York, and I still haven't seen anything vaguely resembling it—anywhere, anytime—in professional sports.

My first major league victory came a couple weeks after Opening Day. It was a chilly Monday night, April 24th, against the Phillies at Connie Mack Stadium. Walt had named me to start against Murry Dickson, who had been around quite a while. He began his major league career with St. Louis in 1939, three years after I was born. At age nineteen, I wasn't the youngest pitcher in the National League—Pittsburgh had a fellow named Art Swanson, who was about three months younger than me. But I was the youngest starter at the time, and I was fortunate enough to win that game, 6–1. I gave up 9 hits, all singles; I struck out 9 and walked 1. The game was scoreless through four innings, then we got 3 runs in the top of the fifth. We went ahead 4–0 in the eighth, then the Phillies scored against me in the bottom of the inning on singles by Frank Baumholtz and Bobby Morgan, followed by Granny Hamner's sacrifice fly. We got another run in the top of the ninth and that was it.

Everybody was terrific to me after the game. Walt mentioned that I had great stuff—"He struck out one of the game's best hitters, Richie Ashburn, who hardly ever strikes out." I had, in fact, struck out Ashburn, who was the Phillies' leadoff batter. I struck out the side in the first inning—Ashburn, Morgan, and Hamner. And Campy said that I was the closest thing he'd ever seen to Ewell Blackwell, which was high praise indeed. Blackwell, who had been

43

called "The Whip" for the way he delivered the ball sidearm, was an outstanding pitcher with the Cincinnati Redlegs before he went over to the American League.

Me? I was excited. Every day was an adventure for me, and this was another new experience. I got back to the hotel and placed another telephone call to Dad and Mom back home in California. Obviously, I wasn't the only one calling Dad. News of my exploits in Philadelphia had been broadcast back to Los Angeles by Bob Kelly, a well-known sportscaster, on KMPC. My friends and family were getting inning-by-inning reports. I've still got that tape stuck somewhere in some closet. Plus, as the years have passed, I've taken some peeks at scrapbooks from my career, and I've noted that a lot of Dad's thoughts appeared in Los Angeles newspapers the day after I won that first game. He was a popular interview that night, and if he was as proud as I was, I'm happy for him, because he contributed a whole lot to my making it in Brooklyn.

About a month later, we were in Pittsburgh and I was slated to start a Memorial Day doubleheader against the Phillies in Philadelphia. The other Dodger pitcher was supposed to be Sal Maglie, a great and grizzled veteran whom Buzzie Bavasi had acquired from the Cleveland Indians for one dollar, the waiver price. Talk about one of the best deals of all time—how about Sal Maglie to Brooklyn for a dollar in 1956? Here was a guy who'd opened the season with the Indians, pitched in only two games for them, then came to the Dodgers and went 13–5. All for a buck.

Anyway, Walt wanted us to get a good night's rest, so he sent Sal and me ahead on the train. It was hotter than blazes, so Maglie and I were perfectly happy to jump into that club car and head toward Philadelphia—Sal with that martini of his, puckering his lips after each sip, and me with my eyes like saucers, just being in his company. I learned a lot about pitching, a lot about baseball, a lot about life from Sal, who was called "The Barber" because when he was on the mound and a batter dug in, he specialized in giving him a close shave.

As soon as Maglie was acquired from Cleveland, The Senator put his locker right next to mine at Ebbets Field, and that was a blessing for me because Sal had a lot of knowledge about the game. Me? I was pretty naive. How naive? Well, on that train ride through the hills of Pennsylvania, with Sal sipping his martinis and me drinking a beer or two, I showed once again just how green I was.

"Geez," I said, "we got a doubleheader tomorrow. Which one are you pitching, Sal, the long one or the short one?"

Maglie just sort of looked at me, took another taste of his drink, and paused, like he was trying to figure out what the hell this kid meant.

"Long one or the short one?" he said. "What are you talking about, son?"

"Well," I said, "we have two games in Philadelphia tomorrow. Do you know which one you're going to start, the long one or the short one? The nine-inning game or the seven-inning game?"

Maglie looked at me for a minute and started laughing.

"Kid," he said, "up here, both games of a doubleheader go nine."

"Really?" I said, dumbfounded. As the rookie in this traveling twosome, I was sort of gearing up to pitch the second game in Philadelphia, the seven-inning game. But Maglie straightened me out. That's the way they did it in the minor leagues, but not in the major leagues.

"Both go nine," Maglie repeated, puckering his lips. Naturally, I felt about an inch tall.

When we got to Philadelphia, it was late in the afternoon and we reported to the Warwick Hotel. We put our bags in the room and headed down for a bite to eat. In those days, we just signed our food bills over to the Dodgers. The major league meal money was something like seventeen dollars or seventeen-fifty, but the Dodgers preferred that we just sign everything over to them—no booze, just meals. Management never quibbled about the amount, at least until the Dodgers started getting a few more players from other teams. I don't know whether they abused the privilege or were just used to the per diem, but the Dodgers changed. The only veteran Dodger I can recall getting in any trouble at all was Campy, who decided to have a little party in his room one Saturday afternoon at Cincinnati. Campy ordered some fancy hors d'oeuvres, and the damage came to something like two hundred dollars. He put his autograph on the room service slip, and caught some grief for it. With the Dodgers, you didn't make a habit of that sort of thing.

At the Warwick Hotel, they had terrific shrimp lamaise. So we enjoyed our meal, and then Sal suggested that we both go out and walk it off before he went to bed. We made a stop and Sal had another martini or two, and then we walked some more and stopped for maybe another drink or two. Before too long, we were both getting tired, so it was time to return to the hotel.

"How do we get back, kid?" Maglie asked.

"You're asking me?" I said. "I don't know my way around Philadelphia. I was just following you."

We wound up taking a taxi back to the Warwick. It was hot as hell again the next day in Philadelphia, but Sal and I made it through our doubleheader. He pitched the first game, and I pitched the second game, and as he promised, they both went nine innings.

During the 1956 season, we were involved in a tense pennant race with the Cincinnati Reds and Milwaukee Braves. It was a fun season, right down to the end. We were home for our final week-end series against the Pittsburgh Pirates. On Friday night, it was damp and foggy on the East Coast, and Jocko Conlan, the veteran umpire, came into our clubhouse at Ebbets Field, trying to figure out what to do.

"This stuff might not lift," he said. "You sure you want to play in this?"

"Heck, no," said Pee Wee Reese. "Call it off. We can play two tomorrow."

The Captain was always thinking. Bobby Bragan, the Pirates' manager, wasn't about to hand anything over to us, even though his team was out of it. He had planned to use Bob Friend, Pittsburgh's ace righthander, in the Friday night game at Brooklyn, then bring him back to start again on Sunday for the last game of the regular season. When our Friday night game was postponed because of fog, we knew we'd only have to look at Friend once, which was a relief, because we'd had a lot of trouble with him.

The next day, Saturday, was a beautiful day in Brooklyn, Ebbets Field was packed, and we beat the Pirates twice. That night I went back home to my apartment—I had moved out of the Bossert Hotel by then—to listen to the broadcast of the Braves' game in St. Louis, where Herm Wehmeier was pitching like there was no tomorrow for the Cardinals and where center fielder Bobby Del Greco was bouncing off walls, making spectacular catches. The tide was turning in favor of us.

The Braves had begun September in first place, with a 2½ game lead on the Dodgers. When Milwaukee went to St. Louis, they still led by a full game and they had their three best starting pitchers lined up for the Cardinals. But Bob Buhl, who absolutely killed us, was knocked out in the first inning of the Friday night game, which the Cardinals won 5–4. That shaved a half-game off Milwaukee's lead over us. Then we went on to sweep the Pirates in Saturday's doubleheader, and we led by a half-game. And then came that Saturday night, when I had my ear to the radio and Warren Spahn, one of the best pitchers ever, was on the mound for the Braves in St. Louis. This was pretty exciting stuff for a rookie like me, even if I was lying on an apartment floor with my ear to a speaker.

Billy Bruton, the Braves' center fielder, homered off Wehmeier in the first inning, but that's about all Milwaukee did with Wehmeier. Spahn, who had a no-hitter going into the sixth inning, gave up a run and it was 1–1 entering extra innings. Del Greco was putting on a clinic in the outfield, chasing down all sorts of potential extra-base hits, and in the end, his big night did the Braves in. The Cardinals scored a run in the twelfth to beat Spahn 2–1, and suddenly, the Braves were one game behind us with one game to go.

On Sunday, we beat the Pirates again at Ebbets Field 8–6 with Don Newcombe pitching and Sandy Amoros hitting a couple home runs, and we clinched the pennant. The Braves and Lew Burdette finally beat the Cardinals 4–2 in St. Louis, but it was too late. The Reds? By the last weekend, they weren't even in it, and that was a team that set a National League record by hitting 221 home runs. They had Roy McMillan, Smokey Burgess, Wally Post, Gus Bell, Ted Kluszewski, Frank Robinson, Ed Bailey, Ray Jablonski—an awesome lineup. They looked like the Chicago Bears football team, they were so physically impressive, and they won 91 games, but they wound up finishing in third place.

I witnessed some memorable feats during my rookie year in 1956. I saw Sal Maglie pitch a no-hitter against the Phillies. I saw Carl Erskine pitch a no-hitter against the Giants. And, of course, I saw Don Larsen of the Yankees pitch the perfect game against us in the World Series. We won the first two games of the Series at Ebbets Field, 6–3 and 13–8. Maglie won the opener, and Bessent won the second game in relief of Newcombe. But the Yankees beat

Roger Craig 5–3 in Game Three at Yankee Stadium. They beat Erskine 6–2 in Game Four, when I made my first World Series appearance—two innings of relief, 2 runs and 2 hits allowed. Then, on a Monday afternoon in Yankee Stadium, Larsen made World Series history with his 2–0 victory over Maglie in Game Five. We got no runs, no hits, no nothing—the first no-hitter in World Series history, and obviously, the first perfect game. Maglie was super, but Larsen, working from that no-windup delivery of his, was even better.

I guess I should have been in awe of Larsen's accomplishment, and it was special. But, as I sat there among my teammates, there never was a thought that day that we were out of the ballgame by any means. Larsen had great stuff, but we had a great lineup. It was only a 2–0 game, and all the Dodgers needed was to get a man on base and then have somebody hit one out. We certainly had the capability to turn around a ballgame, just like that. But it never happened that day. I was impressed by what I was seeing, no question about that. It was quite a thing to be in Yankee Stadium for the World Series during my rookie year against Mickey Mantle and Yogi Berra and all that gang. But we were there on business. And even though we were close enough to drive home after the game, we were definitely the outsiders in Yankee Stadium. The Dodgers were the enemies.

Clem Labine, a relief pitcher by trade, started and beat Bob Turley 1–0 in a great ten-inning pitching duel at Ebbets Field in Game Six, but we couldn't do anything with Johnny Kucks the next day and the Yankees went after Newk and beat us 9–0. That was pretty tough to take, losing the World Series to the Yankees in our own ballpark after we had taken the first two games. But for this wide-eyed kid out of California, it was still quite a year. My parents came to New York for the World Series; that was their rookie appearance on an airplane. They were as much in awe of the big city as I was, and when the President of the United States, Dwight Eisenhower, showed up at Ebbets Field to throw out the first ball before Game One, Dad and Mom were quite impressed. They snapped a whole bunch of pictures that are still part of the family scrapbook.

My folks drove my spanking new 1956 Chevrolet back to California. Meanwhile, right after the World Series, the Dodgers flew to the West Coast and then on to Japan for a series of exhibition games. We spent one night in California in a hotel, and another week in Honolulu playing a few games against the Hawaiian All-Stars. I had a no-hitter working in one game at the Fairgrounds in Maui, but Walt took me out after seven innings and brought Ralph Branca in to finish up. That was the first time I'd ever been taken out of a no-hitter, not that I was upset about it.

"Can't worry about no-hitters here," Walt said with a laugh. "We've got to get all our pitchers some work. Besides, they should have had a couple hits off you. You've been pretty lucky."

The trip seemed to be a series of eight-hour segments in a Pan Am DC-7C, which must have been the biggest plane we could get at the time. From New York to Los Angeles was eight hours, from Los Angeles to Honolulu the same, and it was eight hours from Honolulu to Wake Island, where we had to stop for refueling so we could take another eight-hour trip to Japan. On top of all this, our plane busted its nose gear landing at Wake Island because of all the weight we were carrying. So we had to wait for another nose gear to be flown in from Honolulu and that took—you guessed it—eight hours.

There wasn't much for us to do at Wake Island except sit around the Clipper Club, which was for Pan Am employees. They opened it up to us, and that was about it. It was unbelievable, as though World War II had ended yesterday. There were still tanks and trucks overturned and boats in the bay and propellers and tail sections of airplanes lying on the beach. It looked like a movie set. They had just left it that way after the war. In fact, they wouldn't allow anybody to go through the jungle there without a guide because there were still Japanese mines in place. They didn't know where they were; they just knew they were out there somewhere.

It was so damn hot in the Clipper Club that we vacated after a while, and Pee Wee led an expedition down to the beach, where he took off his pants and went into the water wearing only his shorts. Pee Wee wanted to take a swim to cool off, which didn't seem like a bad idea. Pretty soon, the rest of us were about to join in when we saw some guy running toward us, yelling at the top of his lungs. We couldn't make out what he was saying, until he got real close. Then we could hear very clearly.

"Sharks!" he was screaming. *"Get out of the water! There are sharks in there!"*

Well, I never saw our captain, Pee Wee Reese, move any faster

49

than he did that afternoon. Wouldn't that have been some head-line? "Brooklyn Dodgers Wiped Out by Sharks on Way to Japan." Enough lives had already been lost on this little piece of land, this horseshoe-shaped island out there in the middle of nowhere. It had been a very strategic refueling stop for aircraft during the war and there we were, trying to cool off while waiting for a nose gear to arrive.

When we finally reached Tokyo, we each received $500 worth of yen, which was like trying to jam a softball into your pocket. It was a huge wad. Each of us also had a blue ribbon pinned on us with some Japanese writing across it. None of us could figure out what the writing meant, but after about three days of moving about the city, buying this and that, we had a pretty good idea. All the other players I talked to were just about broke, almost out of yen, like I was. We decided that the printing on the ribbons must have read: "These are the Brooklyn Dodgers . . . charge them whatever you can get."

One of the first functions of our trip was a big cocktail recep-tion hosted by Gen. Lyman Lemnetzer then commander-in-chief of the Pacific, at a beautiful home. We'd each been given a silk kimono to wear—I still have it hanging in my closet—and a little headband. Much as we were supposed to feel at home, there were always some local customs that kind of jumped up at you, espe-cially at a kid like me. Lo and behold, I was in the bathroom during this particular reception and headed right for a urinal. I thought everything was okay, until I was just about done. Then I turned my head, and out from adjoining stalls came Mrs. Evit Bavasi and Mrs. Thompson—the wives of Buzzie and Fresco, two of the ballclub's vice-presidents. Well, I about died. Talk about an awkward situa-tion. We weren't even sure which of us was in the wrong place. I figured out I couldn't have been too far wrong, because there was a urinal in the bathroom. That didn't mean I wasn't shaking in my kimono. Finally, we all figured out that we were all right. They had coed bathrooms over there. I sort of tiptoed back to the party and passed the word around to the guys—watch out!

We stayed over in Japan for just about a month and things didn't start out too well. We lost two of the first three games to the Japanese teams. At this point, our owner, Walter O'Malley, gave Walt a call. They had a meeting during which O'Malley apparently read the riot act to Walt, who in turn read the riot act to us.

"I'm just repeating what Mr. O'Malley said," Walt told us. "He said that some of you guys might think you've had a pretty good year because you won a National League pennant. And some of you guys think you might get raises because of it. Well, fellas, Mr. O'Malley said, 'No way.' Some of you guys might wind up taking cuts if you don't do anything more than you've done over here so far."

At the time, there was considerable pressure on us to play well and win. The Yankees had been there before us, and had done real well, and I'm sure Mr. O'Malley expected the same, which was understandable. We were representing the United States and the National League and Brooklyn and the proud name of the Dodgers. He didn't want us over there thinking we were just on some paid holiday. The idea of a group of American professionals going over to Japan and losing in those days was unthinkable. It still would be in the late 1980s, and the Japanese leagues and players were nowhere near as good then as they are now.

Needless to say, we didn't lose another game after Mr. O'Malley's warning. After losing the World Series the way we did, and traveling halfway around the world, we really didn't need to play any more baseball games, but it was an experience. Carl Furillo wasn't there to sample it, though. Skoonj had put his foot down and said no. Absolutely, no. He said he'd fought the Japanese in the war and he wasn't about to go back there and play baseball games against them. When Carl put his mind to something, you weren't about to change it. He was stubborn, like a pit bull, and when he said he didn't care what the Dodgers did with him, he meant it. As it turned out, they did nothing.

We had a good time. We each received $2,500 and the State Department declared it tax-free, which was nice. A few of the married players took their wives all the way to Japan; a few took their wives as far as Hawaii and rejoined them when we returned to the States. I went solo and had a terrific time. Combined with my salary from the regular season, I was pulling in $9,000—more money than I knew what to do with at that stage in my young life. Then there was the World Series share of $6,934.34 per man—a record loser's share—which was more than my base salary.

My spring training roommate, Jim Gentile, a big first baseman who had hit 40 home runs for the Dodgers' farm club at Fort Worth, was on the trip. He was pounding the ball pretty well over in Japan, too, except for this one day when a tiny Japanese left-hander—don't ask me his name—tied Gentile in knots with junk and struck him out four times. Well, I knew Gentile would be fuming that night, so I called him from the lobby of our hotel, pretending to be a native newspaper reporter.

"You hit no home runs today, please?" I said.

Gentile screamed something into the phone about how you can't hit a home run every day, for goodness sakes.

"The Japanese left-handed pitcher," I went on, "the slow curve, that the reason, please?"

Well, I could just about feel the back of Gentile's neck getting redder, but I kept it up for a few more minutes. Then I said thank you, please, for the interview, and hung up. I couldn't wait to get up to the room, where Gentile was pacing like a caged lion.

"What's the problem?" I said with a straight face.

"*$%&**^! Japanese newspaper reporters!" Gentile yelled at the top of his lungs.

I pitched a bit in Japan, until I pulled a groin muscle on a wet field. You had to play over there, no matter what. You didn't have games called because of bad weather or fog, like we did in Brooklyn during the pennant race. We had 60,000 or so people sitting in the stands at Osaka one day, waiting for us to play a game on an all-dirt field. Jocko Conlan, who had gone over with us, was in charge of the game and after watching a steady drizzle fall for a while, he looked up and yelled out in that shrill voice of his, "That's it! Let's get out of here. We don't play in this rain."

Well, that's when Jocko found out who was really in charge of the game. Those 60,000 people didn't move from their seats. They never said a word, but they didn't budge. We took Jocko's cue and went back into the clubhouse. Pretty soon, though, some Japanese officials dropped by with a couple of interpreters and after a little bit of negotiating, we were instructed to put our uniforms on again. We went back out and played the game, rain or no rain. The fans were terrific. We packed 'em in wherever we played. And we contributed quite a bit to their economy. Japanese tailors would come right up to your hotel room and fit you for a suit. I bought one all-wool job that I decided to wear on the trip home, which I extended to Georgia, where I went to visit Randy Jackson, our third baseman. I was single then. I had no responsibilities, and nothing better to do than to spend thirty-two hours on an airplane—four eight-hour legs. When I got off that plane in Atlanta, the pants on my brand-new suit were sagging a bit. I don't think I ever wore it again.

I bought everything in duplicate, except for that suit. I bought a set of China for myself—why, I have no idea—and another for my mom. I bought a camera for myself, and another for my dad. And so on. I was the typical tourist and the typical rookie, I guess. Two years after leaving California for the first time in my life, there I was, wearing my kimono and buying fine China in Tokyo as a member of the Brooklyn Dodgers. Like I've said, every day was a new adventure. I couldn't possibly have gotten the education I was getting in baseball if I'd decided to go to school.

There was no doubt in my mind then that I'd done the right thing. There's never been a doubt since.

5

A True Blue Dodger

I don't know what I did to deserve becoming a professional baseball player with the Brooklyn Dodgers, but I feel blessed that it happened. I can't remember once feeling like an outsider, even during my rookie year. There was that one time when a group of veterans found me drinking a fifteen-cent beer in Miami. I felt as though I should leave, but they wouldn't let me, and that was the Dodgers.

Just by sitting around and listening to those great veterans talk baseball, you had to learn the game. If you didn't it was because you didn't want to. Simple as that. In Philadelphia, where I won my first game, the visiting clubhouse attendant always presided over a cooler that was well stocked with Schlitz beer, with a few cans of orange and grape drink on the side. A few years ago, I was back in Philadelphia and I saw him—"Ace" was his name—and he brought me inside to his cooler.

"Look at this," he said. "You don't think times have changed?"

Had they ever. The cooler was three-quarters orange and grape drink, with only a few cans of beer. I suppose that proves that the players nowadays don't drink as much alcohol, which is good in a way. It also shows me that these modern players don't hang around the clubhouse and talk baseball the way they used to, which I think is bad. Not only bad, but sad. Now that I'm broadcasting on a daily basis, I can sense that without having to look inside a beer cooler. All I have to do is peek inside a locker room after a game. Some nights, it's like a fire drill. Players rush to take off their uniforms, and rush into the shower, and then rush to get on the team bus headed back to the hotel, or into their private cars. That wouldn't have worked with the old Brooklyn Dodgers that I knew. You wouldn't have wanted it to. The routine in those days was to sit around and chew the fat, before and after games, hashing over the game you just played or were about to play. There was a lot of conversation about baseball, but you don't hear that anymore. I don't know what these players talk about today, but I don't think it's baseball.

For a kid like me, of course, just pulling up a seat next to the Sniders and Robinsons and Campanellas and tuning in was a thrill. Plus, I had the added benefit of having Gil Hodges as my first roommate on the road. When you roomed with Gil, it felt like you were rooming with a saint. He was not only the most impressive person you could ever want to meet, he treated you like an equal. I always had the entree of being Gil's roomie, which meant Gil was in a way always looking after me. If I ever thought about not joining him and the other veterans for dinner or whatever, he would have none of it.

"C'mon, let's go," he'd say. "You're not staying behind. You're going with me." Or, "You're going with us."

Even if I was a tag-along, he never treated me that way. If we showed up and there was a table for four, and it was obvious that I was the fifth, no problem. Gil or one of the other guys would simply go get another chair, and we'd all of a sudden be sitting at a table for five for dinner instead of for four. None of the Dodgers ever treated each other like anything but equals, like friends, like teammates. If there was ever any animosity or hard feelings between one player or another, you never felt it because there was too much professional respect to allow grudges to interfere.

Even when there was criticism, it was the constructive type. For instance, I had established myself as a sidearm pitcher—a pitcher who dropped his arm down and delivered from there, rather than over the top, because it just felt natural to me. It wasn't conventional, but it was comfortable. Well, on our trip to Japan after the 1956 season, Al Campanis took me over to the side one day and started working with me on an overhand curveball, which was something of a Dodger tradition. That was a pitch Dodgers were taught, and even though it was difficult for me—because I had that unorthodox motion—Campanis tried, which was fine.

But I was having a heck of a time with it, because I just couldn't get up there. It was too unnatural for me, and watching me struggle on the sidelines one day, Clem Labine and Campanella dropped over and voiced their opinions. Basically, what they told Campanis was, "Al, he's doing just fine the way he is. Let him throw the way he's used to throwing. Don't change him." That was the last of my overhand curveball experiment. I could throw three-quarters to overhand, but I was also a "hooker"—that's the term used for a pitcher who brings the ball back and then cocks his wrist before starting into his release. One of the old baseball saws is that hookers don't last long, if they succeed at all, but if that was the case, I'd have never won a game, and Bob Gibson of the St. Louis Cardinals wouldn't have, either. Or Jim Bunning, who was a pretty fair pitcher for the Detroit Tigers and Philadelphia Phillies. Or, these days, Rick Sutcliffe, who was Rookie of the Year with the Dodgers in 1979 and won a Cy Young for the Chicago Cubs in 1984.

Pitching is like hitting is like broadcasting. You've got to be you. You can't copy somebody, because when you do and a new situation arises, you find yourself wondering what the person you're trying to copy would do instead of what *you* should do. It isn't that complicated. If you are a pitcher, you have to throw strikes. The Dodgers had a simple device in training camp to help pitchers with their control—the "pitching strings." They were just strings with slip-knots that you threw at to work on throwing to spots. You could adjust the strings to approximate the exact width of home plate and the strike zone, or you could narrow the strings if you wanted to zero in on the outside of the plate, or the inside. It was a great idea handed down from Branch Rickey, but if you ask a lot of baseball people nowadays about "pitching strings," they have no idea what you're talking about.

Another Rickey device was the big black tarpaulin with holes cut in it. It looked like the kind of thing you would throw beanbags at, except that it was for baseballs. The concept was to throw baseballs at the hole that was cut out an inch or two from the plate, or an inch or two below. Then there was one hole for the pitch right down the middle. You could stand out there by yourself, without a catcher, and work on your control for however long you wanted. You'd throw at the holes in the tarp, which was backed up by another big black tarp. You'd get a bunch of balls, and when you'd used them all up, you'd go to the base of the tarp and collect them and start all over again. If it doesn't sound very complex, it wasn't. But it got the job done.

I was what they call a "power pitcher" as a kid with the Dodgers. In 1957, I was clocked at having a fastball of 94 or 95 miles per hour—right there with Sandy Koufax. That might seem exceptional, but for as long as I can remember, the National League has had hard throwers and that period was no different. Bob Gibson in St. Louis, Chris Short, Dick Farrell, and Jack Sanford in Philadelphia, Bob Veale in Pittsburgh, Juan Marichal and Bobby Bolin with the Giants—those were just a few of the flame-throwers during my era. There were others, of course. There were always guys coming up to the National League and throwing smoke. Why there were more hard throwers in the National League than the American League, I don't know. But that's still the case.

One of the best early lessons I got about pitching was from Maglie on how to move a batter off the plate. There were many times when I'd be out on the mound during a ballgame, and I'd peer into the dugout, looking for The Barber. And there he was, giving me a little nod or whistling. That meant it was time to send a "message" to the batter. We talked by the hour about his philosophy of keeping hitters honest, and by the time 1957 rolled around, when I'd had one whole year in the big leagues, I was developing the same ideas as Sal.

Maglie's main contention was that an opposing batter would tip off what he was thinking by the movement of his feet. Pitching and hitting are pretty much the art of deception and outguessing, and if you had an edge in that battle waged sixty feet, six inches apart, you had darn well better exploit it. Sal's theory was, of course, based on the premise that a pitcher had to have decent control—a sound premise, because if you didn't have a pretty good idea where the ball was going, you weren't going to last long in the majors anyway.

Maglie had good enough control to be able to waste a pitch when he was in doubt about what the batter was thinking. For instance, he might throw a ball low and away. Now, he knew it would be called a ball, but immediately after he delivered, he watched the batter's feet. If the batter was stepping in toward the plate, Sal knew he was expecting a pitch out there. If the batter opened up and pulled off the plate a bit, Sal knew he was thinking that the pitch would be inside. So, that gave Maglie an edge. That was one of Sal's little clues—the batter's feet.

The other thing Maglie did was to make sure not to throw just one pitch inside if he was trying to move a batter off the plate. Sal threw two, just for good measure. Again, another sound principle. For instance, let's say Maglie had a no-ball, 2-strike count on a batter. You knew where the next pitch was headed. Sal would brush the guy back, the count would be 1–2, and the batter would think to himself, Well, Maglie's got that out of his system.

But The Barber just might *not* have gotten it out of his system. Maglie would come right back inside on the next pitch. It would be another ball, and the count would now be 2–2, which would seem a lot better for the batter than being behind 0–2. But that didn't bother Maglie. He had such good control, he always felt that he was in command. Who it bothered was the batter, who didn't know what to think because he had no idea what Maglie was up to next. Inside again? Low and away? Fastball? Breaking ball? Now the plate was looking a lot bigger to that batter. He had a lot more to guard against.

I can't say that I was completely new to this business of keeping a batter off-balance at the plate. I'd never thought about it until I reached professional baseball, true, but when I got to Montreal, I observed Lasorda, who would knock his mother off the plate if he had to. And I had Johnny Bucha catching me; I mentioned he was as hard as nails. What being around Maglie did for me, though, was to confirm this idea in my mind and refine it. It was part of the game. I watched Maglie, I listened to Maglie, and it all sunk in. It just sort of clicked. I never said much. I didn't have to. I just listened.

Often, after I pitched a game, we would sit in the locker room or on the train and go over my pitch selection. Sal had a great knack of remembering pitches, even though he wasn't the guy on the mound.

"You remember when it was two-and-one on so-and-so?" he'd say. "Why did you throw what you did there? What were you thinking about?"

"Well," I'd reply. "I wanted to get the count back to two-two. I didn't want to fall behind three-and-one."

"Yeah," Sal'd say, "but if you don't throw a good pitch there, the count won't get to two-two anyway, because the ball is going to be hit. You've got to throw *your* pitch—Not the batter's pitch."

Of course, Maglie was exactly right. Those were things you had to think about. I don't know that all the pitchers with the Dodgers at the time followed Maglie's line of thought. For one thing, several were veterans and more set in their ways. Don Newcombe was 27–7 in 1956. It's not like he needed a lot of help. When he had his control with his hard stuff—which he needed, because he didn't have that great a breaking ball—Newk was as good as anybody. And he'd just as soon knock you down as look at you, too.

Another thing in my favor was that my locker stood next to Maglie's. He knew I was eager to learn and listen and whenever we had some free time, I'd pull up a stool and go to school with Sal the Professor. Was he mean? Oh, my God, yes. When he was on the mound, Sal Maglie was mean. Did he make me mean? I don't know about that. But I do know that, after spending time with him, I decided I wasn't going to let any batters get in the way of my winning a ballgame if at all possible. I wasn't going to win every game, I knew that. But I was sure as heck going to try, and I wasn't going to let a guy beat me. If a batter beat me fair and square, that was one thing. But I wasn't going to do anybody any favors. It naturally followed, of course, that you not only protected the plate, but your hitters, too. If you pitched for the Dodgers, you protected the Dodgers. There was an element of selfishness in that, of course. If the guys in the regular lineup knew you were going to look after them, they would bust their butts to look after you.

"How do you feel about knocking down a batter?" Hodges asked me one day.

"I'll do it, sure," I said. "You have to make the guys on the other team respect you."

"But wouldn't you feel bad if you hit a guy in the head and hurt him?" Hodges went on.

"Nope," I answered.

"Well," said Hodges, "what about if you hit a guy in the head with a baseball and killed him? Would you regret that?"

"Nope," I said. "I wouldn't at all."

Hodges walked away, convinced that I was some kind of killer.

Actually, I had just wanted to put one over on him for a change. As the veteran rooming with a kid, he was forever playing mind games with me—harmless pranks. There was a bit of truth to what I said about being willing to knock a guy down—though not about wanting to hurt anyone—but I thought I'd try to have some honest fun at Gil's expense for a change. I think it worked.

For the 1957 season, I made $7,500—that was a $1,000 raise that actually turned out to be a cut. There was no trip to Japan and, unfortunately, there was no World Series, either.

I had a terrible spring training. Why, I don't know. I just couldn't get anybody out. Toward the end of the exhibition schedule, we were doing our usual barnstorming. This time, we were in Oklahoma City, heading toward Wichita, to play the Braves. We were short on players, because Maglie, Newcombe, Furillo, and Junior Gilliam wouldn't fly. In those days, don't forget, the train was still the way to go. St. Louis was the farthest west we went, and that was our toughest trip. It meant going through Chicago, where, if we didn't stay to play the Cubs, we would have to change trains anyway. There was a little more space in the schedule then, too. We played a lot of Sunday doubleheaders and had a lot of Mondays and Thursdays off, so that allowed for some longer train rides, although we did tend to fly back to Brooklyn quite often from road trips.

Anyway, there we were in Oklahoma City and Walt was a little strapped for players.

"Anybody around here who can pitch and wants to?" he asked.

I couldn't have done any worse than I had been doing, so I started against the Braves and shut them out, 4–0. It was my best game of the spring, the best of a bad lot, and that got me back in the groove. I had had bad rhythm, and I'd been making bad pitches, but it came together in that one game against the Braves. I wound up having a real good season. I won 17 games, lost 9, and finished with an earned run average of 2.69. Podres, who had returned from his year in the service, came back in a big way and led the National League with a 2.66 ERA.

But 1957 belonged to the Milwaukee Braves, who had a terrific ballclub, solid from top to bottom. Their pitching staff consisted of Spahn, Burdette, and Buhl as the big three, plus they had Don McMahon in the bullpen. Talk about a guy who threw bullets.

The everyday lineup featured Hank Aaron and Eddie Mathews and Joe Adcock and Johnny Logan and Del Crandall and Billy Bruton and Wes Covington. Then, just at the June 15th trading deadline, the Braves went out and got the last piece to their puzzle—Red Schoendienst, a smooth second baseman from the New York Giants. He hit over .300 for the Braves that year, and played a great second base for them. You watched him play there, and you swore he was playing a different game. He would shade Campy way over toward the bag, and darned if Campy didn't hit a shot right through the pitcher's box to where Schoendienst was playing. You just couldn't play batters any better than he did, and it didn't hurt that the Braves' pitchers were so good at putting the ball where they wanted it. In August, the Braves mounted a ten-game winning streak and ran off and hid.

So, 1957 proved to me that you can't win every year, even if you were a Brooklyn Dodger. I had my eyes opened in another respect, and that involved Jackie Robinson. I only spent one year with Jackie, 1956, because during that winter, the Dodgers traded him to the Giants. I should say, the Dodgers *tried* to trade him. But Jackie refused and instead retired to take a job with Chock Full 'O Nuts Coffee. I never talked to Jackie about it at the time, but in later years, I ran into him on occasion and I think it hurt him. Jackie had taken a lot of abuse to become the first black ballplayer in the major leagues, and being traded from the Brooklyn Dodgers to our arch-rivals probably was the last straw, a slap in the face.

From the first moment I met Jackie Robinson, I could see that he was an awfully intense man. I could also see the frustrations he had to endure, and the battle scars. Wherever he went, Jackie had to put up with more insults, and he always had to walk that fine line—he had to keep a stiff upper lip, which is why Mr. Rickey had handpicked him, because of Jackie's strong personality and even temperament. Yet, no matter how much crap he took, Jackie had to maintain his competitive edge. Jackie was uniquely qualified. I don't know of anybody else who could have done what he did. There was no crawling out from under a rock for Jackie. He had to be aggressive at all times, because that was his style. And yet, he had to sit there and take a lot of crap. Try that sometime.

A lot of the South wasn't integrated, so Jackie had to put up with problems right from the start of spring training. At Holman Stadium in Vero Beach, there were restrooms for whites and for "colored." The blacks also had to entertain themselves in a nearby town, Gifford, which was black. And the blacks couldn't stay with us at our Miami headquarters, the MacAlister Hotel. But when we took a train through some town where blacks weren't permitted to stay at our hotel, Buzzie Bavasi made sure that we stayed together, anyway. The two or three sleeping cars that were taking the Dodgers to wherever, were just taken off the train and we slept overnight in the trainyard. It was no big deal to the rest of us, and it kept the team together.

I'll never forget a trip we took to New Orleans, where we played an exhibition game in Pelican Stadium. The seats were really close to the action there, and Jackie had an earful. The fans called him the worst possible names, and about the most polite thing I heard was "Gator Bait." It was brutal, and I was always braced for an incident of some sort. If there was a fight involving Jackie, I was damn well sure going to get in there and back him up. But there again, Jackie had to be strong. He had an unbelievable tolerance for aggravation, and who is to say whether stress didn't contribute to Jackie's health problems later on.

We had a few Southerners on our team—Rube Walker and Roger Craig from North Carolina, Don Bessent from Florida, Pee Wee Reese from Louisville—but everybody realized that in Jackie, we had a hell of ballplayer on our team. There was never any problem from within, and if there was, I never knew about it. Knowing Pee Wee, who'd set the record straight on where he stood, he'd have squashed it, anyway. When Reese made it known that he was all for Jackie, that was that.

The rest of the National League got the message that Jackie was here to stay as soon as he broke in, and I heard a fair share of stories about his intensity and drive. But the one I saw in person my only year as Jackie's teammate occurred against the Pirates at Pittsburgh's Forbes Field. Robinson was on first base, running on a line drive to the alley that was chased down by Robert Clemente, the Pirates' great right fielder. He threw in to Bill Mazeroski, the Pirates' second baseman and relay man on the play. When Mazeroski got the ball and turned toward the infield, Jackie had made the turn at third base and was just sort of dancing there. Mazeroski cocked his hand, as if to throw, and Jackie took one step toward the plate—then another step, then another. Mazeroski was glaring at Jackie, holding the ball, and finally, Mazeroski dropped his hands. At that exact moment, Jackie broke for home and scored, beating Mazeroski's throw. It was a great play, a daring play that only Jackie could have manufactured, and I doubt that Mazeroski's ever forgotten it.

That was vintage Jackie. He kept other teams back on their heels. He wanted to beat the other team in the worst way, and he would do it any way possible. I loved just watching Jackie because you could see him getting pumped up. If he could take an inch, he'd take a mile, and I decided early on that here was one guy I was happy to have on my team. Off the field, Jackie kept to himself pretty much. He roomed with Junior Gilliam, who was always raving about how much he learned by just listening to Robinson. When he was around, Jackie was always friendly and like so many of the other veterans, he loved to agitate in his own way. As focused as he was on his job, or his mission, Jackie had a good sense of humor and the ability to laugh. He was also an excellent card player. If he ever relaxed or let his hair down, it was probably when he was playing cards with the rest of the guys.

Walt Alston, to his credit, treated Jackie Robinson just like any other ballplayer. There was a time during an exhibition spin in Louisville when Walt was playing Don Hoak at third base instead of Jackie. Jackie got upset about it, and Alston really let him have it. Roy Campanella, smelling a bit of a problem, went over to Jackie and told him to take it easy. That would have been some confrontation—Walt Alston and Jackie Robinson. Talk about two tough, stubborn SOBs. But it never got to that, of course. Great as he was, Jackie was the ballplayer and Walt was our boss. Alston had to be as happy as the rest of us that Jackie was wearing a Dodger uniform. I only wish that Jackie had worn it longer. He wasn't around after my rookie season. He wasn't around long enough, period. Jackie suffered from diabetes and died at age fifty-three. When they talk about players who had an impact on the game, Jackie is always right there at the top. He did it first and he did it well and who is to say what would have happened had Jackie Robinson not been able to handle the huge task that Mr. Rickey assigned to him? We're certainly not living in a perfect world nowadays, but it's hard to imagine some of the cruel and inhuman things that were accepted even thirty or so years ago. Jackie Robinson looked them all in the eye and went out to play ball. Did he ever play ball.

From a personal standpoint, it was a terrific season. I finally became fully acclimated to the big leagues. I had bought my first new car in Brooklyn, and then I got my first set of golf clubs—brand new from Spalding, with whom I'd signed a promotional contract. I got two free pairs of shoes and golf clubs. That was high cotton. The other guys on the team were always talking about golf, but I could never quite figure it out. I'd look around Brooklyn and think to myself, Where the heck do you play golf around here? I don't see any courses. I wound up keeping the clubs in my apartment and bringing them back to California.

I was in the starting rotation by then, with Newk, Erskine, Podres, and Craig. Maglie wasn't around at the finish. He left us late in the 1957 season for the Yankees. It was a heck of a jump for me, going from 5 victories to 17, but we didn't win the pennant and whenever you win 17 games, you know you must have made a few stupid mistakes that cost you a chance to win 20—which I did. There was one of those games we played at Jersey City when I got beaten after Harry Anderson of the Phillies tied the game in the ninth inning with a wind-blown home run.

I wasn't too happy about that, and I wasn't too thrilled when the telephone woke me up the next morning.

"This is Buzzie," the voice said. "What are you doing?"

"I'm sleeping," I answered. "What did you think I was doing?"

"I'm sorry," Buzzie went on. "But I want you to go over to ten Whitehall Street. You're going in the Army."

"Jesus," I said, "the ball was right by the foul pole and Furillo was right over there and . . ."

By then, Buzzie was laughing.

"Relax," he said. "It has nothing to do with last night's ballgame. You and Sandy are going to be drafted if you don't enter the six-month program."

So, Koufax and I both went over there and got our papers. We were destined for the Army Reserves at Fort Dix, New Jersey, that off-season. That was the winter I first saw snow, another new experience for this kid from the West Coast. Sandy, who was from Brooklyn, actually had to teach me how to walk all over again when there was a coating of snow or a sheet of ice. I was constantly slipping. If it hadn't been for Sandy, I'd have spent that entire off-season flat on my butt. But those six months were good for me. When you wake up at three-thirty every morning, and you realize that some of your buddies are just getting in back home, it teaches you a lot of discipline. The service should be mandatory for every kid in America. You thought you were hot stuff being a major league pitcher, and then you went to Fort Dix and found out that it didn't matter who you were. There were no exceptions.

Besides all the other adjustments I had to make, that was another big change—the weather on the East Coast. In California, when you wake up in the morning and the sun's out, you just figure it's going to be that way all day. And it usually is. In Brooklyn, it was different. It could have rained in the morning, and by three o'clock in the afternoon, I might have been sitting outside in my little backyard getting some sun, pretending that I was back home in the Valley. I never could figure out how people lived that way, not knowing from one hour to the next what the weather was going to be. And the humidity! There was one day in Ebbets Field when it was so sticky that I had to leave a ballgame after the fourth inning because I was about to have heat stroke. I didn't have a pound to spare then, and on this particular day, I not only was working on the mound, but I had to run the bases a bit. When I came back to the dugout, my eyes were fluttering like slot machines. So, the doctor made sure I was out of there—with a lead and only one inning to go before I would be credited with a win! You knew it had to be hot and humid for me to allow that.

It was toward the end of boot camp that we first heard the big news. We were in the mess hall one day when somebody ran up to us and said, "Well, it's official. You guys are moving."

Naive as I was, I didn't know what the guy was talking about. I thought he meant that Sandy and I were moving to another post or something.

"No," the guy said. "The team's moving. The Dodgers are moving from Brooklyn. The Dodgers are moving to Los Angeles."

Well, I was speechless. I used to read the papers pretty regularly and I remembered some stories about the problems Walter O'Malley was having in getting a new stadium built for the Dodgers in Brooklyn. He wanted a ballpark downtown, but the borough officials said he couldn't have it there because it was right in the middle of everything. Right in the produce center and by the railroad station. So, there were some troubles between the management of the ballclub and Brooklyn's civic leaders. But if there was ever a real threat that the Dodgers were actually contemplating a move to Los Angeles, I missed it. At the time I heard it, I thought to myself that this had to be the best-kept secret since Pearl Harbor.

For the record, Danny McDevitt, a young lefthander, shut out the Pirates 2–0 in what turned out to be our last game at Ebbets Field. Gladys Gooding played "Auld Lang Syne," and the few fans who were there—maybe 7,000—were in a melancholy mood. I remember them running onto the field in search of keepsakes, souvenirs, even clumps of grass. Yet, even so, I really didn't acknowledge the possibility that we wouldn't be back there. It sounds strange, I know, but this was Brooklyn and these were the Dodgers. Who would have ever thought of actually moving the Dodgers out of Brooklyn? My second home? My home away from home?

My first consideration was that I was going to my first home, California. But beyond that, I thought about Brooklyn. What about all those people who lived and died with the Dodgers? How were they going to feel about this? And all those friends I'd made in Brooklyn. I might never see them again. It was a very emotional time for me. It was an emotional time for all of us. But I don't think it really sunk in until the next year when we didn't go back to Brooklyn. Maybe I didn't want it to sink in. Maybe that's what it was.

We went to Vero Beach, like we always did, for spring training. But you knew something was strange and different as soon as you put on your uniform. There was an "LA" on the front of the cap. The "B" was gone forever. No more Brooklyn, which was hard to believe for this kid from California, and hard to take. I'll never forget that place. And I'll remember it the way it was, with a great old ballpark, Ebbets Field, not with a bunch of apartments that look like a penitentiary.

6

California Dreaming?

*E*ven though I was born and raised in California, I was like most of my Dodger teammates at the start of the 1958 season—I didn't quite know what to make of this new address of ours, Los Angeles. I had been to the LA Coliseum a few times to watch football games—the Rams, USC, UCLA—and that's exactly what the Coliseum was designed for—football. It was not a baseball stadium, it isn't now, and it never will be.

Actually, we opened the regular schedule up the coast in San Francisco against the Giants, whose owner, Horace Stoneham, had taken his franchise out of New York when Mr. O'Malley pulled the Dodgers out of Brooklyn. We played the Giants at Seals Stadium, a minor league ballpark, and I established a couple of precedents for the Dodgers that day. I was the first man ever to pitch a game for them as a member of the Los Angeles team, and the first man ever to lose a game. I went up against Ruben Gomez of the Giants and we got whipped 8–0 before 23,448 fans—which was absolute capacity for Seals Stadium. The next day we got our first win as the Los Angeles Dodgers, 13–1, but the Giants beat Newk the next day in the rubber game of the first-ever California series.

Later in my career, I would also start and win the first World Series game in California and the first All-Star game, but I wasn't in either fall-classic or midsummer form for Opening Day, 1958. In fact, when I look back on it, 1958 was one totally screwed-up season. It was a wasted summer, really.

All of the veteran Dodgers who had become so accustomed to Brooklyn were at sea in Southern California. I tried to help, and so did Duke Snider, another native, but most of the guys were understandably lost. Guys like Gil had their families rooted in Brooklyn and they stayed there until summer, when school was out and the kids could come west. He wound up living for a spell downtown. Most of the other Dodgers spread out wherever they could find a place to call home. It was like they'd been dropped from an airplane into this strange and foreign land, Southern California, which wasn't nearly as crowded as it is today. But it was still a lot easier to find your way around Brooklyn than Los Angeles, and my teammates were forever asking the same questions.

"Where's a good place to live?" "Where are the good schools?" "Where do you go shopping?" "What's the best way to avoid traffic to the Coliseum?"

The other question you heard quite often, of course, was, "Why did we ever leave Brooklyn?" Naturally, that wasn't our department. That was a matter to be handled by the National League and our owner, Mr. O'Malley. If you'd have asked the players on the Dodgers to take a vote, it might have been 25–0 to stay in Brooklyn. I was born and raised in California, but I would have voted with the majority. There was complete chaos on the ballclub because of our move and I have no doubt that it affected our performance. Players who were used to living at home with their families found themselves living alone in hotels. It was tough on the husbands and tough on the wives, who used to do so many things together. But we lost that community closeness, in part because of the mileage involved. Everything was on top of everything in Brooklyn, but in Los Angeles, we were in the wide-open spaces. We also stopped taking trains and started taking airplanes, and there went another part of the past. A lot of baseball conversation took place on those trains, and a lot of good times.

We were missing more than the familiar surroundings of Brooklyn and Ebbets Field during our first year in Los Angeles. We were missing Roy Campanella, who had been the Dodgers' catcher since 1948. After the 1957 season, during the winter, Campy had gotten into a serious automobile accident. He owned a Cadillac, and he'd taken it in for some mechanical work. In return, he was given a loaner to drive, a car that was a lot lighter than the one he was accustomed to handling. Campy drove around a corner near his home in Long Island one snowy night, the car skidded off the road and ran right into a telephone pole. I talked to doctors after that, and they said that if Campy hadn't been so strong, he'd have been gone. Ninety-nine out of a hundred people involved in the same accident would have died. Campy lived, but he'd been hurt in the worst way possible. He was paralyzed from the neck down and would be for the rest of his life. It was mind-boggling, learning that this robust guy with all that personality and energy never would be able to walk again. That was another dark cloud hanging over us in Los Angeles.

It was a huge transition year, and by the end of the season, you only had to look at the National League standings to realize that it was a totally lost year. We finished with a record of 71 victories and 83 losses, which was just bad enough for seventh place in an eight-team league. The only team we beat out was Philadelphia, and it wasn't by much. The Phillies were right on our heels.

What did I think of the LA Coliseum, our temporary home? Well, there was one day when I was supposed to start and I showed up reasonably early at the park. One of those pre-game contests was on, between the local sportswriters and sportscasters, and damned if they weren't hitting home runs over the left-field screen that was only 251 feet away from the plate and extended from the foul pole 140 feet toward the 320-foot marker in left center field.

Don't forget, this was a huge 90,000-seat football oval they'd plopped us into, and it wasn't easy to carve out the configurations of a baseball field. The left-field fence was so close, you could practically spit on it. The right-field fence was so far away, you needed binoculars to see it.

"It's nothing but a sideshow," I said to nobody in particular that afternoon. "Who feels like playing baseball in this place? If a bunch of writers and broadcasters can hit home runs over that thing, how am I supposed to get out major league hitters like Aaron and Banks?"

Sure enough, I didn't. I couldn't get anybody out, and on the rare occasion when I made a good pitch, the batters would reach out and dink it off that left-field screen, which stretched up something like 40 feet and was supported by these two ugly steel towers. Talk about going from the sublime to the ridiculous. This was it—from Ebbets Field to the LA Coliseum. You'd pitch a left-handed hitter low and away, wanting him to pull the ball on the ground, and he'd just go with it and slap it off the screen. A lot of what should have been routine fly balls became extrabase hits—doubles, triples, home runs. It was awful and so was I. I will admit that the dimensions of the Polo Grounds weren't a lot better. Hank Sauer hit the last home run for the New York Giants off me there, and he still swears it was 450 feet. I remember it as more like 250, but these stories grow with time. There were a lot of 250-foot homers in the Polo Grounds, I know that, but I was too new and green when I got to the Brooklyn Dodgers to complain about anything. I was just happy to be there. I can't say that I felt the same about the LA Coliseum.

Erskine pitched the opening game in the Coliseum, which was packed. We drew 78,672 fans, the largest crowd in National League history, and beat the Giants 6–5 on a broiling-hot Friday afternoon. It was a festive occasion, with Mr. O'Malley on the field before the game, along with Norris Poulson, the mayor of Los Angeles, and Vincent X. Flaherty, a popular columnist with the *Herald-Examiner* who had been a booster of major league baseball there. The Giants beat McDevitt 11–4 on Saturday, in the first major league night game played on the West Coast, and on Sunday, the Giants let me have it again, 12–2. That made me 0–2 and counting.

The Giants and Dodgers took an immediate liking to the left-field screen. In our first series against them, the two teams accumulated 12 home runs; our next three-game series against the Cubs produced 12 more. Baseball people started wondering whether Babe Ruth's record of 60 homers in one season would be safe, although that crazy screen also had its adverse effects. Despite the short porch, Hodges didn't hit as well as many people expected—only 22 home runs. And the weird dimensions practically drove one of our veteran catchers, Rube Walker, right out of baseball. In the first week, he must have hit ten balls that would have been home runs in Ebbets Field but were just long outs in the Coliseum alleys. Not surprisingly, Duke was really handicapped by the dimensions—390 in right, growing to 440 in center. He was the only guy, though, to clear the fence in right center all season. I want to say he did it twice. Campy? If he'd have been with us that first season, he just might have broken Ruth's record. Campy hit those long, high fly balls to left that would have just flown over that screen like nothing. He might have hit 80 home runs in Los Angeles alone.

I didn't have much time to worry about our hitters, though, because I was having enough trouble with every other team's hitters. I was 0–6 with a terrible earned run average before you could say Jackie Robinson. Right about that time, we went into Cincinnati on a road trip. Fresco Thompson, who could be a very funny man but who could also absolutely undress you with his tongue, was there. So was Andy High, the Dodgers' chief scout. Well, there I was, supposedly the lead man of a pitching staff that featured a rotation of Podres, Koufax, and Stan Williams. I was coming off a 17-victory season with expectations that I'd perhaps win 20, and I was already 0–6 and things weren't looking too good. So, Thompson and High took me up to Fresco's hotel suite in Cincinnati and they went at me with both barrels. They chewed me out something awful, questioning the way I was pitching and the way I was thinking. When I tried to give them an answer or an explanation, they jumped all over me again. Finally, I decided to just shut my mouth and take it. I knew they would have to get tired ripping me before too long. By the time I left that room, I didn't know whether I was in Cincinnati or Columbus.

I might have been pressing a bit during the early stages of 1958. I was pitching in my backyard, and even living at home with my folks in the Valley. A lot of friends and relatives came to see me pitch, and when I saw a Punch-and-Judy hitter stand at that plate with one eye on "The Thing," it obviously affected me. Oddly enough, I was a right-handed side-wheeling pitcher who was worried more about right-handed batters than left-handed ones. Unless you had an outstanding changeup like Erskine or Podres, there was no way you wanted to throw one to the right-handers at the Coliseum. They could miss the ball and still get a home run.

"The Coliseum can't help us pitchers," I said in an interview. "It's as simple as that. All it can do is put us all in a hole. Most pitchers will get thrown all out of kilter there because they'll have to make adjustments that knock them out of their natural rhythm. Then you go on the road and try to get back in the groove."

I was taking some heat in the press for my lack of success at the time, and that's the last thing I needed, because I was mad enough at myself. I was getting a lot of suggestions and advice and criticism, and I was getting sick and tired of reading what the second-guessers were saying, and all of that didn't hurt my reputation for having a short fuse one bit. The more I was told that I should forget that screen just over my right shoulder, the more I thought about it. They told us to keep it out of our minds, but if you didn't think about it, you weren't human. I guess there were a few writers in Los Angeles who didn't consider me all that human in 1958 anyway, and Pee Wee tried to be diplomatic about my situation.

"Don's not the type to lose a game and then forget it," Reese said. "He's got to do something, smash something, say something. Maybe it'll make the rest of us realize that it's no high school championship we're fighting for out here this year."

The best thing I could do, of course, was win some games, and after dropping as low as 1–7, I had a much better second half. It was too late for the team to make amends for the way we'd started, though. We were too far buried. At the All-Star break, we were nine games under .500, eight games out of first, in last place. With our team going nowhere, there were the usual changes in personnel that you would come to expect. Newcombe, who had won the Cy Young Award only two years before, was traded in June to Cincinnati for Johnny Klippstein and Steve Bilko, who had been a terrific power hitter for Los Angeles in the Pacific Coast League. But he never did make much of playing "screen-O" in the Coliseum. Pee Wee by that time was forty and nearing the end of his great career. He hit only .224 with us in 1958 and retired after that. Erskine was having elbow problems. He was 4–4 that year and just about done, though he did pitch a bit in 1959. Meanwhile, we were getting an influx of newer and younger players. John Roseboro—whom we nicknamed "Gabby" because he never said much—took over Campy's spot behind the plate, caught 114 games and hit .271 with 14 home runs. Charlie Neal, in his second full year with us, hit 22 homers. Frank Howard, a monster of a man who was an Ohio State basketball star and an $80,000 bonus recruit, made his

Dodger debut with a 2-run homer off Robin Roberts. And Don Zimmer, who'd been up and down with the Dodgers for a few years, played a lot in Reese's spot and hit 17 home runs. I'll say this about Zimmer, too—"Popeye" had the best throwing arm I've ever seen in this game. They talk about Shawon Dunston of the Cubs and what a gun he has at shortstop now. Well, Zimmer's arm was just as strong if not stronger, and it was accurate.

The arms on our pitching staff didn't fare as well as Zimmer's, and I was a big part of the problem. I wound up at 12–13 with a pretty awful earned run average of 4.17. Podres wound up 13–15 and Koufax, who had started strong, finished at 11–11 with an ERA of 4.48 and a club record for wild pitches with 17. That was Sandy's fourth year in the major leagues, and he'd totaled only 20 wins to that point. Still, we were the only three pitchers with double-digit victory totals in 1958. The next best was Stan Williams with 9. That pretty much told the story of our first season in Los Angeles, a season to forget.

And if that doesn't, this will. Charlie DiGiovanna was our equipment manager then, as he was in Brooklyn, and he wasn't about to let a lousy ballclub spoil his year. So, at the end of the season, he went out and got a bunch of chickens and he had them all cooked up real nice. We were going to have a little season-ending party on Charlie, even if we had nothing to celebrate. Well, as it turned out, we had less to celebrate than we thought. Roger Craig was pitching the very last game against Chicago and he screwed up a topped ball down the first-base line. His misplay opened up the floodgates, and we lost another game, 7–4, that dropped us from fifth place all the way down to seventh. We'd been battling the Cubs and Cardinals for fifth, and after Buzzie witnessed our latest misadventure, he came storming down to the clubhouse to give us a piece of his mind. He was madder than a hornet, and what did he run into but this elegant spread of sumptuous chickens set up in the locker room, just waiting to be eaten.

"What are these things doing in here?" Bavasi roared.

"Well, they're for the guys," said Charlie.

Buzzie was livid.

"Get them out of here and I don't ever want to see them again," he went on. "The way these guys play, they don't deserve any chicken dinners."

Charlie didn't want to waste all that good food, so he took the chickens, one by one, and placed them very neatly in the trunk of his car, which was parked in the runway of the Coliseum. By the time us players finally made it to the locker room, there were no chickens for us to eat. We couldn't even have a beer in the Coliseum, because it was dry, so we all took off as fast as we could. There was no reason to hang around, anyway, not after finishing the season in seventh place.

Charlie and The Senator, on the other hand, had work to do. They had to clean up and apparently, in the course of their duties, they had a few drinks. More than a few drinks. Eventually, Charlie drove home, just him and his chickens. The only problem was, Charlie forgot his friends in the trunk the next day and the next day after that, too. As he told it, he was driving someplace a few days later when his nose perked up.

"The car stunk!" said Charlie in his Brooklyn accent. "The smell was unbelievable! I almost passed out. All those chickens sitting there in that heat all those days."

We never did get to eat those chickens, and nobody else did either. But that was 1958 with the Dodgers in Los Angeles in a nutshell. Or rather, in a car trunk.

Buzzie had a reason to be mad, of course. He had more reasons than the chickens, in fact. As soon as the Dodgers arrived in Los Angeles, Duke contracted to do a daily radio show. For some reason, I was summoned to the Dodgers' offices at the Statler Hotel downtown. Dick Walsh, who was Buzzie's assistant, wanted to see me. The offices, like the ballpark, were kind of makeshift. The partitions didn't reach all the way to the ceiling, so if you wanted to, you could pick up on what was going on in the next office.

I was in Walsh's cubicle this particular afternoon, waiting for him to show up for our meeting, when I overheard Buzzie on the phone on the other side of the wall. Buzzie was making a deal with the Detroit Tigers, sending them Sandy Amoros. I heard the whole thing, and when I reported to the ballpark that night, I ran into Duke.

"Boy, have I got a scoop for you, but I don't think you can use it," I said, then explained.

"Oh, gosh," he said. "Would I ever love to use that."

"Well, then, go ahead," I said, changing my mind in a big hurry.

"But you were eavesdropping," Snider decided. "I can't go on the air with that."

Snider was serious, but I knew how I could snap him out of it. Pee Wee always had this trick when he was trying to provoke you into doing something and you were resisting. He would hold his thumb and his index finger about an inch apart and dare you by saying, "You don't have a gut that long if you don't do it."

That's all Duke needed. He went on his show and announced the imminent trade, and as soon as Buzzie got wind of it, he was down in the locker room.

"Where is that SOB?" he yelled.

As Buzzie went charging off, looking for Snider, I grabbed the nearest newspaper and held it right up to my face. I was laughing so hard I was almost crying, and I didn't want Buzzie to see me. As it turned out, he was too busy giving it to Duke in the next room.

"And furthermore!" Buzzie screamed, "If you want to be a broadcaster instead of a ballplayer, just let me know. But you're only going to be one. And when you're ready to decide, you call me in my office."

Buzzie left the locker room in a huff, still hell-bent-for-leather, and then Duke walked around the corner. He looked straight at me with a big smile on his face.

"You son of a bitch!" he said.

I think that was Duke's last big scoop on the radio.

I hit 7 home runs during the 1958 season (after hitting 3 in two seasons with the Brooklyn Dodgers) and that tied the record for a National League pitcher held by Newcombe, who'd hit 7 in 1955. Two of my home runs came in one Coliseum game against the Braves, who were the best team in the league. But I wasn't sorry to hear that our days in the LA Coliseum were numbered. They had to be. Mr. O'Malley didn't move the Dodgers out of Brooklyn so that they could play in a football stadium with The Thing staring down at us from left field. We needed a ballpark of our own, a baseball park. After a lot of referendums and a lot of political in-fighting, Mr. O'Malley got clearance to build a stadium just for the Dodgers in Chavez Ravine, a tract of land covering 183 acres not far from downtown Los Angeles. It was named after one of the city's first councilmen, Julian Chavez, and it was area designated for public housing.

But Mayor Poulson pushed for it as a perfect spot for the Dodgers, and Mr. O'Malley agreed. I didn't know Chavez Ravine from a hole in the wall, but I think I speak for a lot of fans and players when I say that we didn't shed any tears when we learned for sure that the Coliseum was definitely just a temporary site. We'd finished 21 games out of first place in our first season in Los Angeles, and yet we drew 1,845,556 in paid attendance. That was more than the Dodgers ever drew in Brooklyn, including the 1947 season, when Jackie Robinson broke the color barrier to become the first black player in the major leagues. Our average in 1958 also was almost twice what it had been during the Dodgers' final season in Brooklyn. We weren't up to Milwaukee yet, because the Braves were topping the two-million mark with a World Series champion in 1957 and another pennant-winning club in 1958. But there wasn't much doubt that Los Angeles was ready to support major league baseball, even if we were "inept" during our debut season—I think that's the word used by one of my favorite sportswriters at the time, Frank Finch of the *Los Angeles Times.* Inept.

He was right on the mark. We were pretty bad in 1958. In fact, the only member of the Dodger family who had a good year was Vin Scully, the great broadcaster who came with the team from Brooklyn and singlehandedly taught our new fans in Southern California all about the Dodgers and the National League. During the early years in Los Angeles, he was probably a greater asset to the Dodgers than the players. Fans came to the Coliseum in droves, bringing with them transistor radios so they could listen to Vinny's descriptions of the games they were watching in person. It was a strange, but understandable, phenomenon, considering the weird configuration of the Coliseum. In Brooklyn, the crowd was right on top of the action. We could practically hear what the fans were saying, and that contributed to a sense of camaraderie between the paying customer and us, the ballplayers. In the Coliseum, which was hosting meets on an Olympic-sized track when it wasn't hosting football games, there was none of that ambiance. From the bottom to top row of seats, it must have been a good block. The fans didn't only need Vin Scully on the radio to find out what was happening. They needed telescopes. You had no way of getting to know the fans. The only place you got close enough to talk to them was through The Thing in left field. To become better acquainted with the fans in Los Angeles, several of the players from time to time toured some of the major industries in the area. One of the promotional stops I made was to the offices of the *Los Angeles Times,* where I'd worked as a kid.

As for the attitude and knowledge of Dodger fans in the Coliseum, it was unfair to compare them with the fans in Brooklyn for one very simple reason. It was unfair to compare *any* fans anywhere with those fans in Brooklyn. The fans in Los Angeles had had the Hollywood Stars and the Los Angeles Angels minor league teams—they provided good baseball, but weren't the real thing. A lot of former or future major league players came and went there, but it wasn't the major leagues. That was a huge difference. The people of Brooklyn were born and weaned on the Dodgers and major league baseball, and they ate it up. They knew the game like the back of their hand. They lived it. They breathed it.

When you started a rally in the Coliseum, you heard the noise in the background. You knew that the fans knew something was happening, but there wasn't the electrifying buzz that you experienced in Brooklyn. When you look back now, it's really amazing that a huge state like California with all that population didn't get major league baseball until 1958. Only now is there a generation of fans in Los Angeles who can say that they, too, were weaned on the Dodgers.

It took a pioneer to bring this about, and Mr. O'Malley was that man. I have a tremendous feeling for the people of Brooklyn, and I know what they think of Mr. O'Malley. I know how they still hurt. But I have a great deal of respect for him, because in many ways, I think he took a big gamble. So did Horace Stoneham of the Giants, for that matter. Think of it this way. Here were two men who owned franchises in established locations, and their two ballclubs had one of the fiercest rivalries that had ever existed in professional sports, or ever will. O'Malley and Stoneham knew that they would pretty well pack their ballparks whenever the Dodgers and Giants met in Ebbets Field or the Polo Grounds. O'Malley and Stoneham also knew that there always would be a lot of interest in their teams in New York, no matter how good or bad they were.

And then, these two men, O'Malley and Stoneham, just packed up their two teams and this great rivalry and moved them

3,000 miles away. The Dodgers and Giants were maybe an hour apart by car in New York; in Los Angeles and San Francisco, they were an hour apart by jet. O'Malley and Stoneham knew they were going to get certain things in California that they wouldn't be able to get in New York, but still, there were no guarantees. As an example, look at what the Giants have endured since they settled in San Francisco. They've had some profitable years, true, but they've had some tough years, too. Some of their years have been so tough that there have been rumors that they'd eventually have to move again because the Bay Area couldn't support two teams— the Oakland Athletics and the Giants. We've all heard that talk in recent seasons—Giants to Denver, Giants to New Orleans, Giants to wherever.

The Dodgers never had that problem in Los Angeles. As it turned out, Mr. O'Malley probably got a better reception and made more money than he ever anticipated, but that doesn't mean to me that he didn't roll the dice when he pulled up stakes in Brooklyn. There was some atmosphere lost, no doubt about that. The Dodger–Giant rivalry that was so unique back East was re-newed 3,000 miles away in California, and you had the natural dislike between the two cities of Los Angeles and San Francisco. But it wasn't quite the same as what we'd had in New York. I only got a taste of it for two years, but it was a taste I'll never forget. When people ask me to explain how fierce it was, I just tell them to imagine the wildest emotion possible between two ballclubs, and triple it. It's never been like that between the Dodgers and Giants on the West Coast, even at its best.

Brooklyn seemed a world away in 1958, a year to forget for the Dodgers. But I could see that the Dodgers weren't forgotten by Brooklyn any more than we'd forgotten Brooklyn. When we made our first road trip to Philadelphia, a whole bunch of Dodger fans showed up, a lot of them wearing hats with the old "B". They wouldn't have been caught dead with "LA" caps. I felt sorry for the Dodger fans of Brooklyn all over again when I saw them there in Philadelphia, with their long faces. I can't think of any franchise move in professional sports, before or since, to match the impact of the Dodgers' move to Los Angeles.

Maybe, if the Green Bay Packers left Green Bay, it would affect that city as much. Maybe. But the Packers are still there, even if they do play some of their home games in Milwaukee, so we'll never know. I know this. It was awkward for us to play in Los Angeles and it took a long while to get over that feeling.

But time marches on, and somebody was going to bring major league baseball to the West Coast sooner or later. And even as we speak, Dodger Stadium in Los Angeles and Candlestick Park in San Francisco are two of the oldest stadiums in the major leagues.

Crazy but true.

7

1959, 1989, and Gil

*I*n February 1989, the Dodgers had a reunion in Vero Beach to celebrate the thirtieth anniversary of our first World Series team in Los Angeles. It's hard to believe, after finishing seventh the year before, that we climbed all the way into the World Series and won it in 1959. But we did, as no team had done before in major league history.

When I joined the Dodgers in Brooklyn, it was like joining an All-Star team that you figured would never be broken up. Of course, that was naive. By 1959, only seven Dodgers were left from the 1956 team. After three years, we had not only moved clear across the country, but into a completely new era. Another chapter in the wild and zany history of Dodger Blue was being written.

Thirty years later in Vero Beach, we were more gray than blue, myself included, and as I looked around at the bunch of us, I couldn't help but think about one of the people who wasn't there. Gil Hodges.

My former roommate, my second father. Gil Hodges.

In 1972, I was working for the Texas Rangers as a member of their broadcast team. On April 1, the Major League Players Association called a strike. I was down in Texas, preparing for the season to begin, whenever. As it turned out, the strike didn't last too long. The next day, April 2, I was with an old friend of mine, Dick Blue, who used to produce the "Happy Felton Show" on television back in Brooklyn. I had this huge apartment—a townhouse, really—at the Woodhaven Country Club near Ft. Worth. We were just sitting around late one afternoon, shooting the bull, when I thought I heard the name "Hodges" on the radio in the background.

"What did they say about Hodges?" I asked Dick.

"Didn't catch it," he answered.

The news came at the next half-hour, and that's when I heard—Gil Hodges, dead in West Palm Beach, Florida, at age forty-seven, two days before his forty-eighth birthday. He was manager of the New York Mets at the time, and he'd just finished a round of golf with two of his coaches, Joe Pignatano and Rube Walker. Rube later said that they were talking about when and where to go to dinner when Gil just keeled over. Rube said he was dead before he hit the ground. Unbelievable. Here was a man so strong that you figured he was indestructible, so impressive that you figured he would live forever, and he went down just like that at age forty-seven.

The news of Gil Hodges's death absolutely shattered me. I just flew apart. I didn't leave my apartment in Texas for three days. I didn't want to see anybody or talk to anybody. I couldn't get myself to go to the funeral. I couldn't get myself to call his widow, Joan. I couldn't do anything. It was like I'd lost part of my family and I was devastated. When I think of my rookie year with the Brooklyn Dodgers in 1956, when I think of my first World Series championship with the LA Dodgers, whenever we get together as we did for that thirtieth anniversary in 1989, I think of Gil. He was probably the greatest thing that ever happened to me in baseball. I've never been one to label friends as "best" or "next best," but Gil Hodges was as close to me as anybody I've ever met. I respected him so much, and I wasn't alone. Here was a man who went 0-for-21 during a World Series in 1952 and he had people lighting candles for him in Brooklyn. He had priests saying prayers for him at Mass. That's the kind of man Gil Hodges was.

From the first day I shook hands with him in the parking lot at Dodgertown in 1955 until the end, he was one of the most important people in my life. During spring training, the Dodgers' roommate system was a little scrambled. At our McAllister Hotel headquarters in Miami, for instance, Gil would always have Joan and the kids down. So, I spent some time rooming with other players. I was with Dixie Howell in 1956 for a spell, and then

Kenny Lehman. Gil and Carl Furillo had been regular-season roommates for a while, but it was decided to split them up and put Carl with Sandy Koufax and Gil with me. Who made those decisions—Buzzie or Walt or Fresco or all of them—I don't know who or why, although it made sense to put one of the kids with an established veteran.

I'm not sure that I was in awe of Gil, because I was so comfortable around him, but he certainly was impressive. Here was a strapping man whose hand, from the tip of his little finger to the tip of his thumb, measured eleven-and-a-half inches. You never thought he would be sick a day in his life, the way he was built and the way he carried himself and the way he took care of himself. He was a complete gentleman, cordial and polite though very quiet. He was as strong as an ox, and I don't think he knew his own strength. Either that, or he was like Frank Howard, who knew how strong he was but never wanted to show it. It's like a guy carrying a lethal weapon but hoping he never has to use it. I mean, if a Frank Howard or a Gil Hodges ever really got mad, it would have taken an elephant gun to stop him.

There was a night in St. Louis when Gil made a couple of errors in a game against the Cardinals. We went back to the Chase Park–Plaza hotel, where our luggage had been dumped in our rooms that afternoon on our arrival by train—probably from Chicago. In those days, when you made long road trips, each of us owned a suitcase that was more like a trunk. It was a big, heavy thing that contained everything you needed for a two-week excursion, but it wasn't all that easy to carry around.

Well, that night in St. Louis, I pulled out that big long room key and the door opened only a few inches. I couldn't figure out why. Then Gil, who was standing beside me, noticed that our two suitcases were blocking our entry. They were right up against the door on the other side.

"Roomie," Hodges said, "let me get at that."

I stepped aside and watched Gil go to work. First, he pushed the door open, which was no small task. Then he reached in and grabbed those suitcases, one at a time, and picked them up and threw them across the room. He didn't bother using the handles, either. He put his hands around them like you would put your hands around your thigh, and he just tossed them.

"Now, we can get into this cotton-pickin' room," he said. Gil was hot, but he didn't swear. He never did. He didn't have to. He just threw those two suitcases like they were nothing! I was flabbergasted. My jaw dropped and my mouth just stayed open for a while.

"Roomie," I finally said, "you want some of that brownie à la mode?"

"Yeah, order up," he answered.

Whenever we went to St. Louis, Gil liked to have brownie à la mode at the Chase Park–Plaza. He could eat pies and cakes and all that stuff without ever putting on an ounce. Unlike me, he was a big breakfast guy. He'd be up early in the morning—in suit and tie, which was the dress code—and down in the coffee shop, like clockwork. I'd tinker with something small, but he'd have the full treatment—orange juice, bran flakes with a banana on top, eggs and sausage and toast and milk and coffee. And he'd have a few drinks at night on most occasions. And on those rare nights when he made an error, he'd flip a couple suitcases. But he always cooled down and had his brownie à la mode because tomorrow was another day.

I mentioned that Gil Hodges was a total gentleman. And he was. But that didn't mean he couldn't agitate with the best of them. He had a dry sense of humor that he used without batting an eyelash. If you didn't know Gil, there were times when you thought he was so mad at you that you wanted to run away and hide. Either that, or you wanted to hit him over the head with a bat, not that you would ever have dared.

As a rookie, I had to learn a lot of things about life in the major leagues and tipping was one of them. I watched how the veterans tipped—maybe three bucks a day to the clubhouse guy on the road, a buck or two to the porter on the train or the bellhop at the hotel for handling your bags. When I went to dinner with Gil, I watched him tip the waiter. Naturally, being the agitator he was, he often turned the tables on me. We'd be ready to leave a restaurant and I'd put my share of the tip down and then he'd look at me with that straight face of his.

"Are you ready to go now?" he'd ask.

"Well, yeah, I guess," I'd say.

"You're sure you want to leave?"

"Well, yeah, why not?"

At this point, he would be playing mind games, but I didn't know what to do.

"That's what you're leaving as a tip?" he'd continue.

"Yeah, that's what I'm leaving as a tip. Now, let's go."

"Okay," he'd say. "If that's the way you want to be."

Then he'd get up and just walk out and you'd follow him, your brain all messed up. Meanwhile, he's laughing to himself.

Here's another example of Gil the agitator. We were in St. Louis when my daughter, Kelly, was born. It was the start of a long road trip and we were in the dining room at the Chase Park–Plaza when I got word that there was a call for me. I went to the phone, which wasn't far from where we were eating, and received the good news. Don "Popeye" Zimmer was at the table having breakfast, along with Reese and Hodges and myself. They could clearly hear my end of the conversation and how happy I was. But when I returned to the table, they were all talking baseball. They were going over box scores from the previous night's games while I was sitting there on cloud nine, bursting with pride about being a father for the first time. I picked up my fork and resumed eating. Eventually, they all broke up and congratulated me, but you know that Hodges was behind the silent treatment—the same kind of silent treatment that you'll sometimes see a pitcher get when he returns to the dugout after hitting a home run. And I wasn't just a green rookie then. That was 1959 when Kelly was born. I'd been around for a while, but with Gil, you were never immune. You were never safe.

With Pee Wee being such a great captain, I don't know that you could say that Gil Hodges was our leader in the classic sense. But all you had to do was watch how he carried himself, on and off the field, and you knew that his was the right way of going about being a major league ballplayer. Gil was always in control of himself and the situation, which was one way he really helped me. I had a short fuse, particularly when I first arrived on the big league scene, and Gil was very good at monitoring my temper. Most of the time, when I got mad, I got mad at myself—not at anybody else, just at stupid me for making a mistake. Gil was not only my roommate, but the first baseman, and many a time he'd sense that I was boiling out there on the mound about something or other. He'd call time, stroll over, and just say his piece.

"Roomie, get it back together, now," he'd say. "Settle down and don't let this game get away from you."

He didn't yell. He didn't scream. He didn't use a lot of words. Again, he didn't have to. Gil was as solid a citizen as you could meet. He never got himself into awkward situations, though I contributed to a minor problem one night in Pittsburgh. I had lost a tough game to the Pirates and wasn't in a great mood. Frank Slocum, a friend of Gil's working with the commissioner's office, was in town and the three of us went back to the Carlton House for some dinner. We ordered room service, Frank and Gil talked, and I sort of stewed nearby. The phone rang and Gil gave me my instructions. He didn't want to be bothered. He was eating.

"Hello, is Gil there?" the voice inquired.

"Nope, not here," I said abruptly.

"He's not?" the voice asked.

"That's right," I said. "Not here."

I hung up, never even bothering to take note of who was on the other end. The next night, Gil and I were having dinner in the restaurant. I finished and was paying my check when I ran into Walt Alston in the lobby.

"Well, after all these years, I finally got your roomie," Walt said with a laugh.

"What are you talking about?" I asked.

"He wasn't in the room late last night when he was supposed to be," Walt explained. "I finally caught him."

"The heck he wasn't in," I said. "We were both in the room after the game having dinner."

"Not according to you. I called the room and you answered. You said he wasn't there."

"You called the room last night? I don't remember that."

"I phoned, you answered, Gil wasn't there," Walt said. "Finally got him."

At about that time, Hodges came out of the restaurant and picked up on our conversation.

"Looks like I'll have to take some of your money," Walt said to Hodges. "You weren't in the room last night when you were supposed to be."

Gil paused for a moment, then looked at me.

"Roomie, do you mean to tell me that when the phone rang last night and I told you to say I wasn't in, that it was Walt who was calling? And you didn't even know it? If this costs me, I'm gonna kick your butt all over Pittsburgh."

By this time, Walt was practically on the floor laughing.

There was no fine for Gil, fortunately for me. I had heard about Gil in action, and I wanted him on my side. When we were battling the Milwaukee Braves during the 1957 season at Ebbets Field, I hit their shortstop, Johnny Logan, in the back with a fastball. A little imbroglio followed. Eddie Mathews came after me on the mound, and Connie Ryan, Milwaukee's first-base coach, also joined in. I didn't see all of what followed, because I was down on the ground, in a pile of bodies. But I was told that Gil picked Ryan up and flicked him in the air like he was a mosquito. Then Gil kept coming and grabbed hold of Mathews, who was one tough guy. Eddie would fight a redwood tree if he had to, but Gil was too much. Hodges grabbed Mathews by the ankles and dragged him away from the mound all the way to third base, on his face. Then Gil looked at him and said, "Stay right there and don't come back!" Eddie never did make it back to the fight.

Of course, that entire incident was Gil's fault, and if he happens to be reading this up in Heaven, I'm sure he'll have a good chuckle on me all over again. That's what he did when I blamed him for it the first time, right after it happened—he laughed.

After I hit Logan with the pitch, Johnny went toward first and he yelled something at me. And I yelled back. Then he took his lead off the bag and I threw over there, trying to pick him off. But Hodges stuck his glove out and missed the ball, and it hit Logan again! It wasn't just a glancing blow, either. I threw the ball hard, and it hit him hard, and he didn't waste any time heading toward the mound. We met about halfway, and that was the beginning of our rumble.

"Roomie," I told Gil after the game, "if you'd have just caught the damn thing over at first base, there'd have been no problem. I wouldn't have ended up in a fight."

He just shrugged his shoulders and laughed.

I could be a miserable person at times, a no-good SOB if I lost a ballgame, but Gil always made a point of looking after me. If he sensed that I needed to let off some steam, he'd make sure he was around. He knew just how to handle me, sometimes better than I knew how to handle myself.

Gil was a positive influence in another way. He knew when to call it a night and hit the sack. He was like a lot of the veterans. He enjoyed going out and having dinner and a few drinks. But he also valued his sleep and his job and he lived accordingly. I wasn't exactly at the other end of the spectrum. I wasn't a hell-raiser. But if you were rooming with Gil, you didn't want to be out too late because you knew he wouldn't be. He had his couple drinks and then he went back to the hotel to read the newspaper, watch TV, and turn out the lights. When I was single, I was inclined to want to see a little more nightlife, but I found myself getting to bed early just so I wouldn't come in late and wake him up. It wasn't that I was afraid he'd beat me up or anything. I just respected him that much. I didn't want to disturb him, it was as simple as that.

I never barged in at three o'clock in the morning, but there were times when I'd get that gleam in my eye and want to go a little longer than he did. He'd say, go ahead, I'm going up to bed. And I'd arrive a couple hours later, give a knock, and he'd come to the door, which he liked to chain from the inside. He'd let me in, and fall right back to sleep. Every once in a while, the next morning over breakfast, he'd drop a little message on me.

"What time was it that you got in last night?" he'd ask.

"Right about twelve-thirty, maybe one o'clock," I'd say.

"Really? Geez, I thought it was a little later than that."

And you'd sit there, feeling about six inches tall.

Rooming with Gil not only enhanced my major league career, it probably prolonged it. And again, I was lucky to come along when I did. Nowadays, with all these fancy contracts, most players ask for—and get—a single room on the road. Either that, or they can afford to pay the difference between the single they want and the double that the club pays for. All that privacy is nice, I guess, but if you ask me which I'd have preferred as a twenty-year-old kid—a room by myself, or an opportunity to listen to and learn from a saint like Gil Hodges—well, there's no contest. I'd have missed out on a whole lot by not being around Gil as much as I was.

Did he have a temper too? There was this getaway day in Pittsburgh at the Schoenly Hotel. We had played the Pirates and were waiting at the bar late in the afternoon before heading to the train station. Practically the whole Dodger team was there—which, by the way, is another sight you don't see too much anymore. Gil was sipping his Jack Daniels and we all had a drink and after a while, it was time for another round. Well, this bartender was a little slow on the draw. He was pouring drinks as if he was working a health spa. And we were getting thirsty. And we were getting impatient.

Finally, Gil had had enough. He slammed his fist onto that bar and everybody's drinks must have jumped two or three inches into the air. The bartender went higher than that, and when he landed, you could hear a pin drop. The place fell absolutely silent, until Gil spoke.

"Now," he said, "start here with another drink and go all the way down to the end with drinks for the rest of the guys."

The outburst was completely out of character for Gil, but it was very, very effective. Suddenly, the bartender switched gears to fast forward. He hurried as he'd never hurried before in his life. We all got served in nothing flat.

Gil was a tremendous family man, too, and that also made an early impression on me. As a professional ballplayer, living in that bubble, you can lose touch with reality sometimes. You're part of a traveling road show, and there are days when you feel like a vagabond. On some mornings you wake up and aren't sure what city you're in. It was that way then, even though you didn't play as many night games and you didn't take jet planes all over the country at strange hours. But Gil always had his priorities straight, and whenever we returned to Brooklyn, where Joan and the kids were waiting, you could see how important his family was to him. Gil was a great husband and father. He was also a real homebody.

There was never much doubt in my mind that Gil could become an outstanding manager, if he wanted to. There were nights on the road when we'd stay up in the room and read that book *The Sporting News* used to publish—*Knotty Problems of Baseball.* It contained stories and vignettes about weird baseball happenings—situations that tested obscure rules, things like that. We'd go over them and then we'd go over the rule book and see if we could figure out answers and solutions and loopholes. I don't imagine there are too many ballplayers doing that these days, but that was just another way we used to immerse ourselves in the game and

91

nobody was more involved in what he was doing than Gil. I don't remember Gil ever talking about wanting to be a manager, but he was a definite candidate. So was Pee Wee, for that matter, but Reese always said that he "didn't want to put up with all the crap." That was twenty-five years ago. Can you imagine what Reese would think about the way baseball is now?

Gil took the plunge, though, and his first job as manager was with the Washington Senators. One of his players there was Zimmer. One night, according to Popeye, he wanted to stay out a little late. He went to call Gil to ask for permission but realized that he didn't have a dime. So, Zimmer stayed out anyway and the next day he went up to Gil to explain. We sometimes used to call Gil "Gilly" or "Moony" because of that big round face of his, and Popeye appealed to Hodges's sympathetic side.

"Gilly," he said, "I meant to get a hold of you last night, but I didn't have a dime."

Gil looked him straight in the face, dipped into his pocket, and brought out a whole bunch of change.

"Here, next time this will save you a whole lot of money."

He fined Popeye. And that was that.

When Gil moved on to manage the Mets, there was that famous episode with Cleon Jones. He was playing left field for New York in Shea Stadium one day, and Gil didn't think he showed a lot of hustle in chasing down an extrabase hit against the Astros. Rube Walker said he watched Gil leave the dugout and walk toward the mound and then turn and head toward shortstop.

"I thought Gil was cracking up," said Rube.

Hodges kept going, all the way to left field, until he reached Jones. Gil put his arm around Cleon, talked to him for a moment, and then they walked back to the dugout, nice and calmly. Jones was an All-Star and a contender for the league's batting crown at the time, but that didn't matter to Gil. He later announced that Jones was suffering from a muscle pull, but nobody believed it. Gil was trying to reduce any embarrassment felt by Jones. It was also Gil's way of telling Cleon Jones that if he didn't feel like playing hard that particular day, then he should get his ass off the field. And Jones wasn't about to make an issue of it.

"I've played with Gil," said Rube, "I've known him for years, I've sat and talked baseball with him over beers, and I couldn't believe what I was seeing."

That wasn't like Hodges, but he must have become so irritated that he couldn't stand the sight of Jones out there any longer. So Gil went out and got him. He just gave Cleon Jones the hook as you would a pitcher who wasn't doing the job. It surprised me, and yet it didn't surprise me. After I retired, I saw Gil from time to time whenever I was in New York to broadcast a game. We would get on the subject of his ballclub, and I could see that it was eating at him, the way some of his players approached their jobs. Anybody as gifted and as devoted to the game as Gil was, had to be bothered at the sight of a player not giving his all, and Gil had to be doubly annoyed, because he kept so many things inside.

In 1968, Gil suffered what must have been some kind of warning. Late in the season, as manager of the Mets, he was pitching batting practice in Atlanta. He had been trying to shake a cold for a while, and when he returned to the clubhouse before the game, the doctors thought he looked so drawn and tired that they sent him to the hospital. It was announced that he had suffered a mild heart attack.

Whether it was stress or whatever, I don't know, but I remember being in Atlanta at the time and going to see him in the hospital. As his former roomie and a close friend still, I could see that the caliber of modern-day play was getting to Gil. Here was a perfectionist trying to manage a ballclub in an era when a lot of players didn't care. As a manager, what he saw had to be like night and day from what he'd experienced with the Dodgers, who not only were full of All-Star players but players with All-Star character.

Gil was the type of guy you wanted for a brother, the type of guy you wanted your daughter to marry. He was very serious about his business, yet lots of fun to be around. If we had an off-day on the road, we would go to a movie together or better yet, the track. He wasn't afraid to put a bet down on a horse, and you often found Gil puffing away on a cigarette, reading the racing form. Apparently, he started smoking pretty heavily in the Marine Corps. That's about all I ever got out of him about his time in the service. I've heard tales of him being much-decorated during World War II, but he never talked about it. He first came to the Dodgers in 1943, then he spent 29 months in the Marines before returning to Brooklyn. But that was one chapter in his life he didn't discuss. Ever.

If there was one thing about Gil that got my goat, it was the way he drove an automobile. In Brooklyn, we had those eight games a year in Jersey City, plus the games over at the Polo Grounds against the Giants. Sometimes, I'd take my car and pick him up. At other times, he'd take his and pick me up. God Almighty! How could a man who was so smooth and graceful in every other aspect of his life be so clumsy behind the wheel? He was one of those people who had the right foot on the accelerator and the left on the brake, usually at the same time. It drove me bananas.

"Roomie," I would say, "make up your mind. Do you want to stop or do you want to go?"

"I want to keep doing exactly what I'm doing," he'd answer. "Would you like to come over here and drive while I watch?"

"No, but either put your foot on the gas or put your foot on the brake. One or the other. Let's smooth this trip out a little bit."

Then he would do something to agitate me even more. I was from California, where you didn't have to drive that way to get around. Maybe that was Gil's way of handling New York City traffic. I don't know. If he hadn't have been a great ballplayer, he'd have made a terrific cab driver.

Gil was a very intense guy. He was focused on the game when it was time to play, and yet he was able to focus on relaxing when he was away from the ballpark. He spent a lot of hours just lying in bed, taking it easy. I don't want to play doctor, because I'm certainly not qualified. But I do say that Gil kept a lot inside, and I've always wondered whether he kept too much inside. If he had ever gone into a rage, I know I would have wanted to be nine blocks away from him. But maybe it would have been better for his health had he let go more often. I know this much. It was mind-boggling to me when this tremendous specimen of a man died of a heart attack when he was only forty-seven years old. I didn't understand it then, and I'm not sure I comprehend it to this day.

Gil was such a terrific guy that even I occasionally dwell so much on his personality that I forget to emphasize what a great player he was, too. Here was a tremendous fielder who set the standards for other first basemen of his day. Plus, he was an exceptional hitter. For seven straight seasons, from 1949 through 1955, he batted in more than 100 runs. He wound up with 370 home runs and a career batting average of .273, and his last big year was our first big year in Los Angeles—1959, when he batted .276 and hit 25 home runs, despite The Thing in left field that a lot of experts had figured would reduce a lot of his home runs into long singles. He was sturdy and durable. Even at age thirty-seven, he played more than 100 games for us at first base.

As a manager, he left his mark, too. The Mets were a national joke when they started. But in 1969, only their eighth year in existence and his second on the job and just a year after his heart attack, Gil managed the "Amazin' Mets" to a World Series triumph over the Baltimore Orioles—a huge upset. The Mets came from nowhere after the Cleon Jones episode. After five seasons as manager of the Washington Senators, Gil had come to the Mets and injected them with his own brand of positive thinking and professionalism. The Dodgers of 1959 went from seventh to first place to win a World Series. The Mets went from ninth in 1968 to win a World Series in 1969. Not surprisingly, Gil was on hand for both those occasions. The Impossible Dream, twice.

As I look back, I feel as though I accumulated a lifetime's worth of knowledge from being Gil Hodges's "roomie," and yet we weren't really together all that long. I came to Brooklyn in 1956, and we were in Chicago for the last series of the 1961 season when it hit me.

"Have a good winter, Roomie," he said after the final game in Wrigley Field.

"You, too, Roomie. We'll see you in the spring."

"Oh, I don't know about that," Gil said.

"What do you mean?" I asked.

"Well, you know they have this expansion draft coming up," he said. "I'm not sure I'll be around here after that."

The thought shocked me. Gil Hodges, my roomie, not a Dodger? I couldn't really fathom the idea. But sure enough, for the 1962 season, the National League added two new teams, the Houston Astros and the Mets, and Gil was selected by New York. He went back there and played two more years before he retired early in the 1963 season to manage in Washington. He played parts of eighteen years in the major leagues, and I was fortunate enough to be with him for a few of them.

Whenever people get around to talking about the old Brooklyn Dodgers, or whenever we old Dodgers come together as we did for that thirtieth anniversary of our 1959 World Series championship, I think of Gil. My roomie. Those big hands, flipping suitcases and eating brownie à la mode. And that big heart. Will I ever know a better human being or have a better friend? If I don't, I won't feel cheated. He left us too soon, I can tell you that. He left us too soon.

8

Pee Wee and the Duke

*W*hether we were based in Brooklyn or Los Angeles, or playing on the road, the Dodgers talked a lot. This was a ballclub that loved to talk, mostly about baseball, and one of the leaders in conversation was our leader on and off the field—our shortstop, The Captain, Harold Henry "Pee Wee" Reese.

He came to the Dodgers in 1940 and played for them until 1958 with a whole lot of grace and efficiency and class. The reason Pee Wee and I were able to become close at an early point in my career—not that all of us weren't friendly as teammates—was because he had the number 1 jersey and I had number 53, and the way the locker rooms were set up, we wound up near each other. There was another bond we shared—Pee Wee and I have the same birthday, July 23.

As I've said, at the risk of sounding like a broken record, one of the most special things about the Dodgers was the respect with which the players treated each other, regardless of a guy's age or salary or status. I've got to think that Pee Wee was a big reason for that. In a sense, Pee Wee believed that everybody was equal. If you wore a Dodger uniform, if you were one of the twenty-five players on the roster, there was always the chance that you would make somebody else in that same uniform some money. That might seem very cold, and obviously the Dodgers' feelings for each other extended well beyond such financial considerations, but let's face it. Baseball was a business, even in those more romantic days, and the Dodgers used to think of that annual World Series check as part of the deal, part of their salaries.

Pee Wee Reese was our leader and a gentleman. There's no question, despite the Dodgers' array of strong individuals and different personalities, that Pee Wee was our leader. He had a dry sense of humor, and he could agitate with the best of them, and whenever he got under your skin, you could always fire back with his nickname, "Prune." Reese had some wrinkles in his face, so he was "Prune." Duke Snider was "Snubby" because of that short, stubby little nose of his, Hodges was "Moony" because of his big, round face, and I was the "Big Collie," or just "Collie." How I got those tags, I don't really know. Probably because I was just so big and cuddly. HA!

Anyway, Pee Wee wasn't much of a holler guy, but he was one of those guys you would listen to when he did have something to say. You hear stories about those occasions when Pee Wee did deliver a message. There was an instance, before I joined the Dodgers, when the Dodgers had a doubleheader of some significance and Billy Cox came into the clubhouse after the first game and said that he was too tired to play in the second. Everybody was pretty quiet, until The Captain opened his mouth.

"What the hell are you saving yourself for, Billy?" Reese said. "An exhibition game in Altoona?"

Naturally, Cox put on his glove and went out and played the second game of that doubleheader.

I remember one day when I was pitching in Ebbets Field against the St. Louis Cardinals. I don't recall for sure who the batter was. I want to say Bill Virdon. I was in a bit of a jam and Pee Wee drifted over to the mound from short, as he often did.

"Here," he said, "just hold the ball in your glove like this. Don't move it around. It's ready for you, if you want it."

What he was talking about was a spitter. He'd loaded up the ball for me. Somebody on the Cardinals had knocked a base hit, and Pee Wee had gotten the ball in from one of our outfielders. I thanked Pee Wee for the favor, held onto the ball very gingerly, and then reached for the resin bag. Then I went into the stretch, delivered to Virdon, and the ball did nothing. There was no violent movement, no break to it, no nothing. And Virdon promptly spanked it off the scoreboard in right field for an extra-base hit.

Well, not only was I furious about what Virdon did, but I had so much admiration for Pee Wee that I was petrified about how he might react. There was nothing worse than screwing up on the field and then looking over to Pee Wee at shortstop. Sure enough, there he was, glaring at me like I was some kind of a jerk. He had his hands on his hips, and then he dropped his head and just kind of pawed at the dirt with his feet, smoothing it out in front of him. I mean, by saying absolutely nothing, Pee Wee made me feel like I was about four inches tall. That was Pee Wee's way of calling you a dumb bastard without moving his lips, and it was a lonely feeling, I'll tell you. A lot of us younger pitchers felt Pee Wee's wrath in situations like that, but Pee Wee had only one motive. He wanted us to think more, execute better, and win. That's all. That's why he was our leader.

You half-wanted him to come to the mound at a moment like that and talk to you, but on the other hand, you knew by looking at him that he thought you were a big donkey. It was just as well that you kept your distance. He had a great presence, and terrific baseball instincts. Here was a man, who, in his final year, was standing on second base when Duke hit a long fly ball to the deepest part of the Los Angeles Coliseum. The ball was caught, Pee Wee tagged up and scored, all the way from second. Not a flashy guy, Pee Wee, but he got it done.

Pee Wee was awfully finicky about how he took batting practice. It was as though he wanted every pitch on a tee. He didn't want to hit anything off the end of the bat, or off the fists, and it was my mistake one afternoon during spring training to be pitching batting practice in Fort Worth. One ball got away from me, and I plunked Pee Wee in the ribs. The Captain! I'd hit The Captain in the ribs during batting practice! He wasn't wounded in the least, but it gave him a perfect opportunity to agitate.

"You did that on purpose, you big donkey!" he yelled out at me. "Didn't you?"

"On purpose?" I screamed back. "We're on the same team, remember? Why would I do that on purpose?"

"I was taking too many pitches, that's why," he said. "That's why got you mad."

And wouldn't you know it, a few years ago, we had one of those old-timers' games at Dodger Stadium and there I was out on the mound, preparing to pitch to the leadoff batter, Pee Wee. Well, I can't throw hard anymore and I haven't been able to for years.

But I've never been able just to lob the ball, either. I've always had to put something extra on it. And when you get to be my age, not everything works the way it used to. Your hand opens up and every pitch is high and inside. Lo and behold, I threw a ball toward the plate, it was high and inside and damn near hit Pee Wee in the head. Missed him by only this much.

"You big donkey!" he yelled out at me, a big smile on his old prune face.

He stood over the plate the same way he did in his prime, crowding it. That's okay for him. But how am I supposed to have any control after not throwing for so long and then trying to steer the damn thing in so it was an easy strike to hit?

"You big donkey!" Pee Wee yelled again.

Reese had been installed as the Dodger captain many years before I got there, but I never had to ask myself why. As a player, he did everything effortlessly. He made playing shortstop seem almost easy, and he was a solid, capable hitter who batted over .300 only once—.309 in 1954—but knocked in some runs and got his bat on the ball. As a person, I would say Pee Wee personified the "Dodger Way" by the manner in which he carried himself. Pee Wee was born in Louisville, the son of a railroad detective, and he was very much the Southern gentleman. The beauty of a youngster like myself being on the Dodgers at that time was that you had eight or ten great examples to follow, eight or ten teachers of how to play the game and how to handle your role as a Brooklyn Dodger. None was better than Pee Wee. And he didn't become captain just because he was the senior member of the team.

Why it took Pee Wee so long to get into the Hall of Fame, I don't know. But there are a lot of things about that voting system that I don't understand. I can't comprehend the mentality. Each year, every writer gets to vote for ten players. But there are situations where writers put down only a couple names, or maybe even none. There are times when a player will have a lot of votes one year, but not make it, and then get less votes the next year. What's the logic behind that? Can a guy who's retired become a worse ballplayer after waiting a year? How do you manage that? For my own selfish reasons, though, it was good that Pee Wee did have to wait as long as he did because we got into Cooperstown together. That was nice. Real nice. That was a freak year, anyway, because five of us made it.

I mentioned that Pee Wee was a Southerner, and don't think this wasn't taken into account when the Dodgers brought Jackie Robinson up to the big leagues. Again, that was well before my time. But I've heard many a tale about how much Pee Wee supported and helped Jackie. In my first few years, I thought there was a prejudice of sorts against players from California. That seems odd, I know, because there have been so many of us. But I did feel that some players and some members of management looked at us cross-eyed because we were born on the West Coast. Maybe it was partly jealousy. Most of the rest of the country was up to its butt in snow during the winter while us Californians were enjoying the sunshine. But that attitude went by the boards after major league baseball moved to California. It was pretty obvious that, because of the climate, any athlete had a better chance to develop in California than most anywhere else.

Of course, when it came to breaking down barriers, nobody accomplished more than Jackie Robinson. And Pee Wee was right there with him. I would imagine that, with Pee Wee's upbringing in segregated surroundings, at first he might have wrestled with the idea of having a black player come to the Dodgers. I never talked with Pee Wee about it, but he had to be under some pressure to be true to his "Southern roots" about the Robinson situation. But Pee Wee was and is a great family man, a standup guy, and Jackie was coming to another type of family—the Dodger family. Pee Wee wouldn't have had it any other way than to make things as comfortable as possible for Jackie.

I mentioned the "California" backlash I felt (or imagined) early in my career. Maybe that's one reason why I got along particularly well with Duke Snider. We were both from the West Coast, we knew each other a little bit even before I came to the Dodgers, and even though he was ten years older than me, we were cut from a bit of the same cloth. Duke had a short fuse on occasion. I could see that during our trip to Japan during the mid-fifties when we had all bought cameras and were taking pictures by the dozen during one game. Duke had bought a camera, too, but he was fuming because he wasn't able to take any pictures, like the rest of us.

"Come all this way and I gotta play in the game, too," he huffed.

Duke was a great all-around ballplayer, one of three outstanding center fielders playing in the New York metropolitan area before we moved to the West Coast in 1957. There was Mickey Mantle with the Yankees, Willie Mays with the Giants, and Duke with us, and I don't know if you'll ever see a situation like that again in the major leagues—three Hall of Famers playing the same position during the same era in basically the same city. Naturally, that was a source of constant debate around New York: who was better, Willie, Mickey, or the Duke of Flatbush? I'll only say this much. I'm sure glad that we had the Duke around. He could do it all, including adjust.

When we moved from the chummy confines of Ebbets Field to the bizarre configurations of the LA Coliseum, Duke faced a real career crisis. He went from the right-field wall in Brooklyn, which was high but reachable, to a completely different situation in Los Angeles. A left-handed batter, Duke was looking at a short left-field porch and an airport runway in right and right center field. If he'd wanted to be a pull hitter in Los Angeles, he would have been in for some frustrating times. But he made the transition, and that confirmed him as a rare ballplayer. He began knocking balls against and over that screen in left field, and he really never missed a beat.

In 1958, our first season at the Coliseum, Duke hit for a good average, .312, but not for as much power, only 15 home runs. The next year, though, Duke hit 23 homers, knocked in 88, and still hit for a good average, .308. We won the National League pennant and then the World Series, and Duke was a major contributor. I think that tells you a whole lot about Duke. I don't recall ever getting Duke's inner thoughts about the transfer of the Dodgers from Brooklyn to Los Angeles. I'd imagine at first that he was happy at the thought of being able to play in his backyard. But then, he probably took one gander at the LA Coliseum and thought to himself, "Bullshit on this . . . get me back to Ebbets Field in a hurry."

There's a story about the Dodgers' first game in the Coliseum, against the San Francisco Giants. Mays was in town, of course, and he was thrilled at the prospect of zeroing in on that left-field fence, only 250 feet away and 35 feet high.

"They took the bat away from you," Willie told Snider, looking down right field. "You're done, man."

Duke probably couldn't have argued with this at first. From a right-field line of 296 feet in Brooklyn, he was up to 402 in Los Angeles. Center field was 410 feet away. Duke had put up with a fair amount of talk in Brooklyn that he was fortunate to be hitting in such a small park, but people sometimes forgot that Yankee Stadium, where Mantle and Yogi Berra hit, was also 296 feet down the right field line and if you wanted to hit a home run, you didn't have to clear a 40-foot wall like Duke did at Ebbets Field. But Duke made it work in the Coliseum, because he was a great ballplayer. He struck out quite a bit, but he also had the ability to hit a knuckleball. He had the knack of holding his swing and timing it so that he'd be able to crush the knuckleball. He might have been the best I've ever seen at hitting that pitch. Now for a free swinger, who has to resist the temptation to overswing, that's a heck of a talent.

Duke was a terrific fielder, too, with a fine arm and he fit right into the mold of the old Dodgers by being a great agitator. Again, you still see it when we gather for one of these old-timers' affairs. Get the old Dodgers together and we just seem to have more fun than any other group. Roy Campanella said that you have to have a lot of little kid in you to play baseball, and we must have had more than our share. We were very close, and we had one other thing going for us. We won a lot of games. You can get away with more pranks and practical jokes when you're in first place than when you're 30 games out. That was a fact then, and I'm sure it still is now. We wouldn't have been such lovable "Bums" in Brooklyn if we hadn't won all those games, I can assure you of that.

Like most other players during spring training—especially players who were established—I didn't care for those Florida road trips. As a pitcher, I had the extra edge in that I knew roughly when I would be in games. So it was kind of a ritual for me to grab that Grapefruit League schedule from Red Patterson as soon as possible and sort of plan my outings. If I could do most of my pitching at our home base in Vero Beach and avoid as many trips as possible, so much the better, even if we did travel in our own plane. That sounds nice, having our own plane, but if you've ever flown through some of those violent storms they have in Florida, you know it isn't always a day at the beach. As it happened, we just seemed to play in Vero Beach at least every fourth day or so, and I used to pounce on those dates like a lion on raw meat.

Of course, I couldn't always pull it off. One day, Walt wanted me to go over to St. Petersburg to throw. Naturally, I moaned and groaned about the injustice of it all. And to top it off, Alston wanted me to go clear across the state just to throw batting practice.

Well, I thought to myself, if they want batting practice, that's what they'll get—batting practice.

When I got there, I took my share of razzing from the regulars. They knew how I felt about traveling, and when they saw me in St. Pete, they went for my jugular.

"What are you doing here?" asked Junior Gilliam. "Did they make a mistake? This ain't Vero Beach."

"Just get into the cage," I said disgustedly.

Gilliam took a couple swings and that was that. He cleared out in a major hurry.

"No more for me," he said. "That guy on the mound is mad and I want nothing to do with him."

So Duke got in there next, and he fouled a couple off the top of the batting cage. Then he looked out at me.

"Changeup," he requested.

I obliged, and he hit the damndest line drive you've ever seen. It was right back toward the mound, about thigh high, and it must have been going 200 miles an hour. (I told you Duke was pretty good at hitting that off-speed stuff.) I jumped about six feet into the air to avoid the damn thing and somehow, on the way down, I spiked myself and cut my pants from my crotch all the way to my knees. Unfortunately, I didn't avoid the ball, either. It hit me on every part of my body except the roof of my mouth and I fell down on the mound, ass-over-tea kettle. When I finally got up, looking like I'd been to war, the whole team was laughing and nobody was roaring louder than the Duke. His face was beet-red.

Of course, at that point, I was doubly furious. Not only had I had to make a damn road trip to pitch batting practice, but now my teammates were using me as target practice. I grabbed me another ball.

"That's all for me," Duke said, realizing that three pitches from me were about all he wanted to see. He wasn't going to chance a fourth.

"Get your ass back in there!" I yelled from the mound. "This is batting practice."

"I've had quite enough."

"Get your ass back in there!" I yelled again.

"Nope," said Snider. "That's all for me. Thank you very much."

Needless to say, whenever Duke and I see each other, we still have a chuckle about that day in St. Pete. Being Californians, we still get to see each other on occasion. He's retired as a broadcaster and has made it through heart surgery and every so often, we bump into each other at those fantasy camps that have become quite the rage—those week-long sessions where middle-aged businessmen will pay to come to Florida to become "baseball players" for a few days under the supervision of former major leaguers. At the first Dodger one, in Vero Beach, I was managing a team—the Double Ds—and Duke was umpiring. We scored something like 11 runs in the first inning of a game. Duke was getting a little antsy, thinking he might have to be out there for six hours. I loved every minute of it, of course, watching him get madder and madder.

At gatherings like that, or whenever time permits, it's not unusual for Duke and I to have a few cocktails and shoot the bull about old times, much as we did when he wound up his career with the San Francisco Giants in 1964. Alvin Dark was their manager at the time. Also, at the time, Crown Royal was the hot drink. That was the "in" thing, to drink Crown Royals. Fortunately, Duke and I were both at that point in our careers when we could afford Crown Royals.

Anyway, the Dodgers were in San Francisco on a Saturday and I was scheduled to pitch against the Giants the following afternoon.

"What are your plans this evening?" Alvin asked Snider.

"Well," he answered, "it just so happens that I'm going out to dinner with Drysdale."

"Good," said Dark. "I was hoping that would be the case. Here's a hundred bucks. Take the big donkey out on me and get him good and drunk."

"Whatever you want, Alvin. Thanks."

So, Snubby and I went out for a nice meal and a few drinks in a fine restaurant, The Iron Horse, right near downtown San Francisco. Duke announced that he was buying, which was fine with me. What he didn't tell me was that Alvin had given him the money to get me drunk, but, what the heck. A hundred bucks is a hundred bucks. You can't turn down a free meal from an old buddy, right? We had a good evening, and just as it was drawing to a close, I asked Duke where he was headed.

"Down to Burlingame," he said.

"What's down there?" I asked. "Are [wife] Bev and the kids living there?"

"No, I'm just here by myself," he said. "I've just got a little apartment down there near the airport."

"Why bother with all that? I'm rooming with Lee Walls. We've got plenty of space. Why don't you just bunk in with us at the hotel tonight?"

He accepted. I took one of the mattresses off my bed and threw it on the floor. Then I grabbed a pillow and a blanket out of the drawer. Presto. Duke had his very own bed, which was just perfect, because we'd both had our share of Crown Royals, the "in" drink.

The next day was cold and windy, as it tends to be in Candlestick Park, and Duke wasn't in the starting lineup. I could see him over in the dugout, trying to keep warm with his gloves on. And every so often, when I glanced over, he would put his hand up to his mouth and start laughing, like he suspected I was struggling somewhat, too.

Fortunately, we were up about 8–0 come the ninth inning when Alvin sent Duke up as a pinchhitter with 2 out. He stood in the on-deck circle, swinging a couple of bats, anxious to get a piece of me. Naturally, on the first pitch, I loaded one up. The ball must have dropped a foot, he fouled the spitter off, and then he just glared out at me on the mound. I had all I could do to keep from breaking out laughing right there in the middle of the stadium.

With the count 0–1, I gave him a big, fat fastball right in his wheelhouse, as if to say, "Here, it's 8–0, see if you can hit this." But he fouled it off again. He gave it that little characteristic pirouette of his and looked back out at the mound again. Now the count was 0–2, and John Roseboro, our catcher, was grinning behind his mask. You could see his pearly whites shining brightly. He knew this wasn't your ordinary at-bat at the end of a ballgame. He knew something was up and so did Snubby. I wasn't about to let this opportunity escape without loading up another one. I did, nice and moist, and fired it. Duke swung and missed the thing by a foot-and-a-half. Game over.

I came off the mound to shake hands with Roseboro, and he was laughing so hard he could hardly talk.

"Boy," Roseboro said, "is Snider ever mad at you!!"

I went back down the right-field line toward the clubhouse, and then settled in at my locker to talk to a couple of writers. All of a sudden, Miguel "Murph" Murphy, the visitors' clubhouse attendant, kind of ambled over to my stall with something in his hand.

"Note for you," he said.

I put down my beer and opened it up.

"Dear Donnie," it read. "Don't know what the last pitch was when it went by, but it sure smelled like Crown Royal. Love, Dookie."

Not all my memories about Duke are as happy. After the 1962 season, we began to hear whispers that there would be some moves made on the Dodgers. And during spring training in 1963, Duke got wind that he was on the way out, just the way Gil Hodges had gotten wind that something was up the year before. As spring training broke, we all heard rumors that Duke was going to be traded or sold or released, but nothing was firm.

As it turned out, we'd flown all the way to Albuquerque for an exhibition game against the Dodgers' farm club when the news finally became official. Duke had been bought by the New York Mets for $40,000. The Mets, who had joined the National League the year before as an expansion team and had lost 120 games in their first season, had taken on another old Brooklyn Dodger, just as they had chosen Hodges.

Snider wasn't too happy about it. None of us were. Not only was he gone, but they'd made him board that plane in Florida and fly halfway across the United States before they let him know what they already knew. Sometimes, the way they do things in baseball is hard to figure. Baseball can be a very cold business. Apparently, Buzzie Bavasi, our general manager, was so choked up about having to get rid of Duke that he couldn't tell him. Mr. O'Malley, our owner, was left with that task. I don't think Duke was too thrilled about that, either, because Buzzie had been around a long time. We considered him a friend.

For a brief moment, Duke considered just hanging them up and retiring. He was upset at the way he was let go, and it was probably a bit humiliating for him to be sent to New York for cash.

The Dodgers didn't even get a player in return for one of the greatest Dodgers ever. But Mr. O'Malley gave Duke some good advice. He told Duke to go to the Mets and pursue two pretty significant stats that were within his reach. Snider needed just a few home runs to get to 400, and he wasn't all that far from 2,000 hits.

Duke realized that it only made sense. Besides, he was headed back to New York, where he figured to be as popular as ever— which is exactly what happened. He got the hits and home runs he needed and received plenty of affection. A lot of Dodger fans who had been without National League baseball since the team moved became Mets' followers, and it didn't hurt during those trying seasons that the Mets had some legends like Hodges and Snider to help sell the new product. As it turned out, Duke played one season in New York, then the 1964 season with the Giants before retiring to become a broadcaster with the Montreal Expos.

Before he left us that day in Albuquerque, we had a little going-away party for Duke at our hotel. A bunch of us gathered to wish him well. He'd spent sixteen years with the Dodgers, but life goes on, and at least I had the opportunity to pitch against him a couple years later in Candlestick on Crown Royal Day. I wonder if Alvin Dark ever wanted his $100 back.

9

Other Teammates and Characters

*A*s a ballplayer, besides love of the game and the desire to compete, one of the things that keeps you going is the endless succession of personalities you meet. I played with Hall of Famers, then I retired and went into the broadcast booth and worked with Hall of Famers, and in between, I became friendly with some unforgettable characters. If baseball is America's pastime, it's also America's melting pot.

One of the real beauties I rubbed elbows with was Johnny Podres, a lefthander who was as funny as they come. A flake? No. Just loose. We called him "Pointed Head" or "Point." As a pitcher, he was as good as any in a money game. He won the big one for us in 1955, when he beat the Yankees and Tommy Byrne, 2–0, in the seventh game of the World Series at Yankee Stadium. He won a lot of other important games, too, and I'm not saying I'd take him over me for all the marbles, but Johnny was a terrific clutch performer. Right up there with Sandy Koufax, Juan Marichal, Bob Gibson, any of them.

Off the field, he was a free spirit who could cure another guy's bad mood in two minutes. We've all known people who make you crack up just by looking at them. Johnny was one of them. He'd give you his last dollar if you needed it. He loved to fish, and whenever we had a chance during spring training, we'd get a boat and head off on the inland waterways north of Vero Beach. One day, he was going on and on about this great deal he'd gotten on

Ban-Lon shirts. Five bucks each. He'd bought a bunch and was raving about them.

"Five bucks each?" I said. "Christ, Johnny, at that price, be careful. Don't get caught in the rain."

"No, no problem," he insisted. "Great shirts. Look at this maroon one I'm wearing. Beautiful. Even got a pocket. See?"

Howie Reed and Ron Perranoski were with us, along with a bucket of live shrimp, and, of course, a case of beer. You didn't want to get parched throats out there on the boat. Now, for a guy who supposedly loved to fish, Podres had no patience whatsoever. As soon as you came to a stop—Johnny made somebody else drive; he was too hyper to do that—he would drop his line in the water. If he didn't get a nibble right away, he wanted to move on. He never gave the fish a chance to wake up.

That day, Perranoski, our Polish captain, and Podres, our Lithuanian outdoors expert, led us toward this little inlet. We were sitting there, waiting for the fish to come to us, when I looked up and the sky in the distance was pitch black. It was as dark as night, with a silver lining around the clouds. I'd never seen a weather system quite as ominous-looking as that. The wind kicked up just like that, and the temperature must have dropped thirty degrees.

"Guys," I said, "we're a couple miles from shore. We better get the hell out of here."

"Nah," said Podres. "It's just one of those tropical storms. It'll blow over."

"Guys," I went on, "we're gonna get pissed on."

Soon, the drops started to fall. Big drops. Then, kaboom, thunder. That got Podres's attention. Now, he was in a hurry to get moving. Naturally, Captain Perranoski was having trouble starting the boat. Podres was jumpy at this point, so he dumped all the shrimp overboard and put the bucket over his head. That made a nice noise, when the hail stones hit him on the pail. Then there was more thunder, and a bolt of lightning that seemed like it was eight feet away. Podres grabbed hold of the bucket.

"Jesus Christ!" he yelled. "This is it! I'm gonna be electrocuted!"

By some miracle, we made it back to land. It was pouring. We got to our cars, and of course, the windows were down. It was a beautiful day in Florida when we started our little expedition. We opened the doors and the water came gushing out. Thank goodness they were rentals. Thank double goodness the engines turned over and we were able to get back to Dodgertown. There was only one problem. As we headed back to our barracks, I noticed that Podres was bathed in red.

"Johnny," I said, "did you cut yourself? Look at you."

He looked down at his legs, and he turned dead white. He thought he was hemorrhaging.

"Where is it?" he asked. "Where's all this blood coming from?"

"I'll tell you where it's coming from," I said. "It's not you that's bleeding to death. It's that spiffy new Ban-Lon shirt of yours. Five bucks each. What a bargain."

Johnny's wardrobe had been tested and it failed miserably. Not only did his maroon Ban-Lon lose its color, it expanded in the rain to about three times its original size. The thing was hanging down around his knees. It looked like a nightgown. And that nice shirt pocket was down around his waist. It could have been a watch pocket.

"I knew it was a bad deal," Podres said. "What do you expect for five bucks?"

He ripped off his shirt and threw it in the trash. End of bargain.

Johnny, I'm happy to report, is doing fine. He was pitching coach for the Minnesota Twins for a while, then came to the Dodgers as a minor league instructor. He got a little heavy after he retired, and needed open-heart surgery, but he's okay. Probably still fishing, too.

One of Johnny's favorite running mates was Don Zimmer, a real pepperpot and currently the manager of the Cubs. You see Zim's mug today and it's a reasonable facsimile of what he looked like in his youth. That's one face that hasn't changed much.

I've seen a lot of infielders in my day, but I never saw a man with a better throwing arm than "Popeye." None. The man had an absolute gun. He also had a bad run of baseball luck. He was beaned while he was in the minor leagues at St. Paul and was unconscious for something like three weeks. They thought he was going to die. But he made it to the big leagues, where he got hit in the head again by Cincinnati's Hal Jeffcoat in Ebbets Field. I was there. Another inch and he'd have lost his vision. Zim bounced back from that, too, but because of all his misfortunes, he never did become the ballplayer he was expected to be. With Pee Wee Reese at shortstop for us, of course, Zim never had much of a chance. Pee Wee sent a lot of guys back to the minor leagues.

Plus, something was always happening to Popeye. I remember him fouling two consecutive pitches off his foot. The same damn spot. Zim was in such pain that he couldn't make the standing-eight count. He had to crawl back to the dugout at the Coliseum. We didn't give him much sympathy. We were all on the floor laughing.

Popeye hit some home runs in the minor leagues but not a lot in the majors. Eventually, he developed the theory of swinging hard in case he hit it. He played hurt, and he played hard. When we traded him to the Cubs for Perranoski in 1960, Popeye scared me half to death. He stood in there, right over the plate, daring you to come inside on him. He had a motto about that, too: "If you're going to hit me, don't wound me. Get me good. I don't want to lie there quivering. I want to get it over with. Just end it."

After his minor league beaning, Popeye had these plugs stuck in his head to protect him—"to keep my brain from jiggling," says Zim. A lot of people think he's got a metal plate, but they're really like corks. Anyway, after he got dinged again by Jeffcoat, the doctor in Brooklyn took X-rays of Zim's head to check for damage. According to Popeye, the doctor came back from examining the pictures with his eyes like saucers. The doctor was practically shaking. He couldn't believe what he'd seen.

"Which is understandable," said Zimmer. "I forgot to tell him about the plugs I had in there already."

After I retired in 1969 I had some horses running in Del Mar, near San Diego. I was in the turf club and I ran into Podres and Zimmer. They were in the area to play in an Angels' old-timers' game in Anaheim. Whenever they were near a track, Podres and Zimmer managed to find a way to attend. I invited them both to the house for dinner and drinks, they slept over, and the next day, we went to Anaheim for the game. By this time, I had lent them some money because they'd tapped out at the track. On the way back, we stopped at the San Clemente Inn for a beer. There, Podres and Zimmer got the bright idea to go to the dog track in Tijuana. Not me. I went home. At three-thirty that morning, the phone rang. It was Popeye.

"Where are you?" I said.

"Across the border from Mexico," he reported. "Just in the United States."

"How much money you got?" I asked.

"About eight cents."

"Can you make it to your hotel in San Diego?" I said. "If you can, I'll see you at the track tomorrow and I'll bring you some more money."

"Over and out," Zim said. "See you at the track in the morning."

Frick and Frack, Podres and Zimmer, hooked up another night when Wally Moon had a party at his house in Sherman Oaks. We spent some time there, then they decided to head off to Perranoski's place. Podres was driving, with Zim asleep in the backseat. I gave Podres directions, which he didn't quite follow. He got his ramps mixed up as he entered the San Diego Freeway, and was pulled over by the police. Johnny, who didn't like being late to any party, was indignant.

"What's the problem here?" Podres said. "I was only going about fifty miles an hour."

"You're absolutely right, sir," the officer answered. "But you happened to be going the wrong way."

All this commotion woke up Zimmer. He took one look at the police car and closed his eyes again. Podres had to pitch the next night, and he won 4–0. I told you. A money pitcher.

One day during spring training, Buzzie Bavasi got on Wes Parker for playing like he was asleep. Parker said, "You would, too, if you lived across from Podres and Al Ferrara. They have this record player and they blast it every night until three in the morning." Buzzie was furious. He loved Zimmer and Podres like sons because they were so good for the club, but he was hot. He found Podres in the locker room.

"What are you doing, keeping your teammates awake by blasting that music at three in the morning?" Buzzie demanded.

"Don't know what you're talking about," Podres said. "I wasn't playing any music at three in the morning."

"Well," stuttered Buzzie, "it was coming from your goddamn room at three in the morning!"

"It's possible," Podres said, "but I wasn't in it."

Buzzie just stormed off.

Don Newcombe was a huge, happy-go-lucky guy who I always got along with real well. He had this big, long, rocking windup and he threw hard. He featured a little dinky slider, but mostly fastballs, and he had excellent control. Newk had a mean streak in him when he needed it. I saw him and Sam Jones go through both lineups one day in Wrigley Field. Batters on either side were falling like duckpins. Finally, when each pitcher made it once through the order, umpire Jocko Conlan stepped in and said, "Okay, that's it, fellas. Let's go play."

Newk got thrown out of a game one afternoon in Crosley Field, and he wasn't even pitching. He was in the dugout on a brutally hot day with Frank Secory umpiring at the plate and having a tough day. Newk's problem was that he had this loud voice you could hear eight blocks away. That day in Cincinnati, Newk was perched near the water cooler and all he did was laugh. Secory would call a pitch, and Newk would laugh. Finally, Frank had had enough. He threw Newk out of the game for laughing. Newk got up, lumbered behind home plate toward the clubhouse, just shrugged those big shoulders of his, and disappeared.

Newk disappeared one night in Chicago when Buzzie happened to be in town. Chicago was always a tough place, because of all the day games followed by all those free nights. Buzzie knew this and he called Newk's room in the hotel. Roy Campanella, Newk's roomie, answered and said Newk wasn't there. Buzzie found Newk the next day, and Don told him he'd been playing music somewhere else in the hotel.

"Music?" said Buzzie, "Past our twelve-thirty curfew? Well, that'll cost you three hundred."

When the rest of the pitcher's fraternity heard about it, we never let Newk live it down.

"Shoot," said Eddie [Sears] Roebuck, "for three hundred bucks, Newk, you could have hired an orchestra."

Newk, of course, admitted in later years that he had a drinking problem. He cured it, and now works for the Dodgers in community affairs, and is also active in programs that help people beat drugs or drinking. I honestly never suspected Don was an alcoholic when I played with him. The only suspicious thing he ever did when I was there happened in 1956, on that postseason trip to Japan. After pitching once, he hardly showed his face until we were ready to head back home. He got on a scale in the Tokyo airport—a freight scale. He checked in at 270 pounds.

Campy was a jovial sort, too, and to watch him and Newk work together as a battery was a pleasure, especially in 1956, Newk's great year, when he was 27–7. It was like they were playing catch. Campy was a great player and storyteller, too. I could sit and listen for hours when he recollected his time in the Negro Leagues. One time, Campy played two doubleheaders in one day. When it got dark, they hoisted ladders and fastened lights to the top of them so they could see well enough to play.

Campy was in the dugout one day at the Polo Grounds when Junior Gilliam—a quiet, friendly guy we called "The Devil"— bunted foul on Marv Grissom of the Giants. Well, you didn't so much as look at Grissom cross-eyed, let alone bunt on him. Talk about mean. When Campy saw Gilliam bunt, he just covered his eyes.

"Junior, Junior, Junior, what you just done," Campy said. Sure enough, on the next pitch, Grissom put Gilliam down with a little skin-bracer.

Gilliam was a good, disciplined hitter who roomed with Jackie Robinson and probably had a little of Jackie rub off on him. If it hadn't been for him hitting behind Maury Wills, Maury never would have stolen all those bases with the Dodgers. Gilliam also was famous for coming back to the dugout with his scouting report of that day's opposing pitcher. The guy on the mound could be throwing bee-bees 200 miles an hour, but Junior always had the same critique.

"Sheeet," he'd say. "That guy ain't got sheeeet."

In Vero Beach, where the black players never went into town, Campy would eat his dinner and then go out in back of the kitchen, sit down and talk with whoever was around—scouts, the help, other players. They still have that bench in Dodgertown— "Campy's Bullpen." Whether Roy could have blazed the trail for blacks instead of Jackie Robinson, I don't know. Campy had that fatherly image; Jackie had a harder edge to him. Since his accident, of course, Campy has been unbelievable. The man's been para- lyzed for more than thirty years, and he keeps smiling from that wheelchair. Talk about a human being with a remarkable spirit and will to live.

Carl Furillo, alias "Skoonj," was another dandy. Hard-nosed, played the right-field wall in Ebbets Field like nobody else. They called him the "Reading Rifle" from Pennsylvania because you didn't run on him. I saw him throw runners out at first base on balls that dropped in front of him and should have been singles. Amazing. He was forever saying in the clubhouse before the game, "Let's go out and get that check." And yet, he was a warm and decent man. They gave him a night in his honor and one of the gifts to him and his wife Fern was a trip to Hawaii. I'd just gotten married. He turned around and gave it to me as a wedding present. Carl was a bit of a loner. Not antisocial, but he just kept to himself.

I heard the tale about Furillo going bonkers one day against the Giants and charging their dugout in search of manager Leo Durocher. Skoonj broke his hand during the incident. That was before I got to Brooklyn, but I heard the story. You didn't mess with Furillo. We thought we had a real crisis on our hands when we got Sal Maglie from the Indians in 1956, because he and Maglie hated each other. They looked at each other with daggers. We were wondering what it would be like with Maglie in our clubhouse, but typically Furillo was all business. Sal walked in that first day, Furillo went over to shake his hand, and that was that. Pee Wee, our captain, was over at his locker, smoking his pipe, sweating it out. I can still remember the look of relief on Reese's face.

Carl Erskine, Duke Snider's roommate, was a prince. I never saw Erskine take a drink, never heard him utter one profanity. Erskine was the nicest guy in the world; he's a bank president back home in Indiana. The only time I ever saw Carl get into any trouble was one day in LA when he was playing with a boomerang during batting practice. Walt Alston was by the cage watching Erskine in the outfield and Walt got angry. Batting practice came to a halt and Walt cussed out Erskine. Of all guys, Carl Erskine! That was the worst thing I ever saw Carl do. In fact, it might have been the worst thing Carl Erskine ever did.

Don Hoak was one guy I never quite figured out. He seemed to be mad all the time. I kept wondering when and how he relaxed. You know, what do you look like when you sleep? He had the reputation of being a former tough guy in the Marines, except that when he went over to Pittsburgh—where he played pretty well—Jerry Lynch and Dick Schofield spread the story that they'd checked the records and found out that Hoak had really been in the Navy, and only in the band. When Hoak heard that, you might as well have stuck an icepick in his heart.

Roger Craig, who was with me in Montreal before we came up to the Dodgers, was a world of fun. We called him, "Slim Summerville." And Frank "Hondo" Howard was an absolute riot. He was a giant of a man who was as gentle as he was big—which was good for the human race. Talk about a guy who didn't know his own strength. Frank was likable and popular and we went a lot of places together, especially during the off-season when a few of us would dabble in show business with people like Milton Berle and Jan Murray. I don't know that us players were all good, but we had fun. For one stretch in 1962, we rehearsed for five solid weeks, then did four weeks of shows, two a night, sometimes three. Tough work. Snider was there, Sandy Koufax, Willie Davis, Wills, Howard, and myself.

We also took Frank along on a couple of hunting trips, where he got all dressed up like the "Marlboro Man" and looked like a real outdoorsman until we all realized that he didn't know one end of a gun from the other. On one of our little theatrical excursions, we paused one afternoon to play cards and have a drink. We couldn't decide what we wanted to have to quench our thirst. All of a sudden, I remembered a vacation I'd taken to Puerto Rico.

"Banana daiquiris," I said. "I had some of those down there and they were real good. Hondo, what about a banana daiquiri?"

"Sounds good by me," Howard said, and Ron Perranoski agreed. We ordered twelve of them. Frank went through his share like they were water, so we ordered twelve more. Then a dozen more, and Frank was still downing his cocktails.

Pretty soon, it was time for us to head to our show. Moose Skowron was along for this spectacular, plus Perranoski and Howard. When their cue came, they were to go onstage and do pirouettes to "The Blue Danube." Real, nice, classy stuff. All went well until Frank, who wasn't feeling too hot, got dizzy from all those banana daiquiris and fell into the drums. The audience applauded. They didn't know any better. They thought it was all part of our act. We knew it wasn't, and so did the drummer. But the people were loving it. It's a miracle Frank didn't put a hole in those drums. As he tried to get out of the band pit, he banged his head on the cymbals. Hondo got another round of applause. The people figured that was part of our routine, too. Good thing we made our living as ballplayers.

One hot afternoon at Vero Beach in 1963, we went for a beer before dinner. Well, a few beers. Then, we headed off to the Palamino Club. It was all couples there, except us five stooges—Lee Walls, Perranoski, Moose, Howard, and myself. At that time, the "twist" was the popular dance, and sure enough, a lot of husbands and wives or guys and their girlfriends were out on the floor, doing their thing.

"You know something, roomie?" Howard said to Skowron. "We ought to get out there and dance."

"Are you kidding?" Moose said. "I ain't dancing with nobody, least of all you."

I smelled an opportunity for a few laughs, so I jumped right in.

"Go ahead, Moose," I said. "Look at those people out there twisting. Nobody knows who's dancing with who anyway. You go out there with Frank, nobody will bat an eye."

"Well, okay," said Moose.

So, there they were, two of the strongest men in baseball—Moose Skowron from Purdue and Frank Howard from Ohio State—in an all-Big Ten twist-off, swinging elbows and bumping people all over the place. Pretty soon, the rest of the dancers got out of there for their own safety, and it was just Moose and Hondo, with the floor all to themselves. What a scene. It was about eleven o'clock then, and we still hadn't had dinner. We'd met for one beer at about four in the afternoon, and wound up going to a dance.

"We gotta get out of here," I said. "I'm calling a cab."

Perranoski wisely had taken off, so it was just us four fools jammed into the taxi. Frank and Moose were in the back with me in the middle. Walls got in front, next to the driver, who must have seen us tumbling out of the establishment and wished he hadn't answered the call. What's worse, the driver had this little Chihuahua in the front seat with him. As soon as the thing saw Frank, it started barking at him.

"Jesus Christ, my head's spinning!" Howard was moaning. "Now, I got to listen to that barking."

And the dog just kept howling, right at Frank.

"God, am I hungry!" Howard went on. "We never ate a damn thing, did we?"

More barking.

"I'll tell you," Hondo said, "I'm so hungry, I could eat that goddamn dog."

With that, the cab driver discreetly grabbed the dog and stuck it under his coat. We never saw the Chihuahua for the rest of the trip.

They were a pair, Moose and Hondo. One afternoon, we were headed to Milwaukee County Stadium during an eclipse. None of us knew exactly what that was, so we turned to our two scholar-athletes from the Big Ten.

"It's when the sun goes out," said Howard.

"No, it's when the moon and the sun collide," corrected Skowron.

I'll say this for Frank Howard. Nobody worked harder to get that big body in shape, especially in spring training. Some times he worked too hard. There was one stretch of exhibition games when he was always about a foot short of reaching fly balls while playing the outfield. Whenever there was a fly ball hit his way, he would invariably have to field it on one hop. We wondered what the hell was going on. Why couldn't this guy move a lick? Turned out, he had a ten-pound weight on each ankle and a weighted belt around his waist. He was trying to lose some weight and get into shape. Alston put a stop to that.

"Frank," he said, "why don't you work on that program some other time?"

Even in tough going, Frank managed to provide a chuckle. In one game at Wrigley Field, Frank struck out and started to walk back to the dugout, all disgusted. Tommy Davis was on deck, and he and Hondo used to use the same batting helmet. Tommy stepped in Howard's path and put out his hand for the helmet. Hondo just shook Tommy's hand and kept on walking. Tommy stood there with his jaw on the ground.

Chuck Essegian, another strong guy, was with us for a while. He and Frank Robinson started jawing at one another one day, so Essegian came out of the dugout after him. It took both Hodges and Howard to restrain Essegian. If he'd gotten to Robinson, Frank might not have survived. In the minors, pitcher Pat Scantlebury went after Essegian with a bat, hit him with it, and broke the bat.

If Essegian was quiet, Norm Larker fit right into the daffy

Dodger mold. When he made an out, he came back into the dugout and rammed his head into a brick wall. And I mean hard. One time, he was the runner on first base and we had a hit-and-run play on. The batter swung and popped the ball up, but Larker wasn't about to stop. He made a beeline for second base, then was halfway between second and third before he saw Bobby Bragan, the third-base coach, who was yelling at the top of his lungs for Larker to get back to first to avoid being doubled up.

So, Larker turned around, darted right behind the pitcher's mound, and made a mad dash to first base. He hadn't touched second yet. "Shortest distance between two points is a straight line," reasoned Larker.

We called John Roseboro "Gabby" because he never said much. But he could catch. We were lucky that way with the Dodgers. From Campy on, we always seemed to have outstanding receivers, guys who could handle pitchers, call a game, throw, and think. They talk about the history of great Dodger pitching. But don't forget that Dodger catching down through the years. Gabby was among the best, even if he did have to wear white tape on his fingers during night games so we could see the signs. His hands were that dark. John also had to have the world's largest collection of bats. He was forever switching off when he wasn't hitting well. If another guy on the team was on a hot streak, Roseboro would borrow his bat. I don't know how Gabby kept track of all his lumber.

We had some fine relief pitchers with the Dodgers, too, like Clem Labine. He came in from the bullpen with his glove rolled up in his back pocket and he'd throw the damndest curveball you ever saw. He had a rubber arm. He'd get up in the bullpen and be ready in no time. In fact, Clem started a few games and pitched great. He won the sixth game of the World Series, 1–0, in ten innings. I liked Clem a lot. He did have that scholarly air about him. Wherever we went, he carried a big thick book. One day on the plane, Labine went to the bathroom and Roebuck cut out two pages from Clem's book. He returned and just kept on reading. Never missed a beat.

We had some characters on the coaching staff, too. Charlie Dressen used to travel with Spanish onions in his suitcases. He liked to make chili. And could he talk. Charlie, of course, managed the Dodgers in 1953, but he wanted a multiyear contract and Mr.

O'Malley wouldn't give it to him. So, Mr. O'Malley brought Walt in, in 1954.

Bobby Bragan, another of our coaches, was a funny man. As a manager with Hollywood in the Pacific Coast League, he used to come out to argue with an umpire carrying a can of soda pop. Or, wanting a game to be halted because of rain, he'd come out of the dugout under an umbrella.

Of all the coaches that came our way, I spent more time with Leo Durocher than any. Leo was a great baseball man and a real charmer, the life of the party. He wouldn't let you sleep. If Leo was quiet, something was wrong. It was through Leo that I got to know Frank Sinatra. He knew only one way to go, first class. He always dressed impeccably, his shoes were shined, and one thing you didn't do with Leo was mess with his clothes. One of us pranksters tied his socks up in knots in Chicago and Leo held a clubhouse meeting. Walt was the manager, but Leo called a meeting and he was fuming.

"If anything like that ever happens again," he said, "I guarantee you that every one of you SOBs will go home in knickers."

I called Leo the "Ancient Mariner" for a little stunt he pulled in Cincinnati. He had a date and he took her to dinner, then suggested that they take a boat ride on the river. Leo was very fair and gentlemanly about the whole thing. He rowed the boat downstream, and then had her row it back upstream. Nice going, Leo.

We had a couple of beauties covering the Dodgers from the local newspapers when we moved to Los Angeles—Bob Hunter, who we called, "Chopper," and Frank Finch. Bob worked for the *Herald-Examiner* and Frank for the *Times* and we had many a cocktail with them, too. Frank is famous for one story about the day he arrived at a ballgame a little late, like in the seventh inning. He asked a fellow from another paper to give him a "fill"—in other words, to read back the scorecard on the previous six innings so Frank would know who got the hits, who made the outs, and so forth.

Well, in an effort to provide Frank a little more than just the bare bones, this gentleman suggested that one player had made a spectacular catch in the field.

Frank stopped his pressbox lodge brother cold by saying, "I'll be the judge of that."

The sad part of these recollections is that so many past Dodgers have endured personal tragedies in their families and others are gone. Skoonj is dead, so are Hodges and Walt Alston and Gilliam and Robinson. But you can't replace memories. Those old Dodgers were unique, and you'll never convince me otherwise. I'll be the judge of that. If I had a wish, it would be to play at today's prices, but with the guys I played with back then. As long as I'm making wishes, I might as well make a big one.

The Great Holdout

f people don't remember me for my reputation as a headhunter, which I wasn't, or for my scoreless streak in 1968, then I guess they peg me as one half of the infamous Drysdale–Koufax holdout. Or was it Koufax–Drysdale?

The 1965 season was a good one for the Dodgers and for Sandy and me. We won the World Series in seven games against the Minnesota Twins. Sandy pitched two shutouts over them, including a 2–0 masterpiece versus Jim Kaat in Game Seven. I lost the first game, but won the fourth. It was a nice end to a fun summer during which Sandy was fabulous—he had a 26–8 record with a 2.04 earned run average and 382 strikeouts in 335⅔ innings. Unbelievable. I was 23–12 with a 2.77 ERA and 210 strikeouts.

In those days, players' salaries weren't common knowledge like they are today. Which was fine by me. What I make is none of your business, and what you make is none of my business. You didn't see each club's payroll printed in the newspapers like you do now. Sandy and I, therefore, didn't have a handle on what everybody else was earning, but we did know we wanted more than we were getting. He was paid $85,000 for the 1965 season and I got $80,000 and, considering the way things went, I guess you'd have to say we were in a pretty good bargaining position, even in an era when they didn't throw money around like they do now. Also, we were in an era when there was no free agency. You were

123

bound to a club for life with the reserve clause, unless your club traded you and your reserve clause to another team. Or you retired. Or you got sold. Those were your options. Was that fair? No fairer than a lot of things in professional sports today, like the college drafts in the National Football League or National Basketball Association. But what are you going to do if you're a player? It's their ball.

Anyway, it was time for Sandy and me to go in and talk about a new contract. I didn't have an agent. Never did. Agents weren't in full bloom then, and even when they did become popular, I did my contracts by myself. Sandy was advised by a terrific fellow, J. William Hayes—let's call him Bill—of Executive Business Management in Beverly Hills. The man we'd have to negotiate with was Buzzie Bavasi, the Dodgers' general manager who was like a second father to us but a tough cookie nonetheless. He didn't like to throw money around any more than any other general manager you'll ever encounter.

One day long after the season ended, I called Sandy and asked him to meet me for dinner. He had been in once to talk with Buzzie and so had I. In fact, the day before I phoned Sandy to meet me, I had chatted with Buzzie. I didn't have any real purpose in getting together with Sandy, other than the fact that we were friends and lived reasonably close by. He was living in Sherman Oaks, and I was in Van Nuys. So, my wife Ginger and I agreed to meet him at this Russian restaurant not far from his house. As soon as we got there, and he had a drink, I could sense that something was troubling Sandy. He wasn't himself.

"Anything wrong?" I asked.

"Nah, not really," he said. "You know, you try to be halfway decent, and people just won't let you be."

"What are you talking about?"

"Well, you know," said Sandy. "You go in and try to get a contract settled so you can relax and prepare yourself for spring training and you run into a lot of bullshit."

"Whatta you mean?"

"You walk in there and give them a figure that you want to earn," Sandy went on, "and they tell you, 'How come you want that much when Drysdale only wants this much?'"

"When did you talk to them?" I said.

"Today was the first time."

"Never before today?" I asked.

"Never."

"Well, I'll be damned," I said. "I went in to talk to them yesterday for the first time, and they told me the same story. Buzzie wondered how I could possibly want as much as I was asking when you were asking for only this."

It didn't take a rocket scientist to figure out what was going on. Buzzie was trying to play us off against each other, not an unusual maneuver for management. Sandy and I were both asking for percentage increases over our current salaries that were similar to boosts we'd received before. My biggest jump, for instance, was after the 1962 season, when I'd won 25 games. I want to say I might have doubled my salary, from maybe $30,000 to $60,000, or something like that.

The problem after the 1965 season, as we saw it, was that each of us would be breaking that magic $100,000-a-year barrier, which was territory Buzzie didn't want to enter. I know it sounds incredible now, with the salaries being what they are, but in 1965, asking for $100,000 wasn't like asking for the moon. It was like asking for the moon plus the rest of the solar system. At least, that's how you were made to feel. Actually, we had our sights set on more than $100,000 each. But the first offers from Buzzie were in the middle-nineties—not much of a hike for two guys who'd won 52 goddamn games between them the previous season.

"You go home and think about it," Buzzie would say. "Remember, I can only go so far. My hands are tied."

"Fine," I would say. "You go home and think about it, too, Buzzie. If we can't get anyplace, maybe we should go to the next level [Mr. O'Malley]."

When we compared notes about our separate meetings with Buzzie, Sandy and I realized that we might be in for one tough haul. Buzzie wasn't going to be in too generous a mood, not that we expected him to be. But it was Ginger, with that keen business sense of hers, who came up with an idea.

"This whole thing is easy to rectify," she said. "If Buzzie is going to compare the two of you, why don't you just walk in there together?"

A hell of a plan. And that's exactly what happened. The next time Sandy and I talked contract with Buzzie, we went into his Dodger Stadium office together. We told him that was what we were going to do and he said, fine. I don't know whether he cared, whether he was nervous or angry. He didn't let on. There also was nothing he could do. And when we hit him with the fact that we knew about his ploy, he just laughed.

"Look, fellas," he said. "I've got a budget to keep here and there are certain things I'm allowed to do."

As the impasse dragged on the next few days, Sandy and I started to hear the old cliché from Buzzie: "Why don't you fellas come on down to spring training, and we'll straighten it out there?" That was another pretty clever tactic. If you're a ballplayer who hasn't signed a contract, there's nothing that will soften you up faster than heading off to Florida in late February to put on the uniform again and get around all the teammates you haven't seen for months. Sandy and I knew that. We weren't about to bite at that.

Meanwhile, I had been talking to Bill Hayes, and he recommended that Sandy and I hold firm to a package deal for three years that would have cost the Dodgers about $1 million for both of us. Again, teams wouldn't bat an eye at that number in today's market, but in 1965, no pitcher was making over $100,000 a year. Willie Mays was there, so were Stan Musial, Ted Williams, and Mickey Mantle. Maybe Hank Aaron was in there, too. But no pitcher. And there we were, two pitchers, wanting to make the grade. The Dodgers wouldn't budge.

Time passed without any discussions or meetings whatsoever. Finally, Buzzie called one day and suggested that it was getting late. I agreed and we decided to huddle at the Hollywood Roosevelt Hotel. The three of us—Buzzie, Sandy, and I—sat at a corner table in the middle of the afternoon with practically nobody else around. Sandy scribbled some numbers down on an envelope and Buzzie flinched again. We came down from our original demand of $1 million, to closer to $900,000. But there were still too many obstacles. Buzzie didn't like the money amount, or the concept of the three-year commitment, and he sure as hell wasn't too thrilled about the fact that Sandy and I were holding firm together.

As spring training drew near, Buzzie asked Sandy and me if we were going to take the plane to Vero Beach. We both said no. We were staying home. I tried to work out as best I could, throwing to a friend of mine, Eddie Sacks, who used to be a catcher in the Phillies' organization. We went up to Pierce Junior College in

126

Woodland Hills just about every day. The baseball coach there, Bill Ford, had been my coach at Van Nuys High School and I told him that I didn't want anybody to know I was there. There was no problem in that department, but believe me, there's nothing like spring training for getting into shape. Those little sessions at Pierce Junior College just weren't taking the place of Dodgertown.

Sandy was working out on his own, too. Meanwhile, we stayed in touch with Bill, of course. Though we had been getting nowhere with the Dodgers since the end of the previous season, the minute Sandy and I failed to board that plane for Florida—on February 26—our absence became big news. And Hayes was just amazing. He had the greatest instinct for judging how the wind would blow. He could practically name the day that certain publications would take the Dodgers' side in the dispute, or ours. It was uncanny how he predicted what would be said or written and when.

Sandy and I decided that we would try to lay low during the entire episode, however long it lasted, and we pretty well stuck to our guns. There were hundreds of phone calls to my house and Sandy's and Bill Hayes's office, but we didn't go public with any opinions or progress reports. All the information was stemming from Vero Beach, where the Dodgers had set up camp. The party line was that the Dodgers' franchise had a salary structure to maintain, and that we were being unreasonable, and so forth. At the outset, public sentiment seemed to be with Sandy and me. But then when the writers settled in at Vero Beach, where they might have been wined and dined on occasion by the front office, they printed more and more of management's side of the story. I don't fault the press for that. If only one faction is talking, it's pretty difficult to present opposing views. There were lots of columns and articles written about how we were victims of baseball "slavery." And there were other stories wondering why the Dodgers were being so stubborn because it was obvious the team couldn't win without us.

Sandy and I added no fuel whatsoever.

"Hello, may I speak with Don?" the voice would say on the other end of the telephone.

"Sorry, he's not here," Ginger would answer.

And that was that. Sandy and I read about how greedy we were, how unfair we were being to the rest of the team, and so on. Even the editorial cartoonists in the Los Angeles papers had a field day with the cross-country disagreement. But Bill kept saying that the worst thing we could do was negotiate through the press, and I knew he was correct. We wouldn't have accomplished anything by getting into a pissing match with Buzzie or anybody else in the Dodger hierarchy. Plus, it got to the point where the writers grew so tired of recycling the Dodger point of view that they began questioning it. On top of that, with all the statements that were coming out of Vero Beach, sometimes one version of club policy would contradict another. By staying quiet, Sandy and I took some lumps but at least we didn't have to provide daily updates on our mental and physical health.

Every once in a while during spring training, Sandy or I would get a call from Buzzie, wondering whether we had altered our plans. Also, we'd get calls from guys like Johnny Podres, asking us what we were doing and kind of urging us to come on down to Florida. I can't prove that Buzzie put them up to it, but that might have been the case. Then again, our teammates were our friends and they had to be thinking the same thing that Sandy and I were thinking—when is this thing going to be resolved? Or, *is* it going to be resolved?

At one point, Sandy and Bill and I were having a little skull session and Sandy said he was just going to retire rather than endure any more aggravation.

"Easy for you to say," I told him. "You're single. I've got a wife and a child. We went into this together, and we're going to see it through."

Sandy didn't argue with me. I don't know that he was as serious about quitting as he was just plain annoyed. Me, I was more frustrated than anything. It was becoming pretty clear than Sandy and I weren't going to go crawling back with our tails between our legs, and it seemed just as apparent to us that the Dodgers were going to be stubborn, too. There was even a point when we got Mr. O'Malley on the telephone and asked him if he would mind if we sought employment elsewhere, like with Gene Autry, who owned the California Angels.

"You want to go see Gene?" Mr. O'Malley said, very dispassionately. "Fine, go ahead. Of course, we have rules in baseball that prohibit you from doing such a thing."

Of course, Sandy and I knew that Mr. O'Malley was absolutely correct. We had every right to sit out and not get paid, but as far as being able to sign on with another major league team, well, we didn't have a snowball's chance in hell. No other owner would touch us, and if anybody dared to try, he'd have been stopped before he started.

Eventually, the thing got to be a little ridiculous. I think we all agreed on that, which is probably the only item that both sides did agree on. At just about that time, Bill Hayes got together with some of his lawyer friends and they found some piece of legislation that had been passed by the California courts because of disputes between the movie studios and actors and actresses. Bill had told us about personal service contracts for Robert Cummings and Olivia de Havilland, whose deal sounded a lot like ours. Motion picture stars, like baseball players, were held as property of one studio for life until the California ruling. It stated that personal-service contracts were illegal after seven years. The state of New York had a law that personal-service contracts were illegal past ten years.

So, here was a law saying that you could be in the employ of a particular California company for seven years, after which that contract had to be renegotiated. It was a law enacted to protect talent from being abused or exploited by their employers. It prevented the studios from getting too fat off the actors and actresses without compensating them properly and it did not regard option years as years on the contract. In other words, it was Hollywood's version of the reserve clause being overturned, which is exactly what happened to baseball's reserve clause in the mid-1970s, too late to help Sandy and me. But it had to happen, because for all those years, we played under illegal terms. That's what the court finally ruled, that the baseball reserve clause was un-American.

Bill and his friends unearthed this statute late in March and somewhere along the line, Mervin LeRoy, a prominent film producer who was a friend of Mr. O'Malley, got wind that Hayes had been checking into the personal-services contract issue. Sandy and I were ready to go to court to challenge the Dodgers on the validity of the contracts they were holding us to—we were unsigned for the 1966 season, but, under the reserve clause, obligated to the Dodgers, bound to them for perpetuity. We were prepared to sue major

129

league baseball and the Los Angeles Dodgers to become free agents. Hayes instructed one of his partners, Richard Hume, to prepare the briefs.

This, remember, was nine years before the landmark ruling in December 1975 by arbitrator Peter Seitz, who decided that Dave McNally of the Montreal Expos and Andy Messersmith, a former Dodger who went on to pitch for the Angels, had complied with their obligations by playing one year beyond their 1974 contracts and therefore were free agents, available to the highest bidder. That verdict completely changed major league baseball and went a long way toward creating a balance between management and labor. If you've followed baseball at all, you know the reverberations Seitz's opinion has caused since. But in 1966, Sandy and I were basically on the same track, prepared to do the same thing. And I think Mr. O'Malley must have realized we were on to something, because it wasn't a week after Bill Hayes made his discovery that our holdout ended. I'm convinced that was the major reason why the Dodgers moved, because we knew they had found out about Bill Hayes's little discovery. I can't prove it, but my guess is that the Dodgers realized they were playing with fire and that if we went to court, they might lose us both and get nothing in return. Besides, it wasn't that we were bad guys or bad players. We'd won 49 games during the previous season and 3 more in the World Series, and we were just trying to get what we thought we deserved.

Chuck Connors, the former Dodger turned actor and a great baseball fan, helped get the ball rolling a bit when he found out that Buzzie had slipped back into town from Florida. He called him and urged him to meet with us, and then Chuck called me. Then I phoned Buzzie and we arranged to meet at a restaurant called Nikola's, near Dodger Stadium. I called Sandy and told him about our conversation and he said that he didn't care to partake, he had something else to do. But Sandy did tell me that if I thought there was substantial progress, that we would get pretty much what we were looking for, then go ahead and tell them it's a deal. Sandy trusted me with his vote.

So, I met with Buzzie. We talked about my getting $115,000 for the season and Sandy getting $125,000.

"How do I know Koufax will agree to it?" Buzzie asked.

"Sandy told me to be the judge," I said. "But I'll call him anyway."

I went to the phone booth and told Sandy that I was happy with the numbers. He said, fine, if I was happy, he was happy. I went back and told Buzzie it was a done deal, and he said that he'd call Mr. O'Malley with the news in Vero Beach. Meanwhile, he wanted me to call Sandy back and make sure he'd be at Dodger Stadium for a press conference in about an hour. We showed up there, the place was packed, and that was that. The Drysdale–Koufax tandem had ended its job action. That night, Sandy and I flew to Phoenix to join the team, which was heading west from Florida for the start of the regular season. We had only a few days of spring training, and it didn't help me one bit. Claude Osteen was the opening day pitcher for the Dodgers, and I got off to a terrible start. I wasn't in shape, and neither was Sandy, but at least the damn thing was over.

I was so tired and frustrated by the whole thing that I can't say for sure how I felt at that press conference. I don't remember what I wore or what I said. I think it came out in the newspapers that neither side won, which is partly true. Sandy and I got just about what we really thought we would get in the beginning and all that we did was blow five weeks of spring training. And as Buzzie said when peace was reached, "Look at all the publicity we got the last month." I wanted to kick him right in the butt when I heard that, because I figured there were better ways to get ink, but that was Buzzie—always looking to have a laugh, which is probably why I like the man so much to this day. Sandy has said since that my unusually close relationship with Buzzie probably had a positive influence on the holdout situation, and Sandy's probably right.

At the press conference to reveal that we were still Dodgers, management showed a little levity. The program began with the revelation that Chauncey Haines, a "distinguished organist of the motion picture industry," had been hired to play the lovely Dodger Stadium Wurlitzer that season. Oh, and by the way, they added as an afterthought, Koufax and Drysdale would also be back to join the starting rotation.

Strangely enough, I felt sorry after it was all over for Mr. O'Malley. We had put him in an uncomfortable spot with all his peers. Mr. O'Malley was one of the most powerful and respected

131

owners, and I'm sure he didn't care for the fact that we held out as long as we did. I'm also sure, after the deal was done, that he probably took some grief from other owners for allowing not one, but two of his pitchers to crack that $100,000-a-year barrier. Something like that just raises the salary levels of all other players, a troubling prospect for baseball owners. Now, when I say that I felt sorry for Mr. O'Malley, don't take it to mean that I thought in any way that Sandy and I broke his bank. On the contrary, the Dodgers were making a lot of money, tons of money, then as now. In 1965, with a payroll that was nowhere near what the payroll is now, we drew more than 2.5 million fans to Dodger Stadium. That was the official count. In the National League, no-shows aren't counted. That means, if somebody buys a ticket but doesn't go to the game, his seat is considered empty when the paid attendance is recorded. But that seat is paid for, and that guy doesn't get his money back. It goes right to the vault of the ballclub, and the Dodgers had a pretty hefty vault.

Mr. O'Malley was more than just a boss to us. At least he was to me. And he did say that he considered Sandy and I almost like sons. He said he was concerned about what we were doing to our careers and our reputations with that holdout. He said he was concerned because he had gotten some very negative mail about us during the disagreement. (That's when Sandy told him, "Mr. O'Malley, you're seeing only half the mail. You should see the letters we get.") Whatever, I always had the highest respect for Mr. O'Malley and Buzzie, and our brief separation in the spring of 1966 didn't change a thing. Although I must say that I've read some accounts of the holdout, such as Buzzie's in his autobiography, "Off The Record," and it doesn't quite mesh with events as I remember them. Buzzie left out a few details, like Bill Hayes's findings on the personal-service contracts.

Bill had warned us that it would be an emotionally draining period, and he was right. He was also right when he said that if we took a stand, we'd have to hold our ground, no matter what. There's not much doubt in my mind that a key to the whole thing was that Sandy and I did it together. We were both valuable to the pitching staff, but if we hadn't stayed away together, it might not have worked. If one of us had gone to spring training and signed, the Dodgers would have let the other one dangle and twist in the wind. It was tough enough for us to hold out. Without the strength we gained from doing it together, holding out would have been unbearable. I presume that Buzzie figured that out, too, because in his book, he also wrote that he would never, ever tolerate a package situation again. Drysdale and Koufax came along at the right place and the right time and they took advantage of it, but never again. *Never!*

I felt some pressure when I returned to the ballclub, but nothing I couldn't handle. Certain members of the press got in their last licks, and the fans in Los Angeles had their say, especially when I got knocked around a fair bit during the early going. But that was understandable. The other players on the Dodgers were happy to see us, because it was better for our chances to win again, and they had to know that the higher Sandy and I drove the salary structure, the better it was for everybody. Management wasn't going to lose any money on us, that was for sure. We didn't hold anybody up. But the deal did pave the way for better money for others. The only players who might have been upset that we settled would have been a couple of young pitchers who'd hoped to take our places and had probably hoped we'd sit out all summer.

I brushed off the whole episode, as I tend to do with just about anything that leaves a bad taste in my mouth. Sandy, though, wasn't quite as willing to forgive and forget. I think he stayed miffed for a while. He didn't like to be beaten in a ballgame, and he certainly didn't like to be embarrassed. I think our tug-of-war with management embarrassed him. My personality allowed me to say, screw it. Sandy let the whole thing get under his skin a bit. It wasn't easy. It was the toughest period I've ever gone through in professional sports. I would not recommend it to anybody, particularly someone who can't deal with going days without an inch of progress. Whatever the situation is in the morning when you wake up, that's the way it's probably going to be when you go to sleep at night. Not a lot of action. We were lone wolves in those days, because you didn't buck management in 1966 the way you do now. Not in major league baseball, anyway. It was take-it-or-leave-it then, and by doing what we did, we were ten years ahead of our time. In all of our conversations with judges and lawyers, the feedback we got was virtually unanimous—if we went to court, we had a heck of a good case. And I was just disgruntled enough at that point that I was actually looking forward to going to court!

Was I prepared to play no baseball at all in 1966? Absolutely.

I allowed for that possibility in my mind. We even made contingency plans. About a week before our signing, we announced that we had joined up with actor David Janssen to do a movie. (As I said earlier, this holdout featured some strange twists.) Sandy and I assumed that we wouldn't be with the Dodgers during the summer, so we geared up to do a movie instead. It was to be called *Warning Shot*, directed by Buzz Kulik. Janssen was going to be the star, Sandy was going to play a detective sergeant, and I was going to be a television commentator. We had planned to start filming at just about the time the baseball season would begin. Sandy and I had signed contracts and all systems were go.

Bill Hayes had other plans for us, too. He'd had feelers from Paramount and Screen Gems about getting me to sign a long-term contract. Hayes also had an exhibition tour of Japan lined up for Sandy and me—thirty to sixty days that would pay "six figures." None of these bonanzas ever came true, because we went back to playing baseball. I didn't regret putting on my uniform instead of the pancake one bit, and I think Sandy felt the same way. At the press conference announcing our theatrical plans, Sandy didn't look too thrilled. And at the press conference announcing the end of our holdout, one of Sandy's first remarks was, "Thank God I don't have to act in that movie." The studio released us from our commitment, though we did fulfill our obligations to appear in a television show, "Hollywood Palace," during the first week of the season.

As it turned out, Sandy and I got big raises and in some circles, were considered pioneers. I don't know about that. Buzzie later went on record as saying that he didn't feel too good about how it all wound up, but he'd had no choice. It was getting late, and Mr. O'Malley had told him to get us into uniform. After the team's banner season in 1965, Buzzie figured that the player payroll would have to increase by $100,000. As it turned out, according to Buzzie, Sandy and I got $70,000, leaving $30,000 for the other twenty-three players.

Buzzie did also admit that Sandy and I were box office. Somewhere it was estimated that Koufax meant 8,000 extra fans in the ballpark when he pitched, and 3,000 extra when I pitched. If you say that each fan spent an average of $4.50 on a ticket, parking and food, that would mean $36,000 extra every time Sandy pitched and $13,000 every time I went to the mound. Multiply that by, say, twenty starts for each of us during the season just at Dodger Stadium, and what do you get? Well, you get the message. The Dodgers did very well on the deal, thank you. They always did. Of course, Buzzie did try to have the last word. He never put much stock into those ballpark figures. His argument was that if either Sandy or I pitched, but the rest of the Dodgers stayed home, how many fans would come to the stadium then? Okay, Buzzie.

Sandy and I did give in on our original request of three-year contracts, but we never really expected that, anyway. The Dodgers' stance was that, if we could guarantee them we'd be healthy and productive for three years, they'd have no problem with a multi-year contract. But guarantees like that were impossible, which is why they were against multiyear deals. Heck, Walt Alston even went on a year-to-year basis from 1954 until he retired in 1976. That was the way it was in those days, and the Dodgers had a point. Mr. O'Malley and Bavasi knew that Sandy's arm was hurting a bit. After the 1966 season, he retired.

I've got to give credit to Bill Hayes for the way he handled the holdout. He was fair and firm with both sides. Bill was an outstanding attorney in motion picture circles and didn't need to advise a couple of athletes. He had enough clients. He worked with Sandy and me out of friendship. After our settlement with the Dodgers, Bill must have received hundreds of inquiries from other sports types, but he turned them all down except for Don Klosterman, the pro football executive.

The end of our holdout did affect the National League pennant race. While we were sitting at home during spring training, the odds in Las Vegas were something like 4–1 or 5–1 against the Dodgers repeating. But after we signed, the Dodgers became 8–5 favorites to win another pennant, which we did. I had a better second half than first, but I still finished at 13–16. Sandy was sensational, maybe even better than the year before. He won 27 and lost 9 and had a 1.73 earned run average. We were swept in four games of the World Series by the Baltimore Orioles, getting shut out in the last three. It wasn't a real happy ending to the season, but at least Sandy and I had a season. There were a lot of days during spring training when it looked like we were going to be playing television commentator and detective sergeant instead of baseball.

Obviously, for Sandy to quit baseball after winning 53 games and losing only 17 in the previous two years was a tough blow to the Dodgers. But he was a remarkable guy, and there was no turning back when he said he'd had enough. Sandy's word was his bond, and besides, he was hurting. At the time he left, he was an unbelievably dominant pitcher, although most people forget how much he struggled at the start of his career.

When I got to my first spring training camp in 1955, he was wild. You could see he had a great arm, but he had trouble throwing strikes. But he was a bonus baby, so he had to stay with the big club. Those were the rules. There's no question in my mind that those two years were pretty much wasted as far as Sandy developing his craft. I don't know how he feels about that, but instead of being spotted in the major leagues—he won 2 games in 1955, 2 in 1956, and only 5 in 1957—he could have been developing better in the minors. He showed signs of brilliance but there was no way you could predict greatness for him, because of that one factor—his control, or lack of it. He stood there pitching to those strings in spring training, and he not only missed them, he missed everything. I saw him miss the cage in batting practice.

It was so bad that Sandy was going to flat quit. He was that frustrated, and it was Buzzie who talked him out of it, I think in the runway of the Coliseum. Then, during spring training in 1961, we were going over to Orlando to play against the Minnesota Twins. Sandy sat on the plane over there with Norm Sherry, his catcher for the day and his roommate. Norm had a good baseball mind, and he tried to talk to Sandy about backing off a bit. In other words, when Sandy fell behind the batter on the count, he had a tendency to muscle up more than ever, to overthrow. Norm's suggestion—and I guess it wasn't the first time he'd ever made it—was that Sandy try to get command of his body, develop some rhythm, and take the "grunt" out of every windup. It couldn't get any worse, in other words, so try relaxing out there a little bit on the mound. Every pitch didn't have to be 100 miles an hour. Don't force the fastball. Throw a curve once in a while when you get into trouble. Pitch to spots. Pitch, period, instead of throw.

Well, that created the monster. Sandy took it to heart, and soon became a completely different pitcher. He finally developed a style, an idea, and he just exploded. He came into his own. He won 18 games that season, 1961, and was having a hell of a year again in 1962 until he developed that problem with the index finger on his left hand. First it went numb on him, and then the skin started to tear away. It turned out to be a circulatory problem, and Sandy wound up winning only 14 games (he lost only 7) but if he'd have been around all season, we would have won the pennant in a cakewalk. As it was, we blew a lead and lost to the Giants in a playoff.

But in 1963, Sandy was fabulous again, winning 25 and losing 5. The next year, he was 19–5. And then there were two more great seasons. You take what he did from 1962 until 1966, and you might not ever see a comparable five years by any pitcher ever again. I mean, he was unbelievable. For a stretch of seasons there, we were billed as the "Big Two," Koufax and Drysdale, and it was fun. I don't know if Sandy enjoyed watching me pitch, but I sure as hell enjoyed watching him do his thing. He was something.

Sandy also was a lot warmer and more outgoing than most people realized. During that winter we spent in the Army at Fort Dix, he and his family in Brooklyn were very good to me. I went over there a lot for dinner, which was nice for a guy who was 3,000 miles away from home and experiencing his first real winter ever, learning how to cope with snow and ice. Sandy had the car and he would drive from Fort Dix to Brooklyn, too, and it never failed. When we were about five minutes out of Fort Dix, I fell dead asleep on him in the shotgun seat. He could turn the radio on full blast and it didn't bother me a lick. I was gone, out of it, until we hit Brooklyn. I wasn't much of a companion, but I did get my rest.

Sandy came across to the public as a quiet, introverted guy, a churchmouse. That was the picture painted of him by the press, but Sandy didn't care to let his hair down around the press, or in a crowd of people. You had to get him off to the side or out for a beer before he started telling jokes in that great Jewish accent of his. A funny, funny man. Occasionally, Sandy would be knocked for being a recluse, but my answer to that was, "Who is one person to say how another person should live?" Sandy was a great guy, and still is. He's keeping pretty much to himself, living in Vero Beach, Florida, and working for the Dodger organization. Every once in a while, I'll see him, and Sandy's the same as ever. He'll have a few cocktails with you and lay a few jokes on you.

I was sorry to see Sandy call it a career, but he had that arthritic elbow, and he was gone in a flash after the 1966 season. He never cheated the Dodgers, that's for sure. When he matured,

137

he was as good a pitcher as I ever saw. Make that the *best* I ever saw. When Sandy Koufax got the ball, you always allowed for the possibility that he'd throw a no-hitter. There always was that expectation, because he was that dominant. I don't know how you can top that.

11

The Scoreless Streak

*I*f you'd have told me that I'd make any kind of history during the 1968 season, I'd have told you to think again. The 1967 season wasn't exactly a banner year for me—I had a good earned run average of 2.74, but my record was 13–16. There was even mention in a couple newspapers that I was trade bait, because I was on the downside of the baseball mountain.

Then during spring training of 1968, at an exhibition game in the Houston Astrodome, I jumped up for an overthrow while covering third and felt a little pop, felt something snap in my right arm. I never thought much about it, though as I look back, that injury might have been the beginning of the end for me. That, and the continuing wear and tear on my arm—which affects all pitchers sooner or later.

Our team that year didn't hit a whole lot. In fact, our starting pitchers during that brief era—Sandy Koufax, Claude Osteen, Bill Singer, Stan Williams, and myself—all fell in the period when Dodger teams didn't hit a lot. I came in at the tail end of an era that featured a Brooklyn team with a terrific offensive lineup, and then after a lot of my contemporaries left, in came Steve Garvey and Ron Cey to hit a bunch of home runs. There were Dodger teams shortly after I retired that had five guys in the lineup hitting 30 home runs a season. It would have been nice to pitch for that crew, but, believe me, I'm not complaining.

We hit enough to win some ballgames. The thing was, we just

didn't scare anybody. Gene Freese put it all in perspective. He was a pretty good infielder during the sixties with the Reds, Phillies, Pirates, and White Sox and he was quoted once as saying, "I hear the Dodgers just came into town. They're taking batting practice in the hotel lobby." You get the idea. The 1927 Yankees, we weren't. Freese also had another one: "Watching the Dodgers take batting practice is like watching a silent movie." Cruel, but true.

I joined in the gentle jabs, too. During the 1964 season, I went to Washington, D.C., for a day to appear at a government affair to honor some war veterans. I had just lost the night before in Philadelphia, 1–0 or 2–1, and Sandy was going the next day. The reporters found out where I was in Washington, and I got a couple of calls.

"Did you hear about what Sandy did?" one of them asked.

"No," I said. "What happened?"

"He just threw a no-hitter against the Phillies," the writer told me.

"Great," I answered. "Did he win?"

I had some basis for making the remark, besides our team batting average. A few years earlier, Harvey Haddix of the Pirates had a perfect game through nine innings at Milwaukee, but he still lost to the Braves in extra innings. So, these things do happen, and that pretty much was the frame of mind with which we approached each game we started during that era. You'd better think about pitching a shutout, or giving up at most 1 or 2 runs, if you had any ideas about winning. That mindset can do wonders for a pitcher's ability to concentrate and bear down, although I'd much rather go out there in the first inning with a 5–0 cushion. I'm not a numbers guy. I'm not a person who's hung up on statistics. But if there's one part of my career that I'm proud of, it's that I wound up with an earned run average under 3 per nine innings—2.95 to be exact. That means that most of the time, I did my job. I kept the Dodgers in the game to the point where we had a chance to win.

Fittingly enough, my scoreless string that created such big headlines in 1968 began with a 1–0 victory over the Cubs and Ferguson Jenkins in Dodger Stadium on May 14. I beat Dave Giusti of the Houston Astros 1–0 four days later, and then Bob Gibson in St. Louis on May 22 by 2–0. At this point I had twenty-seven straight scoreless innings, and a couple of trends were developing. We didn't score many runs, and the pitcher I went up against on each occasion was outstanding. Jenkins and Gibson were two of the greatest competitors you'll ever see, and Giusti was pretty hard to handle, too.

That third game of the streak in St. Louis was on a bad night. The weather was lousy, and the field was wet, but the Cardinals had a good team and Gibson always meant box office. The Cardinals had a big advance sale, so they were going to do everything possible to get the game in and they did. We got 3 hits, St. Louis got 5, and we won.

My next start was May 26 in Houston, and I pitched my fourth shutout in a row. I beat Larry Dierker of the Astros 5–0—we got 5 whole runs!—and it was then that I remember people starting to take notice. Some of the writers dived into the record books and came up with the fact that Harris ("Doc") White of the Chicago White Sox had pitched five consecutive shutouts in 1904. That game in Houston was not without incident. Grady Hatton was the manager of the Astros at the time, and Al Barlick was the umpire that night. He was one of the greatest umpires ever—he was inducted into the Hall of Fame in 1989—and apparently, Al was asked to go out and check me for foreign substances, to frisk me.

"Look," Barlick said, coming out to the mound from behind the plate, "I've got to look around here. Don't worry about anything."

He didn't seem too serious about his mission. He asked me to turn around and look like I was being searched and all that. I obeyed, and then he went right back to work behind the plate.

"Let's play," he said. Case closed. I had nothing to hide at the time, and furthermore, I don't think Al was too thrilled about being told how to run a ballgame. He was a very strong individual. When I first came up to the Dodgers, part of my education was listening to veterans like Hodges and Pee Wee and Duke talk about the umpires in the National League. You learned how far you could go with certain guys. Larry Goetz, for instance, you didn't dare look at cross-eyed. No way. Artie Gore, you stayed clear of him, too. I found that out with my own two eyes. One night in the Polo Grounds, Maglie got mad at something and threw his glove to the ground. Before it landed, Gore gave him the thumb. Bingo. Get outta here. Barlick was much the same. That's the scouting report I had on him. Don't mess with Al. A terrific umpire, but let him handle the ballgame. He handled the situation in Houston just the

141

way he wanted to. He put on a little pantomime at the mound, and that was it.

Oddly enough, an umpire figured in my next start, on May 31 against Mike McCormick, a pretty good lefthander for the San Francisco Giants. We had a 3–0 lead going to the top of the ninth inning at Dodger Stadium. Willie McCovey walked, Jim Ray Hart singled, and then I walked Dave Marshall to load the bases with none out. Marshall was a left-handed hitting outfielder, the same guy who later that summer would break up a no-hitter I had at Candlestick Park. There were 2 outs in the eighth, and he got a base hit, but I hung on to win my 200th game.

Herman Franks, the manager of the Giants, put in Nate Oliver to pinch-run for McCovey at third base. Dick Dietz, the Giants' catcher, was the fourth batter in the inning. I went 2-and-2 on him, and then our catcher, Jeff Torborg, called for a slider. It didn't slide. The ball just sort of grazed Dietz on the left elbow. He was all set to head toward first base, forcing in Oliver from third and ending my streak. But Harry Wendlestedt, the plate umpire, ruled that Dietz hadn't tried to get out of the way of the pitch, so Dietz stayed right there. It took a lot of balls on Harry's part to make that call, but I felt he was absolutely right. Dietz had made no effort to avoid the pitch, and that was confirmed to me the next day. Juan Marichal, the Giants' great righthander, told me that Dietz had said in the dugout before he came to bat, "If it's anything but a fastball, I'll take one and that will end [the streak] right there." In other words, knowing that a hit batsman would bring in a run, Dietz was willing to get in the way of a pitch.

After Dietz was ordered to stay at bat—the count was then 3-2—he fouled a pitch off, and then hit a shallow fly to left field. It was too shallow for Oliver to score on, and when Jim Fairey caught the ball, that made it bases still loaded with 1 out. Ty Cline was next up, pinch-hitting for shortstop Hal Lanier. Cline hit a hot smash toward Wes Parker, a fine glove man, at first base. Parker dug the ball out of the dirt and fired home for the force out at the plate on Oliver. Two out, bases still loaded, shutout still intact.

Jack Hiatt then was sent up to pinch-hit for McCormick. Hiatt popped up to Parker at first, and the game was over. We won 3–0 and I had pitched my fifth straight shutout. Well, Dodger Stadium went whacko. There were 46,067 fans that night, and they made enough noise for twice that many people. It was almost like a World Series celebration. I had no trouble grasping the significance of my accomplishment then, even though, in all honesty, it hadn't affected me that much to that point. I always operated on the theory that you break down a ballgame—inning by inning, batter by batter, pitch by pitch. I never did put much stock in streaks that lasted over days or even weeks. What's done is done. Let's get on to the next thing. That was my game plan. My idea always was to throw the fewest number of pitches possible, pitch to the fewest number of hitters, and get it over with. If you shut the other team out in the first inning, then think about shutting them out in the next.

It was contradictory to my nature to worry about the big picture, so to speak. I was more into focusing on a particular batter or situation. Naturally, whenever you're a starting pitcher and you get the ball in the first inning, your goal is to give up nothing. That's a given. And naturally, you don't ever expect to give up nothing for five games in a row. My rule of thumb was that if I allowed the opposing team more than 3 runs a game, I wasn't going to win. Against studs like Gibson and Marichal, you knew damn well that you could give up 3 runs or less in a game and lose. Bob Friend was in their class, and so were Chris Short and Jim Bunning and Fergie Jenkins. Maybe it was my imagination, but it always seemed that other teams set up their rotations to give us their best pitchers. Everybody liked to beat the Dodgers and kick us while we were down, which was an indication of how much success we had had. It was forever the Dodgers vs. the top guns.

When Dietz was first hit by the ball, I didn't have an immediate reaction. It was so close that I couldn't really tell from sixty feet, six inches away whether the ball had hit him or the bat. But, after he took one step toward first base, he was called back so quickly by Wendlestedt that there wasn't much doubt in my mind what was happening. I knew the rule, of course, stating that a batter had to make an honest attempt to avoid being hit, and it was obvious that Harry was exercising his right to make a judgment call. Peanuts Lowrey was coaching third for the Giants and he didn't agree with the decision any more than Herman Franks. They came out and screamed and argued and the game must have been delayed twenty-five minutes. I saw that figure in one of the newspaper

143

accounts of the game—twenty-five minutes—and all during that delay, the fans were having a ball watching the Giants jump up and down.

There was an incredible buzz in the ballpark, and part of the reason was that the fans were not only enjoying what they were watching, they were also listening to Vin Scully on their transistor radios, describing the scene. Los Angeles fans made a habit of taking in Vin's broadcasts while they were at the ballpark. It not only added to their enjoyment but to their knowledge of what was happening before their eyes. And that night, during that delay that seemed like an eternity, Vinny was reading the specific rule to the listeners. Hell, he could have read the whole rule book while those sparks were flying.

Dietz, Herman, and Peanuts were all going nuts right around home plate while I stood out there on the mound, trying to stay loose and warm by playing catch with Torborg, our infielders, whoever wanted a little exercise. Nobody said anything to me. There was nothing to say. It was bizarre and when it finally ended, Franks had been ejected. It's hard to imagine, if you weren't there, that one pitch could create such a fuss. After all, when the smoke finally cleared, the Dodgers were still leading 3–0 and the Giants still had the bases loaded with 1 out. The only thing that had changed was the count on Dietz and, hell, if I hadn't have thrown a strike on the next pitch, or another strike on the pitch after Dietz fouled one off, the Giants would have scored, anyway.

That's what I always kid Herman about. I get along with him well, and we've seen each other countless times since. He's forever calling me a lucky SOB because of Wendlestedt's call, but I always come right back at him. Herman, I say, you fancy yourself a great manager. If you were, how come you couldn't get even 1 run out of having the bases loaded and none out? I mean, where was that managerial genius of yours that night in Los Angeles? Herman, a pretty fiery guy, just grumbles when he hears that. He called Wendlestedt "gutless" in the newspapers the next day, but you've got to know Herman. He's likely to say just about anything when he's hot under the collar.

It was interesting, too, to see how our manager, Walt Alston, operated that night. In the seventh inning, with a 2–0 lead, he put our best defensive players in the game. For instance, he moved Parker in from left field to play first base for Kenny Boyer. But in

144

the ninth inning, with the bases loaded and none out, he played the infield at double-play depth to protect the victory. He didn't play the infield in to protect the shutout. I wouldn't have expected anything but that from Walt, who had his priorities in order. The reason we were out there that night was to beat the Giants, not to pad my scoreless streak. When we were fortunate enough to do both, Walt was among the first to sprint out to the mound to shake my hand. He was asked later about the controversial play involving Dietz.

"I never saw the play called before," Walt told the writers. "But then, it's the first time I ever saw anyone get deliberately hit by a pitched ball."

So, I had the National League record of five straight shutouts and I had tied Doc White's major league record. My next assignment was on June 4 at Dodger Stadium against the Pittsburgh Pirates. In the second inning, I struck out Bill Mazeroski to break King Carl Hubbell's league mark of $46\frac{1}{3}$ consecutive scoreless innings established thirty-five years previous. Then I continued on to work a complete 5–0 victory over Bunning, extending my string to 54 straight scoreless innings with my sixth straight shutout. It was calmer in the ballpark that night, but I had a pretty good outing. I gave up 3 hits—one by our former shortstop, Maury Wills—and I did hit Manny Mota in the helmet with a pitch.

I also had some great support in the field. Paul Popovich, our second baseman, had helped me get that fourth straight shutout in Houston when he turned a hard-hit ball by Lee Thomas into a double play. In fact, Popovich made two fine plays that night on tough hops in equally tough circumstances. They were still playing on that old dirt infield in Houston, and it was hard and crusty. It was like a goat ranch. Against the Pirates, Gary Kolb doubled in the sixth inning and advanced to third with 2 away. Wills hit a little chopper toward Popovich, who got Maury at first on a close, close play. Everybody knows how fast he was. That could have been a run right there. Not long after all this happened, I got a congratulatory telegram from Doc White, who was living in Florida.

On June 8, my next start, we faced the Phillies and another top pitcher, Larry Jackson, who was particularly tough on the Dodgers. In the top of the third inning, our Kenny Boyer at third base made a real nice play on a hard-hit ball by Roberto Peño and threw him out. That enabled me to break the all-time major league record of

56 straight scoreless innings established by Walter Johnson. Another standing ovation. But, my streak came to an end awhile later, at 58⅔ innings.

I came into the game with 54 and made it until the fifth, when Tony Taylor and Clay Dalrymple singled. Taylor went to third on the hit by Dalrymple. I low-bridged Roberto Peña, the next batter. He went down in the dirt, and I eventually struck him out for the first out. Howie Bedell was the next batter and he lifted a fly ball to medium left center. Len Gabrielson, our left fielder, went over and caught it, but there wasn't much doubt that Taylor would score from third. He was an excellent baserunner and there was no chance to throw him out. The streak had ended and I think my first reaction was one of relief that it was over. I knew it couldn't go on forever, and it had gone on a whole lot longer than I expected. When Taylor came in, the fans in Dodger Stadium gave me a nice standing ovation and I don't remember how I responded. I might have tipped my cap. I might have just turned around and looked at the outfield or bent down to tie my shoe, as I often did. Or I might have done all of the above. I just don't remember.

When I was finally ready to pitch again, there was Jackson at the plate with a bat in his hand and he did a really classy thing. He sort of looked out at me on the mound and tipped his cap, as if to say, "Nice going." He didn't make a big show of it. He just made that little gesture, and then went about his business of knocking the dirt out of his spikes and stepping in to face me. But it was a nice thing to do. I nodded back, and went back to work.

Gene Mauch, who has become a great friend of mine, was the young manager of Philadelphia at the time. He was coaching third base, too, and Gene was pretty good at agitating. He was always looking for an edge against the opposing team, and no sooner had I come off the mound after that fifth inning when the streak ended than plate umpire Augie Donatelli came up to me. I had just about gotten to the third-base foul line on the way to our dugout when Augie sneaked up on me and grabbed my hat.

"What the hell are you doing?" I said.

"Just checking you out," he answered. "Just making sure everything is okay."

Then he ran his fingers through my hair.

"What the hell is this all about?" I asked. "Get away from me."

"Don't you talk like that to me," he said, and he was right.

Augie Donatelli was another of those umpires who didn't take any guff, but I wasn't really in a mood to mind my manners, so I kept on yapping.

"I'll tell you whatever I want to tell you," I snapped. "Usually when someone runs their fingers through my hair, she gives me a kiss, too."

And I stared at him, with my lips puckered.

"Get outta here," Donatelli said. "Go back to the dugout. You're okay. There's nothing wrong with you. Get your ass out of here."

Obviously, Mauch had engineered the whole thing. He didn't say a word while the streak was intact, but the minute it ended, he protested. So Augie came after me and found nothing. That's baseball, folks. It was a nice experience. And Ginger and I got a dog out of it, though not for long. Toward the end of the streak, some friends of ours from Vero Beach sent us a dog. We called him "Shutout," but we didn't have much chance to enjoy him. We were living out on a ranch at the time, and Shutout never quite got acclimated to all those wide-open spaces. Whether he just ran off or ran into some rattlesnakes, I don't know, but Shutout didn't stay around. He was a pure-bred with great papers, but we just couldn't keep him tied up. Maybe curiosity got the best of Shutout. One day, before he disappeared, Shutout came home with his nose all bloodied, so there was a chance he eventually encountered something he couldn't handle. We still had our German shepherd named "Pitch," and our jumping horse, "Full Count." We had everything covered.

People have asked me many times whether I had ever pitched better than I pitched during that scoreless streak, and the answer is yes. I've pitched better single games, like the 1–0 victory over the Yankees in the World Series or the game against the Cardinals when Curt Flood led off with a single and I retired the next twenty-seven batters in a row. And I probably had stretches when I actually threw the ball as well or had just as much stuff. To go 58⅔ innings without yielding a single run, you have to be doing something right, true. But you have to have some luck, too. There has to be a combination of both, and I had it.

In those seven games that constituted the streak, I gave up 33 hits, which tells me I had something going. We had 50. I didn't get a lot of lusty hitting behind me, but as I said before, I got just enough. We wound up the season with a 2.69 team earned run average, but our batting average was just .230 with only 67 home runs! That was a period when I did quite a bit of pinch-hitting. In 1965, I got up 130 times, hit 7 home runs, and batted .300 to lead our team in batting average. But that was the way it was, and pitchers had to accept that fact. We didn't have a lot of thunder. As I look back, the best games I pitched during that stretch probably were the first three—against the Cubs, Astros, and Cardinals. But the one I thought about most was the game against the Pirates, because they gave me all sorts of trouble.

The 1968 season was dubbed the "Year of the Zero," for more reasons than my streak. My streak had recently concluded when Gibson came into Los Angeles on July 1 on a tear of his own—he had 48 straight scoreless innings in his pocket. He was right on my tail, and who did he face on a Monday night in Dodger Stadium but me. Matter of fact, one of the first times I'd ever been held out of a start so Walt could juggle the rotation was then, so I could pitch against Gibson. It was quite a confrontation, with 54,157 fans in attendance.

But we put an end to Gibson's attempt in the very first inning. With 2 out and his streak at 48⅔ and counting, Gabrielson singled to right and took third on another single by Tom Haller. With a 1-2 count on Ron Fairly, Gibson fired a wild pitch, scoring Gabrielson, who took a big leap toward home plate and landed on it with a thud. Gibson's pitch was a slider down and in the dirt. He overthrew it and the ball bounced over catcher Doc Edwards's shinguards. After the game, Gibson was nice enough to say that the "shutout streak belongs to Don Drysdale." But as somebody was quick to point out, while we won the battle of zeroes, we were losing the war. We were seven games out of first place going into that night, the Cardinals beat us 5–1, and then won the next three games to sweep the series, too. They ran off and won the National League pennant going away, and Gibson survived the traumatic experience of his wild pitch pretty well, too. He won 22 games, lost only 9, and had an earned run average for the season of 1.12, which is unbelievable. An ERA of twice that was considered fabulous. How does a pitcher pitch for sixth months in the heat of summer and allow only 1.12 runs per nine innings?

Now, if you're going to ask me another question—what did I know about Howie Bedell?—my answer would be, not much. I never remembered even seeing him. He was a left-handed hitter who played a little bit for the Milwaukee Braves several years before and then all but disappeared until he showed up that night to bat against me. I had no idea how to pitch to him, and I don't know that anybody on our team had any idea of his strengths and weaknesses. There weren't a lot of Howie Bedell scouting reports lying around.

One day, years later, I was broadcasting for the California Angels. Buzzie Bavasi, my old boss from the Dodgers, was with the Angels then and so was Bill Rigney, a former Giant manager. We were just hanging around the office in Anaheim, and we got to talking about that scoreless streak. Somebody asked how many runs Bedell batted in during that 1968 season and Buzzie had a tongue-in-check reply:

"It probably was Bedell's only RBI of the season. Let's get that record book out."

We looked it up, and sure enough, the only run Bedell knocked in during 1968 was the run that ended my streak. Bedell batted only nine times, had only 1 hit, and that sacrifice fly. Buzzie got a real good laugh out of that.

I can't say that the pressure of the streak really got to me, though I did have my superstitions as the thing went on and on. I wore the same sweatshirt at the ballpark at Dodger Stadium, and for road trips, where we had to dress a little better, I brought the sweatshirt along with me. As it turned out, all but two of those games were in Los Angeles, so I didn't have to worry too much about my wardrobe. There were a few other items that I didn't want to touch, like underwear and socks and that sort of stuff. Nobe Kawano, our clubhouse man, knew well enough to stay clear of washing my clothes after I pitched a shutout. And after pitching six in a row and not washing some garments that really needed it, believe me, there were a lot of people besides Nobe steering clear of me. This was in the middle of the summer. Some of that stuff got pretty moldy.

As the number of shutout innings mounted, the press became more and more interested, but that was never a problem. I've never had any real trouble with the media, and 1968 was no different. On days I was scheduled to pitch, I would talk to the writers if they got to me early, before batting practice. After that, I didn't have much to say until after the game, win, lose, or no decision.

149

Batting practice for me was a good way to loosen up and also to concentrate on the game ahead, and the writers respected that just as I respected the fact that they had a job to do. I was a pretty loose guy and, don't forget, in 1968, there wasn't nearly the number of writers and broadcasters there are today. I don't really know how it's happened in the last twenty years, but the press corps has multiplied. That's good for baseball, good for sports, because it's more exposure. But it can get a little hairy, and when Pete Rose was chasing Ty Cobb's all-time hit record a few years ago, I don't know how he kept his sanity. He had to hold press conferences every day, before and after games. During my streak, I was only the center of attention on days I pitched. I could vanish for three days in between starts, or use those three days to do the bulk of my interviews.

That much said, I don't understand a lot of these modern-day athletes who claim that they don't have time to grant interviews or that interviews create too much pressure and break their concentration. If answering a couple questions about yourself affects your pregame preparations or postgame rituals that much, then I've got to wonder what you're all about. I've got to wonder where your head is. But, then, I'm an old-school guy who grew up in a more graceful period when writers weren't considered the enemy so much as they were thought of as part of the professional sport scene.

I'm not trying to trot out any false humility here, but I wasn't all that impressed by what I did during the scoreless streak. I can watch another sporting event now, or I could watch a Sandy Koufax as a teammate, and be awed. But I wasn't all that taken by what I was doing in 1968. I think more about it now than I did then, because that streak is probably the one thing I'm remembered for most. When you're around fans and they start talking baseball, that seems to be the thing they associate with me. "The Streak." That and my reputation for being mean, or the fact that I was durable and didn't miss a turn. Maybe that's what I'm proudest of, that I took the ball.

Strangely enough, at the outset of the 1968 season, I was beginning to think of life after baseball. My arm was hurting on occasion, and the consistent velocity I used to have wasn't always there. It would come and go. One day you had it, one day you didn't. I could feel the toll all those years were taking on my arm.

I could feel it during the streak, when my arm was a shade sore. During spring training, I even went on record with one writer as saying that I'd consider retiring early to be a manager—if the spot was there, I might hang 'em up. I was starting to realize what all players in all sports realize, that you're not indestructible. There was a time when I really did think about managing—I still do once in a while—but I'm not sure I've got the temperament. Specifically, the patience.

Thanks to Vin Scully, Mr. O'Malley provided some lasting momentos of that streak. Vinny kept referring to all those innings as a "string of pearls"—like Don Drysdale has added a forty-ninth pearl to his string. When it ended, Mr. O'Malley gave my wife Ginger a strand of fifty-eight pearls with a beautiful locket of diamonds and emeralds with a "2/3" engraved on the locket. I didn't get any bonus or any other material goods, which was fine. I didn't expect anything. The Dodgers always had a clause whereby anybody who pitched a no-hitter would get $500. That's not a lot of money, but I didn't have to worry about it, because I never pitched one.

Whenever you do something that fans and writers seem to get all worked up about, there's always a frame of reference that helps you put everything in perspective. During The Streak of '68, I didn't have to look far. On the same night I pitched that sixth straight shutout, Senator Robert F. Kennedy was at the Ambassador Hotel in Los Angeles on the campaign trail. He was ahead of Senator Eugene McCarthy in the California Democratic presidential primary. When Senator Kennedy heard about the ballgame, he announced the score to a ballroom full of supporters. He congratulated me and they cheered.

Two hours later, he was killed by an assassin's bullet. So much for the importance of all those shutout innings.

Warming up in spring training as a Brooklyn Dodgers rookie in 1956.
(National Baseball Library, Cooperstown, N.Y.)

Manager Walter Alston congratulates me after I won my first major league game as a starter, 6–1 over the Phillies on April 23, 1956. A great moment I'll never forget.
(UPI/Bettmann Newsphotos)

The 1956 National League champion Brooklyn Dodgers.
Front row (L to R): Sandy Amoros, Coach Joe Becker, Coach Billy Herman, Coach Jake Pitler, Manager Walt Alston, Captain Pee Wee Reese, Clem Labine, Carl Erskine, Dixie Howell, Gil Hodges, and Carl Furillo; Second row: Traveling Secretary Lee Scott, Duke Snider, Sandy Koufax, Chico Fernandez, Charlie Neal, Gino Cimoli, Ken Lehman, Randy Jackson, Jackie Robinson, Dale Mitchell, and Trainer Dr. Harold Wendler; Back row: Clubhouse Custodian John Griffin, Rube Walker, Ed Roebuck, Don Drysdale, Roger Craig, Don Newcombe, Junior Gilliam, Sal Maglie, Don Bessent, and Roy Campanella. Seated in front: Charlie DiGiovanna.
(Los Angeles Dodgers)

Some teammates who taught me "the Dodger way": Pee Wee Reese (pictured with Miss Gladys Gooding, the Ebbets Field organist).
(Los Angeles Dodgers)

Roy Campanella (left) and Sal Maglie (center), who taught me a little about intimidation.
(Los Angeles Dodgers)

Jackie Robinson, an example for everyone.
(Los Angeles Dodgers)

My roommate and friend, Gil Hodges.
(Los Angeles Dodgers)

Carl Furillo, the "Reading Rifle."
(Los Angeles Dodgers)

My buddy Dookie, Duke Snider.
(Los Angeles Dodgers)

Three executives who contributed to the Dodgers' success: E. J. "Buzzy" Bavasi, Vice-President and General Manager; Walter F. O'Malley, President; and Fresco Thompson, Vice-President in charge of Minor League operations.
(*Los Angeles Dodgers*)

Don Newcombe holds me back from a fight with Milwaukee Braves' shortstop Johnny Logan in 1957. Logan was mad because I hit him in the back with a pitch.
(*UPI/Bettmann Newsphotos*)

A tale of two stadiums: Ebbets Field in Brooklyn (*UPI/Bettmann Newsphotos*) and the new Dodger Stadium in Los Angeles, opening day in 1962. (*UPI/Bettmann Newsphotos*)

Getting ready to start the third game against the Yankees in the 1963 World Series, with Johnny Podres (center), the second game winner, and Sandy Koufax, who won the first. *(UPI/Bettmann Newsphotos)*

After winning that game 1–0, coach Joe Becker (left), outfielder Lee Walls (second from left) and manager Walter Alston (right) are as happy as I am. *(UPI/Bettmann Newsphotos)*

The 1963 World Series ended with Sandy celebrating a 2–1 victory and a four game sweep of the Yankees. *(Los Angeles Dodgers)*

A sampling of my non-baseball adventures: losing my grip on a six-shooter during my first try at acting in an episode of "The Lawman" *(AP/Wide World Photos);* and guest starring in a segment of "The Brady Bunch." *(AP/Wide World Photos)*

Some scenes from the 1965 World Series against the Twins: Getting ready to fire one in.
(*UPI/Bettmann Newsphotos*)

Scrambling to field a bunt in the first game, which I lost 8–2.
(*UPI/Bettmann Newsphotos*)

Celebrating with Lou Johnson (left) and Wes Parker after winning Game 4, 7–2.
(*AP/Wide World Photos*)

I had some disagreements with the umpires over the years. He's probably checking me for
"foreign substances" or telling me not to throw inside.
(Charles Segar Photo)

Here's a good sequence of my pitching motion, hooking the ball behind me and then coming at the batter from the third base side.
(*Los Angeles Dodgers*)

During our 1966 holdout, Sandy and I considered offers from the movie industry. Here we are with Buzz Kulik, who was set to direct *Warning Shot,* where I would play a television commentator and Sandy would portray a detective. As Sandy said after we signed, "Thank God I don't have to act in that movie."
(*AP/Wide World Photos*)

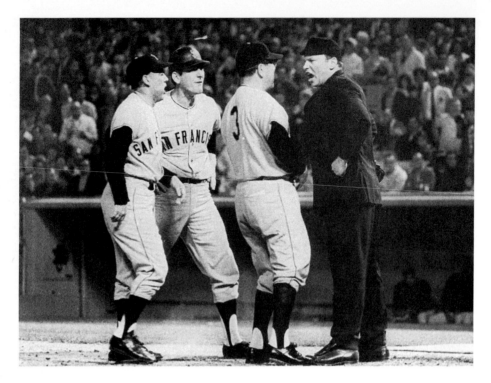

Key moments in my 1968 scoreless-innings streak: during the fifth consecutive shutout, Giants' manager Herman Franks (right), catcher Dick Dietz (center), and coach Peanuts Lowrey argue that Dietz was hit by a pitch, which would have forced in a run. Ump Harry Wendlestedt says Dietz didn't try to get out of the way, and makes him resume his turn at bat. Dietz flied out and the streak continued.
(National Baseball Library, Cooperstown, N.Y.)

Roberto Pena of the Phillies grounds out to Ken Boyer at third base for the first out, helping me break Walter Johnson's record of 56 consecutive scoreless innings.
(National Baseball Library, Cooperstown, N.Y.)

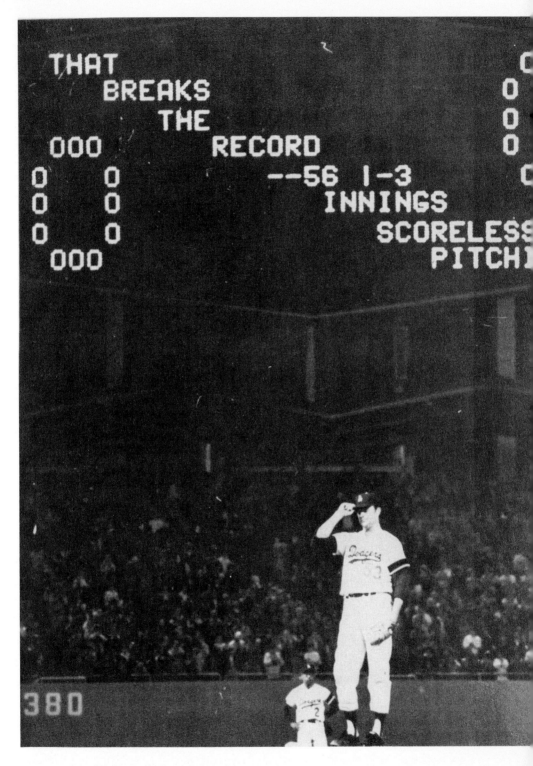

The scoreboard behind me tells the story.
(*National Baseball Library, Cooperstown, N.Y.*)

With my fellow Dodgers broadcasters Vin Scully and Ross Porter. *(Andrew D. Bernstein/Los Angeles Dodgers)*

Happier than ever: Here I am with (clockwise from left) daughter Kelly, Donnie Jr., wife Annie, and son Darren in my lap.

12

The Other Buzzie

I've given you the cold and calculating side of E. J. "Buzzie" Bavasi. Now, let me give you his human side. Like Gil Hodges, Buzzie was like a brother or a second father to me. Buzzie could kick me in the butt one minute over something I did, and the next, he would pat me on the head. Buzzie had four sons of his own, so he knew how to handle players, some of whom he called "boys." When he got upset with me, he called me "Donald." When he became really angry, he called me still other names.

Buzzie had a job to do. He had to run the Brooklyn Dodgers, then the Los Angeles Dodgers, and it wasn't an easy task by any means. But most of the time, he managed to keep his head on straight and maintain a pretty good sense of humor, too. He was an old-school baseball executive who grew up in the game, climbing from the very bottom of the ladder to the top, and he just loved baseball. He breathed it, unlike so many of the three-piece pinstripe suits you see in major league offices nowadays.

As I've said before, Buzzie gave me some of the best advice I ever got when he signed me to that first contract at 215 Montague Street in Brooklyn. He told me how it was easier to get to the major leagues than it was to stay, and if it sounded trite, it wasn't. All I had to do was take a look at the Dodger system then. There were 600 or 700 players in our minor league organization, and down in spring training, you'd have sworn that 500 of them had toeplates on. In other words, 500 of them were pitchers, just chomping at

153

the bit. That might have been my imagination, or paranoia, but if there were ten spots to be had on the staff of the big league club, it always seemed to me like there were 50 young guys in Dodger blue waiting for each one of those jobs.

Buzzie liked to have a little fun with you, which seems like a lost art in today's game. I had won 17 games during my second year in Brooklyn, 12 more than my rookie year in 1956, so when I went into his office that winter, I was prepared to ask for a healthy raise. I was in the New York area in the off-season doing time with the Army Reserves, so I had plenty of time to drop in to shoot the bull, even when money wasn't the subject.

"Well, how much do you want for next season?" Buzzie began.

Now, I was a general manager's delight at that point in my career. I was very naive. I made the $6,500 minimum my first year, and got a raise of $1,000 my second. I really had no idea what I was entitled to for the 1958 season.

"I was thinking about a ten-thousand-dollar raise," I said.

"Oooh, Jesus Christ!" groaned Buzzie. "What did I ever do to you? Do you want to get me fired or something? I have a budget to maintain here. I mean, if it wasn't for me, you'd have gone into the Army for two years. They were going to draft you. It was me who got you into the reserves, and now you come in here asking for all that."

Naturally, I felt like a midget, which is how I was supposed to feel—like I'd walked in there, pounded on Buzzie's desk, and demanded the crown jewels.

"Ten thousand dollars," I said. "I think that's fair."

"Oooh, no, no, no," Buzzie said. "I'll tell you what I'll do. We'll settle it right here and now."

Buzzie then ripped up three pieces of paper and wrote a figure on each. He told me to pick one, and whatever salary I picked, I'd get. I told him I didn't gamble like that. He said, "Well, you are now. If you don't know how to gamble, you're going to learn now, kid."

"What did you write down?" I asked.

"I'm putting down seventeen thousand on one slip of paper. And I'm putting down two other figures on the other two pieces. I'm not telling you what the others are. Now, you just pick one. I've got to leave the room for a minute. I've got something to do. I'll be right back."

Now, naturally, I was curious as hell. I was trying to peek at all the pieces, but he'd crumpled them up. Of course, I was absolutely petrified about opening them, for fear that he'd walk in and catch me red-handed. Finally, he returned to his desk.

"Well, which one did you pick?" Buzzie asked.

"I haven't picked one yet," I said.

"Hurry up. I haven't got all day. I've got other things to do."

So, I held my breath, like a kid does when he doesn't want to eat his spinach but knows he has to in order to keep peace at the dinner table. I closed my eyes, reached down, picked up a piece of paper and opened it.

"It's for seventeen thousand two hundred-and-fifty dollars," I said.

"Jesus Christ!" Buzzie screamed. "You've killed me! You're going to get me fired."

Of course, it was all a charade. I was sweating bullets, thinking he might have written $10,000 or $12,000 on those other pieces of paper. As it turned out, he'd put down $17,000, $17,250, and $17,500—all right in the ballpark. He'd just wanted to play with me a little bit. That was Buzzie's idea of a good time. He loved to get his jollies that way. Many a day, he'd just pick up the phone, ask you what you were doing, and tell you to get down to his office right away. Your first reaction was to think that something was wrong, that you'd been traded. But it was usually just a case of Buzzie wanting to chat about anything. That was his style. In many ways, that was Mr. O'Malley's way of operating, too. His door was always open if you had a problem, or if you had no problems at all. The old days. You never ever saw Mr. O'Malley or Buzzie in the clubhouse, but you always knew they were around, available and watching.

Throughout the years, I've tried to negotiate with one principle in mind. If you want five dollars, don't ask for ten. Ask for five. Buzzie came to understand that, so we never really had a problem. Even the holdout wasn't a problem with Buzzie or Mr. O'Malley or the Dodgers so much as it was a problem with the salary structure of baseball. That's what Sandy and I were really fighting.

Anyway, there was another year I went to Buzzie and asked for

$2,500 more than he was willing to offer. So, he told me to sign the contract as it was, and then he'd throw in an IOU for the extra $2,500. I agreed. It seemed like a strange way to do business, but we did a lot of crazy things. He wrote out on a little piece of paper, "IOU $2,500, E. J. Bavasi." I put the piece of paper in my wallet, and sure enough, at the end of the year, the money showed up in my paycheck.

Well, it must have been two years later that I was cleaning out that old wallet and I stumbled across that piece of paper. I still had the IOU, and I decided it was my turn to have a little fun. So I went down to the ballpark to shoot the bull with Buzzie, and during our conversation, I brought up the $2,500. He had completely forgotten about it. I showed it to him, and there was no way he could get around it. The note was right in front of him, in his handwriting.

"I guess I have to pay you," he said. He called for Edna, his secretary. Then his memory kicked in, and he told Edna not to bother.

"Goddamn it, Drysdale!" Buzzie roared. "I paid you this money two years ago. Get your ass out of here with those old notes."

Buzzie played the office trick on other Dodgers, too. Don Newcombe had a great season in 1956—he was 27–7. He came in to sign a new contract, just like I did. Buzzie's office had those frosted-glass partitions that didn't extend all the way to the ceiling. His office wasn't quite closed off from the other cubicles. So, before Newk showed up, Buzzie told Edna to write up a contract for Roy Campanella.

"But Mr. Bavasi," she said, "you did Mr. Campanella's contract the other day. He already signed it."

"I know that," Buzzie answered, "but draw up another one and put in a salary of thirty-eight thousand dollars."

She did and Buzzie conveniently set it on his desk. In came Newcombe.

"What do you want?" Buzzie inquired.

"I want forty thousand," Newcombe said.

"Jesus Christ!" Buzzie exclaimed. "That's a hell of a lot of money. Do you want to get me fired? I've got a budget to maintain here. What did I ever do to you?"

"Well," said Newk, "I think I had a hell of a season."

"You did," agreed Buzzie. "But forty thousand's still a lot of money. Wait here for just a minute. I've got one other thing to do. I'll be right back."

Campanella's phony contract just happened to be lying right there on the desk and I just know that that sneaky SOB Bavasi must have had a stool somewhere that he could climb up on and peek over the partition to watch his players squirm while he laughed his ass off. That had to be Buzzie's form of amusement, peering over those glass partitions while we all went through hell. As the story goes, Newk was sitting there by himself when he saw this contract on the desk in front of him. He kind of turned his head sideways, and then upside down, contorting himself in every way possible to get a look at the money figure. Eventually, he saw the name Roy Campanella, and the figure, $38,000.

Newk had to be thinking, Geez, here's Campy, a three-time Most Valuable Player making only $38,000 and here I am after only one big season wanting $40,000. On cue, Buzzie then returned to his desk.

"Now where were we, Don?" Buzzie continued. "You wanted how much, forty thousand? That's an awful lot of money."

"Well," Newk said. "How about thirty-five thousand?"

"Oh," said Buzzie. "That's a lot different. That's fine. That's a deal."

In fact, Campy probably was well into the forties, but Buzzie just had to do his thing, and he did it well. You think about all the great accomplishments of those Dodger teams and then realize that, when we arrived in Los Angeles for the start of the 1958 season, our highest-paid player was Duke Snider at $50,000. That's just the way it was. And really, it was that way everywhere. Warren Spahn of the Braves, one of the greatest lefthanders in baseball history, a man who won 363 games, told me that the most he ever made was $85,000. In today's market, he would get $2 million a year—easy. Fans who think players are making too much money today don't remember the "good old days," when owners and general managers had us right by the throat.

There was also a time when Buzzie Bavasi fired me. That's correct, he stone-cold fired me. Buzzie's son Peter had gone down to Albuquerque to become general manager of the Dodgers' farm club there. Peter was learning the ropes, just like his dad had, and we were scheduled to go there to play an exhibition game. But this was right in the middle of the 1965 season, when we were fighting for a pennant. We lost a tough ballgame at Dodger Stadium, and as I was taking my uniform off, I started complaining to a couple of my teammates about having to take a flight to New Mexico to play this stupid exhibition game. I made note in my little diatribe that if it weren't for Peter Bavasi, we'd never be going. We'd have a needed day off instead of this meaningless, goddamn game against Albuquerque.

It was just my luck that Morton Moss, a writer for the *Los Angeles Herald-Examiner,* happened to be walking by my locker when I was letting it all hang out. I didn't even see him, but he heard me. Did he ever hear me. The next day's headlines screamed: "DRYSDALE BLASTS BAVASI!" I was in the airport, preparing to get on the flight, when I saw that banner. I knew damn well that the headline wouldn't be the only thing screaming at me before the day was over. When I got to Albuquerque, I put on my uniform so fast, I almost got a hernia. Then I headed for the outfield to shag flies, as far away from home plate as I could get without leaving the ballpark. My only problem was that I knew I'd have to come in eventually for the start of the game.

Buzzie had gone into town a day early with his wife to share in all the hoopla with the city fathers about the Dodgers' arrival, but that didn't matter. News travels fast. The story in the *Herald-Examiner* had been picked up by the wire services and it was all over the country. It was only a matter of time before I got my earful, and it came in the runway between the visitors' dugout and the clubhouse. There was Buzzie and he was hot. He ripped me for what I'd said, and I defended myself by saying that what I had said was not meant for publication.

"You still said it," Buzzie went on. "You dumb son-of-a-bitch."

"What did you call me?" I said.

"You dumb son-of-a-bitch," he repeated.

"You call me that one more time," I said, "and I'm going to knock you right on your ass."

"Is that right?" he said. "Well, you're not only a dumb son-of-a-bitch—you're fired!"

Buzzie then dashed into our clubhouse in a rage and yelled for Lee Scott, our traveling secretary, to write a plane ticket for me back to Los Angeles. Scotty didn't know what to make of it and neither did some of my teammates.

"Where the hell are you going?" Johnny Podres asked.

"I'm going home," I said. "You heard Buzzie. I've just been fired."

Podres started laughing like hell.

"Buzzie didn't mean it," said Podres. "You know Buzzie."

"You heard him," I insisted. "He told me I was fired. Scotty, where's my damn plane ticket?"

At this point, Scott told me that Buzzie wanted to see me. I was real hot. I told him I didn't want to see Buzzie. Scott persisted. He told me to go see Buzzie, who was sitting in the stands behind home plate with his wife Evit. He was on the left, Evit was beside him, and there was an empty seat next to her. I walked up and sat down beside Evit. The game was just about to start.

"Hello, Evit," I said.

"Hello, Don," she answered.

At this point, Buzzie leaned over and said to his wife, "Ask him why he said what he said to that writer."

Then Evit leaned over to me and repeated the question.

"Tell him that I never said what I said to the writer. I said it was not for publication."

Evit leaned over to Buzzie and told him what I'd told her.

"Ask him if he's sorry," Buzzie instructed Evit, which she did.

"Tell him that I'm sorry," I said to Evit, "and while you're at it, ask him if I'm still fired."

She went through the whole routine again.

"No, you're not fired," said Buzzie, finally talking directly to me. "Now, get the hell out of here."

I got up from my seat, said I was sorry to Buzzie once more, and had just about made it out of earshot when I heard him growl, "Where are you going now?"

"I don't know," I said.

"You're going with Podres, Perranoski, and Miller back to the hotel, aren't you?"

"How did you know?"

"Because I know you guys," Buzzie said. "Now, don't get yourself in any more trouble."

"Thank you very much," I said, "and good-bye."

And that was that.

Then there was the time in 1959 when I lost both games of a doubleheader in Pittsburgh. I got whipped as a starter, 9–2, in the opener, then came back to relieve in the second game and dropped that one, too, in extra innings, 4–3. During the long, hot afternoon, whenever I was out there on the mound, I heard Charlie Dressen, one of our coaches, whistling to me from the dugout. I couldn't figure out what he was trying to do, and I asked him in the clubhouse afterward. It turned out Charlie was trying to "whistle" instructions to me—you know, do this and do that.

Well, that was the last thing I needed after losing two ballgames in one day during a pennant race, so I ripped into what I called the "sickening second-guessing" that was going on on our ballclub. "Any pitcher can have a slump," I fumed, "but what gets me is having to lose and then getting second-guessed about losing. Everything on our club is our fault. I never hear anything said if an outfielder drops a ball or a guy gets picked off first base. All you hear about is bad pitches. Why don't they tell a guy first, and not later? If they want somebody to do something, hell's bells, tell him about it. I have no use for anybody who waits until it's too late to say you should have done this, you should have done that. All it does is create bad feelings and that's what happened with me. I'd rather be fined than have them sit there and second-guess me behind my back."

My outburst certainly didn't hurt my growing reputation as a hothead, but I did cover my tracks. I was sticking up for our pitchers, but I absolved all other players. I also said that I wasn't pointing the finger at our manager, Walt Alston, because he was always up front with me. And I wasn't knocking our pitching coach, Joe Becker, whom I called the "greatest critic I ever had." I also said that I had absolutely no problems with Greg Mulleavy or with Pee Wee Reese, who was also on our coaching staff that season. By process of elimination, that left Dressen as the target. I didn't get that specific, but I did say, "If the shoe fits, wear it."

All of this appeared under the byline of Leonard Schechter, a writer for the *New York Post* who caught me at a bad time. He'd bumped into me at the Warwick Hotel and I just reiterated what I'd told Charlie. I had Rocky Nelson of the Pirates 0–2 and I threw the next pitch inside. Nelson stepped back, stuck his bat out, and hit a chopper on that brick infield of theirs over Gil Hodges's head at first base for a single. That was my fault? Then after the game, I had to hear about what I did wrong from all the second-guessers. If talk could win games, we'd be in first place by 17 and so on. Sometimes I got so angry at the dugout experts that I half-felt like walking off the mound and giving them the ball to see what they could do. All of this was in the *New York Post,* but again, news travels fast. When we arrived in Philadelphia from Pittsburgh, stories about a rift and dissension on the Dodgers were all over the East Coast and back home. And I was the bad guy, the guy with the big mouth. President Eisenhower had just had a heart attack, but I'd chased him all the way to page three in the Los Angeles papers.

"DRYSDALE BLASTS DODGER COACHES!"
"DRYSDALE SOUNDS OFF!"
"DRYSDALE BLASTS OFF . . . BIG DODGER RHUBARB!"
"DRYSDALE BLOWS TOP IN BLAST AT DODGERS!"

Naturally, the press was anxious for a reaction from Buzzie and naturally, he wasn't about to let the controversy just slide by. He sent me a plaque, of all things. It read: "To be seen, stand up. To be heard, speak up. To be appreciated, shut up." The thing was all wrapped up like a gift. I was so mad when I opened it up that I could barely see, but I put it in my locker for safekeeping after I cooled off. There are days even now when I think about Buzzie's message. He also dispatched a telegram to my apartment in Van Nuys. It read: "Took a day off to watch the Rams. Understand you put your foot in your mouth again. Kelly Jean has more sense. My love to Ginger, not you. Buzzie Bavasi."

Walt Alston, to his credit, backed me and said there was no problem on the ballclub. He said that I was a terrific guy and a fine competitor and he gave my words the benefit of the doubt as "constructive criticism." To the rest of the world, Buzzie said that he planned no disciplinary action but that he would meet with me as soon as the ballclub returned to Los Angeles. He did, and the storm clouds passed. Buzzie knew my personality and he knew where I was coming from. I just wanted to win, the same as everybody else on the Dodgers, and fortunately, we did win the pennant that season, beating the Milwaukee Braves in a playoff.

There was another time when we had a doubleheader in Wrigley Field. Sandy and I were the starters, we beat the Cubs twice, and it took us less than two hours to finish each game. We didn't have the Dodger plane on that trip, and we had to wait until ten o'clock that night for our commercial flight from Chicago to Los Angeles—a big, Continental jumbo jet with plenty of space. But we were out of the park by five, so we had some time to kill downtown and we spread out. Sandy, Doug Camilli, Leo Durocher, and I weren't that hungry, so we stayed around the clubhouse for a while before heading out to the President's Club—the private club for Continental—at O'Hare Airport. We just sat there having drinks and eating peanuts well into the evening, enjoying ourselves immensely.

The hours passed, and before long, we were getting calls in the President's Club warning us that we'd better head out for the gate to catch our flight. Well, by that time, we needed a van to get us to the plane. We weren't allowed to have any liquor on that flight, but I just happened to take a seat next to Podres, who just happened to be carrying a small bottle of Scotch. I didn't know where Johnny had been since the end of the doubleheader, but obviously he was well prepared for the long flight home. We played gin, Johnny sitting next to the window with me on the aisle. When Walt came down the aisle to "say hello," Johnny tried to hide the bottle, but by then he must not have been thinking too clearly. Instead of putting the bottle behind him, Johnny was "hiding" the damn thing right out in the open, where all Walt had to do was open his eyes.

Meanwhile, Leo was feeling pretty well in the pink, too. Here was one of Walt's right-hand men, a coach who knew we weren't supposed to drink on the flight, but Leo was walking up and down the aisles, driving the stewardesses daffy. "We win two today in Chicago," Durocher kept saying, "get some whiskey for my boys, girls. We win two today in Chicago." I don't think Walt was too thrilled about that display. The strongest thing Walt ever drank was a whiskey sour.

We got back to Los Angeles, and the next day, the phone rang. It was Buzzie, wanting to know what I was doing. I told him I was just sitting around, and he asked me to come down to his office at the ballpark. I thought nothing of it, until I arrived and saw Leo sitting there.

"How were you last night?" Buzzie asked.

162

"You mean on the plane?" I said. "I was fine. I was sitting in the back, playing cards with Johnny."

"Oh, yeah," said Buzzie. "Johnny and his bottle of Scotch."

"How'd you know he had a bottle of Scotch?" I said, laughing.

"Because the dumb bastard was so drunk he couldn't figure out where to hide the damn thing, that's how. But don't worry about Johnny. I'll talk to him in due time. I want to know if you were with Leo."

"With Leo where?" I said.

"Were you in that private Continental club at the airport in Chicago?" Buzzie asked.

"Yup."

"And who was with you?" he continued.

"Well, dammit, Buzzie. You seem to know everything else about last night. Why don't you figure that out too? I'm not going around telling tales on my teammates."

"Okay," said Buzzie, "I'll tell you who you were with. You were with Koufax and Camilli. And, of course, Leo. I know that because Leo told me."

"If you knew all that, then why did you ask?"

"Never mind that," Buzzie said. "I'll tell you what. I'm fining you five hundred dollars and I'm fining Leo here a thousand because he's been a manager and should know better."

"Fining us for what?"

"For drinking," Buzzie explained.

"We couldn't drink on the plane," I said. "That's the rule. And I *didn't* drink on the plane. I drank in the damn Continental Airlines private club and if your stoolpigeon Leo here didn't know the president of the airline, I wouldn't have been in the President's Club in the first place."

That got Leo's dander up.

"Now, wait a goddamn minute, Don," Durocher said. "You guys wanted a place to have some whiskey after the doubleheader and you didn't want to go eat so I found you that nice place at the airport to have a few drinks. And now you're blaming me for that?"

Buzzie couldn't have asked for more. Not only had he brought us both in there to agitate us, but now Leo and I were fighting. Buzzie finally just broke out laughing and kicked us both out of his office. He never fined us, either.

Buzzie was more than just fun to be around. He was a great,

great executive. He was as good with a pencil as anyone you'll ever see. He could make figures talk. He also had tremendous instincts for running a franchise. There was one period when he wasn't too happy about what was going on in the Dodger farm system. So, he called a meeting of all the scouts and instructed them to go out and sign a hundred or so ballplayers. Al Campanis, who was then the team's scouting supervisor, couldn't believe his ears. He told Buzzie that would blow the budget. Buzzie told him not to worry about any budgets. That was Buzzie's concern, not Campanis's. The scouts went out and signed a bunch of players, and the Dodgers got some outstanding talent out of that group. That was the old Branch Rickey theory. When all else fails, sign quantity and maybe you'll get some quality out of the results.

Buzzie was one of the reasons why the Dodgers had such great camaraderie during his tenure, and don't you believe otherwise. He never put on a uniform, but in many respects, he set the tone for the feeling of closeness the Dodgers had. When we were stuck in those barracks at Dodgertown during spring training, with nothing really going on around Vero Beach except baseball, Buzzie would think of something to get our attention. He might gather the fastest kids in camp together and stage a race, just for the hell of it. He'd have the major leaguers mix with the minor leaguers, then he'd have the scouts get out their stopwatches to clock everyone, and then he'd find Zimmer and Hodges and have them get a big pool up. Of course, Buzzie would still be looking for the edge himself. And he made sure that he had all the necessary inside information. One year, he staged his race and all of us picked Maury Wills to win. But Buzzie knew about this other kid in camp, Willie Davis. Well, Maury got off to a good start, but when Willie got moving, it was all over. "Three Dog," as we called Davis because of his uniform number, "3" ate Maury up by leaps and bounds. Buzzie liked to go to the track, but even when he wasn't looking at horses, he liked to have his tout sheet.

Buzzie gambled with players, yes, to a point, but to my mind that was part of the makeup that made him such a successful general manager. A successful general manager needs to be a bit reckless on occasion. You can't just stand pat. You have to take a flyer once in a while. You have to play a hunch, and live with it. You can't always go by the book. You have to be unconventional, and Buzzie was all of that. He was very colorful, with a lot of charisma. There aren't many Buzzie's left anymore. The old guard is fading fast, and the new button-down GMs are moving in. They all seem to look the same, they all seem to act the same. I'm not saying they aren't capable. I'm just saying they're a different breed—a much different breed.

I don't see any young and frisky Buzzie Bavasi's out there on the horizon. I think that's sad.

13

My Other Bosses:
Alston and Mr. O'Malley

*A*fter I'd retired as an active player and had my second broadcasting job with the Texas Rangers, I was working a game one afternoon in Arlington, Texas, when the electronic scoreboard in the outfield flashed one of those baseball trivia questions:

"Which player spent the most consecutive years playing for the same manager in major league history?"

I had absolutely no idea what the correct solution was to that riddle, until they put it up a few minutes later.

"Don Drysdale, pitcher for the Brooklyn and Los Angeles Dodgers, played all fourteen years of his career under manager Walter Alston."

Well, you could have about knocked me over with that one. I would never have guessed me, but in a sense, that speaks volumes about how lucky I was. Not only did I play for the best organization throughout my career, but I played for a terrific guy like Walt Alston. He fit every definition of the strong, silent type of man, but that's no knock. No way. I've always maintained that if you couldn't play for Walt, you might as well pack up your gear and find another line of work.

Walt was a man's man. He wasn't a Dick Tracy who watched your every step off the field and checked your room at night to tuck you into bed. He didn't hound you during games. He didn't beat you over the head with advice and he certainly wasn't a rah-rah type like Tommy Lasorda, his successor with the Dodgers. Walt only expected you to play hard and to know how to play the game, and more and more, I think that was his pet peeve as the years went along. When he first joined the Brooklyn ballclub as "Walt Who?" in 1954—the manager nobody knew—all the Dodgers knew how to play. But by the time he left in 1976, I think it was evident to Walt—and a lot of other major league managers, for that matter—that the caliber of player had changed drastically. It wasn't that the modern-day players didn't have talent. It was that they hadn't spent as much time in the minor leagues learning the intricacies and nuances of the game. Primarily because of expansion, players come up to the big leagues in a lot bigger hurry now, sometimes in too big a hurry. They simply aren't ready.

From time to time, we felt that Walt was getting a gentle nudge from the front office to use some Dodger prospects. Walt would resist, but every so often, he'd put a kid in there—ideally in an exhibition game. If the kid showed he could play, fine. If not, Walt wanted him sent back for more seasoning. That was Walt's way. His philosophy about pitchers was just as basic—either throw strikes or be gone. Walks would drive him nuts. He was forever giving the umpires a piece of his mind if they didn't make opposing pitchers come to a full stop from the stretch position. When we had all those rabbits, like Junior Gilliam, Willie Davis, and Maury Wills, Walt always wanted to make sure they got an extra step toward stealing a base. Opposing pitchers naturally were aware of our speed, so they would tend to hurry their deliveries and come close to balking.

If you were a pitcher, the least you were expected to do was to be able to execute a simple sacrifice bunt when needed. After one particularly dry streak, Walt gathered us all together and let us have it. We had screwed up so often that we were going to work on bunting, a half-hour each day, two of us per day. He sent us down to the bullpen at Dodger Stadium, where he had set up a machine that looked like a bazooka. It wasn't the usual iron-mike-type pitching machine; this one just shot balls out of a chute like one of those Roman candles. Problem was, there was all that gravel on the ground out there, and the balls got scuffed up, which affected the way they came out of that gizmo.

Well, I was down there doing my duty one afternoon and I squared around to bunt. Damn, if the third ball didn't float out of that rotten machine all crazy, like a knuckleball. I was a sitting duck. The damn thing hit me right in the chin. I took the bat I was holding and broke the friggin' thing into eighteen different pieces and walked back to the dugout. There was Walt.

"You through already?" he said.

"Screw you and your friggin' bunting and all that other crap!" I roared.

"What's the problem?" Walt asked, in his typically low-key way.

"That SOB machine of yours just fired a friggin' ball right at my chin!" I answered. "Those balls are all chewed up and they're flying all over the place. You're gonna get one of us killed!"

Walt loved it. He nearly keeled over laughing.

"Go put some ice on it," he said. "You're the one pitcher I've got who knows what to do with the bat, and you're the one who gets hurt."

Walt was extremely well organized. From the first day of spring training, he had his agenda written down on a pad. It was that way for the rest of the season. Walt didn't waste a lot of time, words, or actions. He must have gotten that idea of preparation from his days as a schoolteacher. But he didn't have a classroom session every day. On the contrary, meetings weren't his thing. He'd have maybe one a month, but when he did, boom. He let things build up inside of him, then he'd call us together, and he'd just blow. I mean, I'm talking serious combustion. He'd go down his list of complaints about the way we were playing, sometimes going down the roster player by player, and then it was over. Just like that. He got it off his chest, he held no grudges, and see you in another month or so.

We had such a meeting in Jacksonville, Florida, one spring training after an exhibition game. The master plan that day was for us pitchers to throw the "first sign after 2" from the catcher. In other words, if the catcher flashed "1-1-2-1," we were supposed to throw "1," or a fastball. If it was "1-1-2-2," we were supposed to throw "2," or a curveball. We played the Braves that day and lost and didn't look too inspired. Even though it was a nothing game, Walt wasn't too pleased. He told Lee Scott to allow one bus to take off from the ballpark with everybody aboard but the pitchers and catchers.

"The pitchers and catchers," Walt said, "will be staying right here. They might stay an hour. They might stay two hours. They might stay all night. I really don't care how long. I don't give a shit. Because you can take that 'first sign after two' and stick it. We're gonna have to do a better job than that. And if we miss the plane until you figure out a better system, I don't give a shit."

I don't remember whether we caught the plane that day. All I remember is that we caught hell.

Not all our meetings were quite as grim. There was a day in Milwaukee when Walt was in one of those moods. There would be a kind of hush in the clubhouse, a sense of expectation, and then you knew something was up when Walt lit a cigarette. He would take a couple deep draws on it, his hands would quiver, and then his veins would stick out in his neck. Then he'd amble over to the clubhouse man and whisper to him to get everybody out—writers, broadcasters, whoever didn't belong in the inner sanctum.

Oh, shit, I'd think to myself. Here it comes.

It came that afternoon at Milwaukee in the form of an inquisition of Johnny Podres, our freewheeling left-handed bachelor who could make a statue laugh just by looking at it. Well, Walt wasn't laughing that day. We'd had an off-day there on the way from Chicago. Before the meeting, he'd come up to me in a real quiet way and told me he might want me to pitch.

"It's Johnny's turn," I said.

"I know that," Alston snapped. "I'll take care of that. I just want you to know that I might call on you."

"Whatever you want," I answered.

Then Walt turned toward Podres.

"John, I've got a question to ask you. Did you have a girl in your room last night?"

"Oh, no, Skip," Podres said. "I've gotta pitch tonight."

Walt took another drag on his cigarette and shook a little bit.

"Now, John, we've known each other a long time. And I want you to tell me the truth. Did you have a girl in your room last night?"

"Oh, no, Skip," Podres repeated. "I didn't have a girl in my room last night."

Once more, Alston paced. There wasn't a sound in the clubhouse besides his footsteps, and by this time, the rest of us were trying to hide our heads to keep from breaking up.

"John," said Walt, "I'll ask you one more time. And I want you to tell me the truth. Did you have a girl in your room here last night?"

Silence. Finally, Johnny spoke.

"Well, okay, Skip. I did have a girl in my room last night. *But I didn't screw her!*"

With that, of course, we had all we could do to keep from falling off our stools in front of our stalls. The place just erupted in laughter, and even Walt had to bite his lip.

"Okay, John," he said. "I appreciate your telling me the truth. But from now on, if any of you guys gets caught with a girl in your room, it'll be a five-hundred-dollar fine."

That night, a profile in courage, Podres went out and beat the Braves, 4–2. He came back into the locker room, happy as a lark, and he turned to Snider.

"Geez, Dookie," Johnny said. "What pressure! I told you I could pitch under pressure."

The writers nicknamed Alston "The Quiet Man," and Walt was indeed that. You never saw him much away from the ballpark. He kept to himself. He wasn't a drinker. If he did anything, he had dinner on occasion with his coaches on the road. Walt wasn't one to drop into a bar and buy the players a round. As the years passed, I got to the point where I kidded around more and more with him. Maybe that's because he became looser or more mellow. Maybe it also stemmed from the fact that I'd been around him so long. After a while I could read him pretty well, and he could read me just as well.

Once on a road stop in Atlanta, we happened to be staying at a hotel where there was some sort of huge convention. It was just Walt's luck that his room was practically next door to the group's hospitality suite. There was drinking and laughing and loud music into the night, and finally Walt had had enough. He called the suite and asked them to tone it down. That didn't cut it, so he called again. It was the wee hours but the party wasn't ending, so Walt tried once more.

"Look," he said. "I've called the front desk, and I've phoned you twice, and still there's a racket. If you don't shut it down, I'm going to grab four or five of my biggest and strongest players out of bed—I don't care what time it is—and we'll come down there and make sure the noise stops."

I know about this conversation because I heard Walt com-

171

plaining to Lee Scott the next day on the bus from the hotel to the ballpark in Atlanta. And I now suspect that if Walt had wanted any reinforcements, I'd have been his first choice. That's why I had to laugh, sitting in that seat behind Walt. A year or so later, I explained why.

"Walt, you remember that trip to Atlanta when you couldn't get to sleep because of all that noise down the hall?"

"Hell, yes," he said. "That was the worst. In fact, I was this far from calling your room that night for help."

Then he looked at me with a half-smile.

"I wouldn't have found you, would I?" he asked.

"No," I said. "You wouldn't have found a bunch of us. You'd have been all alone fighting in that hospitality suite. But we're thinking of getting you a gun so you can send up a flare if you're ever in that kind of jam again."

Walt was from Darrtown, Ohio, a small town about an hour's drive from Cincinnati. He returned there every off-season to do his woodwork and play with his grandchildren and shoot pool. What a pool player he was! I saw his house in Darrtown once. I think we had an off-day before a series with the Reds, so I took a drive out. The whole scene was typical Walt. Nothing flashy. It says something for Alston that, despite his fame in a fast-track and glitzy place like Los Angeles, he never got into that star-conscious syndrome. When the season was done, he went back to his roots and he stayed there until spring training. He didn't hang around Southern California for the Hollywood parties. He didn't care one bit for all the bright lights. He was courteous and decent to all the West Coast types, but Walt was all country. He was Darrtown, Darrtown was Walt.

Essentially, Walt Alston had no ego. Here was a man who had one of the most coveted jobs in baseball, managing the Dodgers, and he held it for twenty-three years. Yet, all he ever got by way of security was twenty-three one-year contracts. That was Dodger policy and it didn't bother him a bit. If they had chosen not to renew him at any time, Walt would have gone back home and done his thing. It wouldn't have devastated him. Walt was also a man surrounded by people like Leo Durocher, Dressen, Bragan, and Lasorda who either had managed before or were waiting to manage. Again, if he ever felt threatened, Walt never showed it. He was too much of a man to be looking over his shoulder.

172

Not that Walt wasn't involved in some tense times, a few involving me. In the 1965 World Series against Minnesota, I pitched the first and fourth games and it was my turn to pitch the seventh. But Walt went with Sandy, who threw a shutout. How could I argue that? I'd back Walt on that selection if it happened all over again tomorrow. Three years before, a year when I went 25–9 and won my first and only Cy Young Award (there was only one Cy Young for both leagues at the time), Walt came under fire when we had a very good team but ended up in a playoff with the Giants despite winning 102 games during the regular season and despite having a four-game lead with eight days to play. To make matters worse, we lost the playoff.

We dropped the first game in San Francisco, 8–0, to Billy Pierce, who beat Sandy Koufax. If Sandy hadn't gone down in the middle of the season with a circulatory problem in his pitching hand, there wouldn't have been a playoff. There wouldn't have been a pennant race, period. But that's a another story. Walt announced that he was going to start Stan Williams in the do-or-die second game instead of me. I snapped and was quoted as saying, "What's Alston saving me for, the first Grapefruit League game? It doesn't matter anyway. Buzzie hasn't told him who's pitching tomorrow yet." Yeah, I guess I was a little bit angry.

As it turned out, I did start Game Two, which we won, 8–7, no thanks to me. I gave up 5 runs in 5 1/3 innings. In the third game, we led 4–2 at Dodger Stadium entering the top of the ninth, but the Giants tied it. Williams, on in relief of Ed Roebuck, threw a wild pitch and then Walt ordered Ed Bailey walked to load the bases and set up a force out at any base. Again, I was quoted as saying, "That was one of the dumbest moves I've ever seen." On a 3–1 pitch, Williams walked Jim Davenport to send in the go-ahead run. We lost, 6–4, the Giants won the pennant, and Walt became the center of speculation. He was supposed to be replaced by Durocher, or by Bobby Bragan, or by Charlie Dressen, or by Pete Reiser. Pick a name. Buzzie Bavasi, who was running the show, picked none. He unceremoniously signed Walt to another one-year contract, and for all my heated remarks, I was glad about it. We won the pennant by six games in 1963 and won the World Series in four straight over the Yankees. I won the third game in Los Angeles by 1–0 over Jim Bouton, and it might have been the best game I ever pitched. I gave up 2 singles to Tony Kubek and a bunt single to Mickey Mantle, struck out 9 and walked 1. The next day, we got only 2 hits—both by Frank Howard—but Sandy Koufax beat the Yankees, 2–1, and we swept to conclude a terrific season. After we won it all, Junior Gilliam said, "They can't call us choke artists anymore."

We had made amends for 1962. The moral of the story is: only the sturdy survive, and nobody was sturdier than Walt Alston.

I'm not talking only mental toughness, either. Walt was one of the strongest men physically I ever met. I don't say he managed out of intimidation, because that wasn't his style, but none of us ever wanted to test him. *None* of us—not even a guy like Gil Hodges, who could break you in half if he wanted to. Walt had this little game he played with a bat. He'd hold it up sideways with both hands, and dare you to grab it, twist it vertically and, take control of it. I saw Walt challenge just about everybody with that trick—including Hodges—and he never lost.

For all his reputation as a tough guy and a taskmaster, though, Walt never felt compelled to do things just to prove he was in charge. If you were pitching the next night, Walt always let you do your work and then go on home to get your rest. You didn't have to hang around the ballpark the night before just so he could say he had everybody in tow. That was a given with Walt. I don't know how much of that you see anymore. Some managers seem to want to keep tabs on all their players all the time. The only point where that varied was in the mid-sixties when the Dodgers were a little short of offense and Walt started using me as a pinch-hitter. Even if I was starting Tuesday night, I might be called on to hit during Monday night's game. So I couldn't leave the ballpark. No big deal. I liked to hit, anyway.

Was Walt a good manager? I think so, absolutely, but I was biased. They say the greatest strength a manager can have is knowing his pitchers, and Walt knew us like the back of his hand. In spring training, he left everything up to his pitching coach, Joe Becker, and later, Red Adams. But once the bell rang, that was it. Walt took over. It was the pitching coach's job to get you in shape and watch out for any sore arms, but the actual handling of the rotation and staff was Walt's territory. Walt was also pretty adept at handling criticism of his pitchers. Many a time, the vultures would come after me when I wasn't going well. I recall being booed one night in the Coliseum during the 1961 season, when I went only 13–10 and Cincinnati finished in first place. I got racked up by the Reds in an early June outing, and the fans let me have it, but Walt stood right by me.

"Don's getting a lot of bad breaks," Walt said. Yeah, a lot of my pitches were running into a lot of bats. But I appreciated the skipper's support.

My other boss during the Dodger years was Walter O'Malley, but I never referred to him as Walter or Walt. He was Mr. O'Malley. He may have been a mysterious figure to a lot of other people in baseball, but Mr. O'Malley wasn't that to the Dodger family. As a rookie, and for a few years thereafter, I was careful to keep my distance. But even then, in my "listening" years, I realized that he was very approachable for a man of his stature. He always told his players that he was available if we had a problem, and that wasn't just talk. If you had a baseball-related question, he was there. If you just wanted to ask him about the stock market or an investment possibility, he was there. One bit of early advice he gave to me was this: don't try to get cute with the government. Ever. Pay your taxes fair and square. The few extra hundred dollars you might pocket by trying to cut corners just wasn't worth it. That probably was one way Mr. O'Malley had of telling us we were Dodgers, that we were professional ballplayers in the spotlight, and that we'd better do things the correct way.

Podres and I tested Mr. O'Malley's open-door policy one dreary day during spring training in Vero Beach. The rest of the ballclub had gone somewhere else to play a game, Johnny and I were left behind, and we really had nothing special to do. Nothing, that is, except go down to Gulfstream Park near Miami. We all had the next day off, so it was a perfect time to get away and relax. Our only problem was cash flow. It was toward the end of spring training, and we were damn near busted. Buzzie was off with the team and so was Lee Scott, our traveling secretary.

"What are we going to do?" wondered Podres.

"Only one guy left around here," I said. "The boss."

"Mr. O'Malley?" said Podres, his eyes as big as saucers. "You mean, you wanna go ask *him* for money to go to the racetrack? Geez, I don't know about that."

"All he can do is say no and throw us out of his office," I reasoned.

It was a major move for us, one requiring a great deal of

courage, but after about an hour of procrastinating, we finally got up the nerve. We called Mr. O'Malley's office from the clubhouse. Edith, his secretary, said he'd see us in about twenty minutes. Podres and I walked over there real slow, each one wanting the other to get a step ahead. We might as well have been stepping on broken glass.

"Kind of a lousy day," Mr. O'Malley said, greeting us. "I can't even play golf. But it must be better over on the other side of the state. Just talked to the team and we're going to play. Now, what is it I can do for you?"

I took a huge gulp.

"Mr. O'Malley," I began, "we have tomorrow off, and Johnny here and I . . . uh . . . we thought we might like to go down to Miami."

"Oh, what a nice idea."

"Yeah," said Podres. "We thought we'd . . . uh . . . go down to Miami and go to the racetrack."

"That sounds like fun. I don't see any reason why you can't," Mr. O'Malley said agreeably.

"Well, there's one catch." Johnny paused. "We don't have any money."

"Oooh," said Mr. O'Malley. "Money. That's what you're after. You mean I get to make a decision around here? Everybody else must be gone. I will get it back, won't I?"

Mr. O'Malley called down to the auditor—he called him "The Commander"—and within minutes, we each had $200 in our pocket and were on our way.

Mr. O'Malley was always kind to us and to the other office employees. In spring training, he always arranged for a little group outing to Jamaica, or some other exotic place. He wasn't one to be seen in the clubhouse, because he obviously felt that wasn't his turf. But if you wanted to find Mr. O'Malley, he wasn't difficult to locate. When he wasn't in his office, he often rode around in his golf cart. He was an engaging sort, but was also the boss, and you knew that. He had that habit, in deep conversation, of dropping his head and peering at you over the top of his glasses. He could deliver a message that way without saying a word. I had many discussions with Mr. O'Malley, particularly when I was the Dodgers' player representative dealing with management-labor relations. Obviously, Mr. O'Malley was on the opposite side from me, but he never acted like we were adversaries. Quite the contrary. He was always exploring ways to improve the lines of communication between them and us. Mr. O'Malley was always interested in making things better. He was not the type to sit back and watch the world go by.

In that vein, it was Mr. O'Malley's idea to have a Dodger plane take us around the country during the season. We had to bite the bullet on those coast-to-coast trips that lasted seven or eight hours, including a refueling stop, usually in Grand Island, Nebraska. But it was a nice touch. At a time when most ballclubs were flying commercially, we knew our plane would always be there. And you treated it as you treated your own living room, or better. You didn't leave newspapers and sandwich wrappers behind you when you landed. You didn't put your feet up on the seat, either. Not on the Dodger plane, you didn't. When you get off a charter flight nowadays, it can look like a war zone.

For financial reasons, I imagine, the plane was kept in Las Vegas, where there's no state tax. And in later years, when we weren't using it, the Angels would rent it on occasion. It was a real blessing, especially after an extra-inning ballgame when you knew you didn't have to rush.

I suppose there might have been a tendency to become spoiled by the Dodgers, or to think that perhaps it was done their way in every other place in the major leagues. But the best antidote for that was when a player or two would come over to the Dodgers in a trade. Then, you would hear all the tales of how they did it in other cities and you had to realize how privileged you were to be wearing that Dodger Blue. You knew the Dodgers were first class. You knew that they were different, and it was Mr. O'Malley who set the tone.

In 1959, we were caught in a streak of bad weather in Florida. It rained for five straight days and five straight nights in Vero Beach, and Buzzie started worrying. He got together with Mr. O'Malley and told him that we were going to blow all the benefits of spring training if we didn't get some games in, and soon. And this was after a terrible season in 1958, when we finished seventh during our first year in Los Angeles. You wouldn't have thought management would have been in a good mood about anything.

But Mr. O'Malley heard Buzzie out and got on the telephone with Bobby Maduro, who was a big man in Cuba's baseball ranks.

Then Mr. O'Malley called Gabe Paul, who was running the Cincinnati Reds. Mr. O'Malley got all our players and staff together, loaded us up on the plane, and flew us to Havana. Then the plane turned right around and went back to Florida to pick up the Reds and fly them to Havana. It never rained a drop for four days there, we played games and got in shape and we never missed a beat of spring training. Whatever cost was involved meant nothing to Mr. O'Malley. He would spend money if he thought it was worthwhile. He would spend money to make money, which I believe is what all successful owners have to do. It's hypothetical, but we won the pennant that year by beating the Milwaukee Braves in a playoff. If we had lost one more game during the regular 154-game season, we'd never have made it to the playoff, or the World Series. And you've got to ask yourself if those few days in Cuba didn't make the difference. Mr. O'Malley, whose only desire was to get a good return on his money, spared nothing and got a good return on his Havana expenses.

Mr. O'Malley has died and the baton has been passed to his son Peter, who has maintained the Dodger way. If you've ever been to Dodger Stadium, you know what I mean. The park opened in 1962, but you can practically eat off the floor. First class, all the way.

14

Was I Mean? Well . . .

*W*hen I was playing, I was forever hearing about what an ogre I was, forever reading remarks like the one from Pittsburgh's outstanding short-stop, Dick Groat: "Going to bat against Drysdale is like going to a dentist appointment."

And now that I'm damn near a senior citizen, I still hear it. Charlie Fox, a veteran baseball man, recently came up to my wife, Annie, and said with a big smile on his face, "Oooh, you should have seen your husband when he was in his prime . . . was he ever a mean bastard!"

That sort of talk still amazes me, not because I'm unaware of my reputation, but because I never thought much of it when I was earning it. I'm not trying to play dumb or naive here, because it's a fact. When I pitched, there were any number of guys who wouldn't think twice about knocking a batter on his ass. You want mean? Nobody was meaner than Bob Gibson of the Cardinals. Sam Jones was no prince, same with Larry Jackson, and practically every guy on that great Milwaukee staff of the late fifties—Lew Burdette, Warren Spahn, and Bob Buhl. And Vern Law of the Pirates? The man they called "The Deacon"? He'd have gladly drilled you. It just depended on what mood he was in, or what the game situation was.

So, I didn't exactly feel like a lone wolf out there on the mound when I took the position that I didn't give a damn what happened, as long as I got the job done. There are two little categories in the box scores you see in the morning papers. One is "WP" for winning pitcher, the other is "LP" for losing pitcher. There's a hell of a difference between the two and my attitude was, you do everything possible to get the win, everything possible to get that edge, everything legal. Sometimes, I even crossed that line and did a few things that weren't legal. No big deal.

I was called "intimidating," and I wasn't about to dispute that. I never talked about my reputation, but I was very much at peace having others talk about it. Baseball then was a game of intimidation, and if opposing batters figured you were going to throw the ball inside at 94 miles an hour on a day when you didn't feel like you could break a pane of glass, fine. Let 'em think that way. Perfect. I always believed that it was them or us, and nothing was going to stand in my way. Take no prisoners, and if you were going to lose, take down the son-of-a-bitch who beat you, too. Make him feel the cost of victory. That was the Sal Maglie philosophy, and it was good enough for me. I was making a good living playing baseball, more money than I ever thought possible. I liked what I was doing too much to let any guy with a bat in his hand take it away from me.

I wasn't one of those guys who woke up mad on the day I pitched. I wasn't a bear around the house or anything like that. I didn't wake up in a bad mood, growling at my wife. I think if you dwell on a game all day, you can become mentally whipped. I might have started thinking about it when I drove to the ballpark for a home game, and relaxed in the hotel on the road. But when I got to the ballpark, which was my office, and put that uniform on, I guess I worked myself into a frenzy. I had a pretty good temper—and still do on occasion—but I basically kept my red-ass personality at the ballpark. It all locked in when you saw that first batter staring out at you from the plate. Then, after the game, it was over. That's how I developed that "Jekyll–Hyde" label as a guy who was an SOB on the mound, but a pretty decent drinking companion afterward. As the old saw goes, I was the same guy who would "brush back his grandmother" to win a game one minute, and then sing songs at a baseball writers' banquet the next—as I did at the 1963 affair in Hollywood. My assignment was, "One Love," "Give Her Love," and "Secret Love." See that? All love and kisses.

Of course, I do have this record of leading all National League modern-day pitchers in hit batsmen, 154 in fourteen years. That mark is still alive. In 1959, I hit 18 batters, the most for one pitcher in the National League since 1915. Overall, though, Walter Johnson has me beat in the American League by a bunch. He had 206 in his career. But he pitched for a lot longer than I did, and during a different era. Yet, for all those batters I nailed, I can honestly say that I never tried to hurt any of them, never tried to hit any of them in the head—never tried to hit any of them, period. Of those 154 victims, I'd say I wanted to knock down only 15. To only 15 of them was I trying to deliver a little message.

Also, for all my reputation, I got into only one real fight—the brawl I mentioned earlier with Johnny Logan and the Braves in 1957—and that happened because I dinged Logan with a pickoff throw at first base, not a pitch. I got suspended just once, after an incident involving Cincinnati's Frank Robinson in 1961 at the LA Coliseum. Frank was a great hitter, who actually changed his stance after his first year by moving up on the plate and closing his feet. On this particular day, I pitched him inside and he went down. Dusty Boggess, the plate umpire, came out to warn me.

"Shit, Dusty," I said. "What do you want me to do? Lay the ball right down the middle so he can beat my brains in?"

I came right back and threw another pitch inside, and down Frank went again. This time, the ball hit Robinson, and Boggess immediately threw me out of the game. I was suspended for five days by Warren Giles, the National League president, and fined $100. I wasn't too happy about it, and neither was Buzzie Bavasi, our general manager. But there was nothing we could do, except to try to point out how ridiculous it all was. I mean, pitchers all over baseball were hitting batters without being ejected or suspended, but I guess that might have been one case where my reputation hurt me instead of helped me.

So I owed the National League $100 and the next time we went into Cincinnati, I decided to pay my debt in person. I went to a bank and got $100 worth of pennies in those rolls, emptied them out, then put all the loose coins in a sack, and delivered them to Mr. Giles's office at the league headquarters in Carew Tower. I dumped the sack on his secretary's desk, she gave me this little smile, and I took off in a hurry. I was pretty proud of myself when I headed back to my hotel room, but I wasn't there too long before the phone rang. It was Mr. Giles's secretary.

"Mr. Giles would like to see you," she said.

I went back to the office and had a bit of a conversation with Mr. Giles. He told me to be careful about the way I was pitching, and I told him that I wasn't going to change my philosophy of keeping batters off the plate. It was all very amiable.

"And by the way," Mr. Giles added, "I want you to take those pennies of yours and roll them back up for me."

Fortunately, I had the paper rolls back in my room. I took the sack back to the hotel, and sat there for hours, putting the damn pennies in their containers, cursing all the way. Thank God I saved those containers or I would still be back in that Cincinnati hotel, rolling up $100 worth of pennies.

My first official warning had occurred a year earlier in San Francisco against the Giants. I came inside on Willie Mays, and he went down. That wasn't unusual for Willie. He went down often. He didn't do it to be a showboat. That was just his style. Some people pass another automobile on the highway by ten inches; other people want to be on the safe side, so they pass it by ten feet. Willie wanted to be on the safe side, although umpire Frank Secory came after me.

"Watch it," he said. "Don't be coming inside like that."

With that warning, I was automatically fined fifty dollars, according to the rules. I didn't care about the money.

"What the hell are you talking about?" I asked. "Jesus Christ, you're a former pitcher. Can't you tell when I'm throwing at somebody and when I'm not?"

"You're throwing at Mays and cut it out," he came back. "That'll be fifty bucks."

"Well, screw you," I said. "You better make it a hundred, because this next pitch is going in the same goddamn place."

I threw the next pitch inside—same spot—and Mays stepped back and fouled it off. That proved my point. I looked in at Secory and just raised my arms, as if to say, "Well, was I trying to hit him there?" I never did pay that fine.

Later that season, I had another episode with umpire Stan Landes. I threw a pitch that hit Joe Cunningham of the Cardinals in the right elbow. This was in the third inning of a game at the Coliseum; Cunningham, who was on a real tear at the time, had hit a home run off me in the first. When Cunningham went down, Solly Hemus, the St. Louis manager, came onto the field like he wanted to punch me out. I don't know if you remember Solly

Hemus, but he was at least thirty pounds lighter and nine inches shorter than me.

Anyway, Landes came out and had a little discussion with me.

"You better look out where you're throwing that ball," he said. "That's a warning."

"Well, you can take that warning and stick it up your ass," I snapped. "You're standing there telling me what I was thinking, that I wanted to hit the batter. How do you know what he's thinking? Was he looking for a pitch outside and did he just step into a pitch that was inside? Cunningham's one of the toughest guys in the league to pitch to because he does that all the time. He steps into the plate. If you're so smart, find out what he was thinking. Did you ask him where he was looking for the pitch?"

"I don't have to ask anybody anything," Landes said.

"Well, I'll tell you what," I told him. "If you fine me, I'll get a lawyer and I'll sue your ass over this stupid rule and I'll sue the entire National League. How can you tell me what I was thinking, what my intent was?"

I was never fined there, either. I can only guess that Landes, like Secory, realized that I had a good argument.

In 1962, it was Drysdale against the Cardinals again in another controversy. In the sixth inning of a game at the Coliseum, I was the runner at first base. Maury Wills was up and he hit a chopper toward the third-base line. Kenny Boyer, their third baseman, was cheating in. He was a heck of a good fielder, mobile and quick, and he grabbed the ball and threw to Julian Javier at second base to force me. As I went into the bag, I made a pretty good hook slide and I flipped Javier. Nothing serious. I was within my rights. I was trying to break up a double play, fair and square. I wasn't trying to hurt Javier or spike him.

Well, as it turned out, the play was ruled a foul ball. Boyer had picked it up and made the throw, following his instincts as a player should. You continue the play and worry about whether it's fair or foul later.

I returned to first base, and on his next swing, Wills slapped a ground ball to shortstop Dal Maxvill, who tossed it to Javier, again for the force out on me. Javier had a lot more time this time, though, and after he wheeled to relay to first base, I could see that he had other things on his mind than the double play. He backed off the bag and aimed the ball directly at me. I was well on the outside of the basepath, knowing I was already out, and Javier's throw wound up hitting the auxiliary scoreboard in short right field—eighty feet from the bag, and in foul territory. He'd had no idea whatsoever of throwing to first base. He wanted to hit me in the head, and if I hadn't ducked, he would have. I said nothing to him. I got up and went to the dugout.

One inning later, it was my turn. Javier came to bat, and I threw a high, inside fastball right at his chin. He went down like he'd been shot by a cannon, his helmet flying one way, his glasses going up in the air. When he got up, it looked like he'd been in a flour sack. He was filthy. He'd had his shot, and I'd had mine. I just looked at Javier, waiting to see if he had any notion of coming after me with the bat.

Johnny Keane, the Cardinals' manager, was livid. He said afterward that I'd deliberately attempted to injure Javier on the play at second base, and then compounded my felony by deliberately throwing at Javier. At least Keane was right on one count—the latter. Keane went on to say that if I denied that I was guilty on both accusations, I was a liar. Then he issued a challenge, saying that the Cardinals would retaliate against me, sooner or later.

"If they do," I said, "they better make sure they take me out of the park on a stretcher. Because if they don't, if I'm just wounded, I'll take out every one of those sons-of-bitches."

There's one important point here. I didn't hit Javier, nor did I want to. That was part of my philosophy, and it evolved partly from discussions with Maglie years before. If you wanted to brush a batter back or knock a guy down, the place to throw the ball was at his head. A batter would always see the ball that way, and be able to duck. The ball came in at eye level, and it wasn't all that difficult to avoid getting hit. I speak from experience, because I was a batter, too, and with my reputation for being a mean bastard, I faced my share of skin-bracers from other pitchers. But I knew I wouldn't get hit in the head for that same reason—I knew I could see the ball and get out of the way in time. The rest of my body, I didn't really care about. The worst thing that could happen was that you'd suffer a broken bone somewhere. I was fortunate to have a pretty high tolerance for pain. I played with cracked ribs, I had the shingles and I pitched. I was an animal and I expected everybody else to be like me.

So that was one part of my pitching plan. If you really wanted to hit a guy, don't throw at his head. If you did want to hit him, the best place to throw was down and behind him. Whenever a batter sees a wild one coming his way, the natural instinct is to back up. If you throw the ball behind a guy, chances are he'll back right into it. That's just the way it was, and still is.

I also had the belief, as did Maglie, that for every one of my teammates who went down, two players from the other team would go down. Or, if two Dodgers were knocked down when I was pitching, four opponents would bite the dust. I thought that was a nice, orderly way of doing things. I never really talked to my teammates about this little arrangement of mine, but I suspect they appreciated it. When I was on the mound, the Dodgers knew that they were going to be protected. I got some terrific support from Dodger hitters through the years, and some great defensive plays behind me, and I have no doubt it had something to do with the fact that my teammates knew I was behind them until the end. You'd have to ask my teammates about their inner thoughts when I was on the mound. I did see a quote here and there that would lead me to believe they felt good about my presence.

Don't get me wrong. The Dodgers always put out hard for whoever was pitching, but I think they were dead sure I wasn't going to let any opposing pitcher take shots at them without a reply from me.

I didn't like to save my retaliation pitches for the lousy hitters, either. If I felt moved to knock down the opposing pitcher, I would. But that was only one. I still had another to go, and I preferred to hold that one for a big guy in the lineup. If I didn't use one brushback on the other pitcher, then I had two to play with. And if the other team wasn't aware of my addition, that would keep them on edge. Depending on what the situation was, I might wait or I might go right at them. It was like Russian roulette, but the general rule of thumb was, hit 'em where it hurts. Don't waste your time with a guy who isn't hitting his weight unless you really have a good reason.

I remember an exhibition game we played against the Pirates in the Bahamas. We were playing on a cricket field to a big crowd. The people there loved the Dodgers, not only because we were a good ballclub but because we had that history of having black players, starting with Jackie Robinson. On this particular day, though, the fans' loyalties were divided because the Pittsburgh pitcher was Alvin McBean, who was a native son. He was from the Bahamas, and I was pitching against him.

Well, damn if Bob Bailey didn't hit a home run for us just before I came up to bat. And damn if McBean didn't throw a pitch that hit me right in the butt. Now, I'd been thrown at a fair bit during my career, but in an exhibition game? I had trouble figuring it out, except that McBean obviously was pissed and probably embarrassed. There he was, having a tough afternoon in front of his countrymen. I didn't say anything. I tossed the bat aside and took first base.

What the hell is going on here? I thought to myself. Here we are in a nothing game, and this guy hits me in the ass. Well, if he wants to play by those rules, so will we.

The thought of a civil war or a riot never occurred to me. The only thing I went over in my mind while I was standing at first base was, Who's coming up for them next inning? Sure enough, McBean came up with a couple men on base. The Pirates sent him up there to bunt, and it's a good thing he got his bat on the ball, because if he hadn't managed to sacrifice successfully, the pitch would have hit him right between the eyes. I give him credit. I didn't bother throwing at another member of the Pirates to satisfy my quota of two that day because, after all, it was only an exhibition game. Regular season addition didn't apply.

I can't honestly say that the Pittsburgh incident was my only scrap in an exhibition game. There was another one in Vero Beach in 1961 against the Minnesota Twins. Zoilo Versalles hit a home run off me and on an 0-2 pitch to the next batter, I decked Lennie Green. I got a warning from umpire Nestor Chylak, who didn't even know me. He worked in the American League. There was no immediate trouble, but a couple innings later, we met again. I was at the plate waiting to make the tag, and Green was trying to score. I saw Green raise his leg as if to spike me.

"You cock that leg and I'll rip it off," I told him.

Green then had a few choice words for me, and we went at each other. In a matter of seconds, both benches emptied and we had a fine old time. Buzzie had a brief talk with me, and so did Alston. He told me that I was of more value to the club on the mound than I was in the clubhouse. He told me to watch my legendary temper because, the more of these things I got involved in, the greater the chances I had of getting hurt. I wasn't ejected from the game, but I was taken out by Walt himself. Just another shiny day in the Grapefruit League.

Now, let me get another point across here. Some of the best and most effective brushback pitches I ever threw were never intended to be brushbacks. They just happened. The way I threw, with that sidearm motion and the action on the ball, meant that my pitches just naturally ran in on right-handed batters. If you crowded the plate and I aimed a ball toward the inner half, chances are you were either going to have to bail out in a hurry or be hit. I'll never forget the time I hit Ernie Banks with a pitch in Wrigley Field. Doing that in Chicago was trouble, because Ernie was so popular. Hitting him with a pitch was worse than hitting the Pope. But Ernie never made a big thing about it.

"I was looking for a ball away, and his pitch came in on me," Ernie said. "Drysdale wasn't trying to hit me."

And that was that. Instances like that were inevitable. I must have plunked Carl Sawatski on the back of his left knee five times. Sawatski was a pretty good-hitting left-handed catcher. When one of my pitches came in on him, he had the habit of getting his right, or front, leg out of the way in time. But his left leg was planted, and bingo—he'd get nicked. Then there were batters who just froze when they saw a ball coming at them. Our own Carl Furillo was one, and so was Don Zimmer. For some reason, they just didn't react. I was petrified when I had to pitch to Zimmer after he was traded away from the Dodgers. Not only because he was my friend and because he had already been seriously beaned twice in his career. But because he just stood over that plate and stayed there, no matter where the ball was headed. That's probably why he was hit twice in the head, because he had that habit of freezing.

Not all of my brushback attempts were prompted by actions of opposing pitchers or players actually in the game. Every so often when I was on the mound, I heard guys from the other dugout yelling things at me. They might have figured they could remain anonymous, but I had a knack of sneaking a look to find out who was doing the yapping. Lots of times, it was a guy who wasn't in the game. I didn't think that was too brave and I didn't care for it, so every once in a while, I took it out on a guy who was in the game. That was the only way to stop the music. What was I going to do? Throw a high, hard one into the dugout?

187

Also, of course, there were occasions when I felt I had to take care of some personal business. In 1968, before the All-Star Game in the Houston Astrodome, Tom Haller, who was our catcher with the Dodgers, happened to be in the National League locker room when he caught Rusty Staub poking through my shaving kit. Staub was an All-Star from the Astros, a member of my own team that day. But there he was, messing with my shaving kit. I don't imagine that he was looking for a spare razor, either. He wanted to check on whether I was carrying any foreign substances around. I didn't appreciate Haller's report on the invasion of my privacy, but again, I had my chance to deliver a message later in the season.

In a game against the Astros, Staub came up to bat and I sent him sprawling.

"That's for looking through my goddamn shaving kit," I yelled at him. Rusty never said a word.

I never did have much fun pitching in the Astrodome to begin with. They had this huge electric scoreboard in the outfield, and whenever something big happened—like an Astro hitting a home run—this damn thing would show a long and loud cartoon with whistles and horns blowing and animals running across the screen. If you're a pitcher who's just given up a run, the last thing you want is to stand there and watch this crap with your ears ringing, but you had to wait until the damn thing was over. I don't remember the date or the individual, but I do recall taking out my anger one game on the next Houston batter. Whoever it was just looked at me like I was crazy, and I explained myself from sixty feet, six inches away.

"Tell them to cut that friggin' cartoon short," I yelled.

I didn't have any great or novel theories about how to win games in the big leagues. I suppose I thought like most other pitchers. If you were going to get beat, get beat by the good hitters, not the .220 ones. Keep the Punch-and-Judy guys off the bases, so the Henry Aarons and Frank Robinsons and Willie Mayses wouldn't be able to hurt you too badly. You knew the great hitters would get their share of hits. Aaron hit 17 home runs off me, which sounds like a lot, but considering all the times I faced the Braves, it's not all that bad. Mays and I had some memorable confrontations. When he went down after one of my pitches in San Francisco, the place got up in arms. They booed me for hours. When I kept him off the plate in Los Angeles, naturally, I was cheered.

188

I never worried too much about getting batters mad—about waking sleeping giants, so to speak—although if there was one guy who seemed to hit better when he was angry, I'd nominate Frank Robinson. He seemed to make better contact than the rest when he was boiling. On days when I wasn't going well, of course, it seemed like the good hitters were hitting out of order. It seemed like they were up there every third guy.

I don't see all the pitchers in the major leagues, but the only one I can think of offhand who reminds me of some of the guys like myself twenty years ago is Roger Clemens of the Boston Red Sox. He throws hard and he throws inside and if you happen to get in the way, well, your ass is on the ground. He's a hell of a competitor, Clemens is. I think he would fit right in during the fifties and sixties when so many of those games were like sparring matches.

In my current job as a broadcaster, I can pick out probably nine of ten times when a pitcher is trying to hit a batter or brush him back. You can just sense it. But there aren't that many occasions when it happens anymore. There are lots of games when you figure somebody has to go down, but nobody does. Pitchers just get themselves into jams and stand out there getting the living crap beat out of them. It's like banging your thumb with a hammer. It's amazing to me how some of these guys get tarred and feathered in broad daylight without even attempting to back hitters off the plate, but that's the way it is. Sooner or later, you have to declare yourself and say, it's my ball and half the plate is mine. That's the way I pitched, only I never let on which half of the plate I wanted. If I took the half of the plate that a batter was claiming, then there was a hell of a chance of a collision. That's why I've always said, show me a guy who doesn't want to pitch inside and I'll show you a loser.

I have to laugh at people who criticize Sandy Koufax for being too perfect, for never throwing inside with the Dodgers. Nothing could be further from the truth, and if you don't believe me, talk to Lou Brock. He'll tell you about the night he got a walk from Koufax, then stole second and third, and scored on a sacrifice fly. The Cardinals got a run without a hit and Sandy was irate. I was sitting in the dugout with Jim Lefebvre who had just come up to the ballclub.

"Frenchy," I said, "I feel sorry for that man about what he just did."

189

"Who?" he asked.

"Brock," I said. "Sandy doesn't appreciate that sort of thing. Sandy gets mad enough when you beat him with base hits. But when you score runs without hits, look out."

Sure enough, the next time Brock came up, Koufax drilled him in the back with a fastball. You could hear the thud all over the stadium. Brock went down like he was a deer who'd been shot. He got up and trotted toward first base, not rubbing, pretending he wasn't hurt. But he never made it. Brock just collapsed and they had to carry him off on a stretcher.

"Goddamn!" Lefebvre said. "How about that!!"

How about that! Way to go, Sandy.

I don't remember exactly when I got this label as a "head-hunter." It might have been when a magazine writer from Santa Barbara did a story on me one day, took a few liberties, and they stuck a headline on the thing making me sound like a combination of Frankenstein and Dracula. Then there were those remarks from other ballclubs branding me as the "meanest pitcher in either league." I never paid much attention to all the ink, and I never, ever talked about it. I let other people have their say, and every once in a while, my reputation rose up and bit me. When I came out of a hotel or a stadium and a bunch of kids wanting autographs would ask me how many batters I'd hit that day or that season, I wasn't too thrilled about this neon sign I was carrying around on my back. But I knew I wasn't doing anything vicious. I didn't hate opposing batters. I just wanted to win, and brushing them back seemed to be the professional way to do it.

No doubt my physical stature helped me intimidate batters, if that indeed is what I did. I was tall and lanky and all arms. Also, the angle the ball came from was unusual. There weren't many pitchers delivering the ball by way of third base or left field. I'm sure that kept a few guys loose. I know this. The Braves had a guy, Gene Conley, who looked a lot like me. He was a basketball player with the Boston Celtics, so he had some real height on him. I liked to hit and I took pride in it, but I never thought of stepping in there against Conley as a day at the beach. He looked like an octopus out there. You didn't know where the ball was coming from or where it was going and Gene had a bit of an ornery streak in him, too.

But I was never such a villain that I ever attempted to maim an opposing batter. There's a big difference between brushing

190

back a hitter and trying to hit him. There's all the difference in the world. And I wasn't interested in ending anybody's career. I just wanted to keep my own going. I wanted to win in the worst way; I did not want to ship the other guys off to a hospital. I'd prefer to think of myself as one of those players you love to have on your team but hate to have on the other team. And as much as I was blasted during the years, I would hope that opponents realized that I was nothing more and nothing less than a competitor trying to do his job. I think I was respected for being that and, hell, guys who ran into me off the field might even have learned to like me.

I'm sure a lot of critics were flabbergasted when they discovered that I'd applied to be a public relations man with the Meadow Gold Dairies during the off-season early in my career. My first interview was with W. A. (Bill) Hutchinson, who was general manager of the company.

"When I met you, Don," Hutchinson was quoted as saying, "I couldn't help thinking how amazed I was to find you such a gentle, polite young man."

"What did you expect?" I asked. "A convict?"

All I wanted to do as a pitcher with the Dodgers was win, and everything worked out well. In fact, when I was voted into the baseball Hall of Fame in Cooperstown, New York, in 1984, I read the inscription engraved on my plaque. It stated all the particulars—how many games I'd won, how many shutouts I'd pitched, how many batters I'd struck out, and so forth.

But it also said that one of the reasons I'd survived was because I was "intimidating." I guess I was.

15

True Confessions and Good-bye

I was running in the outfield at Holman Stadium during spring training of 1969. The Washington Senators were in Vero Beach to play the Dodgers, and Ted Williams was the new Washington manager. Williams not only possessed one of the most picture-perfect swings ever (it's not only pitchers who can be intimidating), but he's in a dead heat with Frank Sinatra as the most magnetic person I've ever met. Talk about two men who can light up a room just by coming through the door.

That day in Vero, we got to talking about the 1959 All-Star Game in Los Angeles. It was a first for the West Coast, and I got the start in the Coliseum, a nice honor. In the third inning, Williams absolutely crushed one of my pitches and hit it to the deepest part of center field. Willie Mays had to pull it in against the wall. But here it was, ten years later, and Williams's photographic memory was in vintage form.

"You know that pitch before the one I hit?" he said. "What was that? What did you throw me there?"

"Oh, that was a sinker," I answered. "The pitch you just fouled off? I threw you a sinker."

"Yeah, yeah, sinker my ass," Williams said. "I've seen some good spitters in my days, and that was one of the best goddamn spitters ever. And in a friggin' All-Star Game, you threw it!"

I just laughed and headed back to the outfield to do some more running. I couldn't tell a lie then, I cannot tell a lie now. I

193

threw some spitters in my career. Yes, I loaded up a few. Not as many as a lot of people think I did, and not as often. But a few, depending on the game and the situation. Some days, I threw twenty. Some days, ten. Some days, maybe five. To hear some of my former opponents talk, you'd think I wet every pitch I ever threw. In fact, to this day, I run into Richie Ashburn, who's broadcasting for the Phillies, and he always greets me the same way.

"You cheatin' son-of-a-bitch, how are you?" he'll say with a big laugh. Oh, how he used to scream in that batter's box when I served up a wet one. It was hilarious. I did it almost just to hear him moan. Billy Williams of the Cubs used to get aggravated, too, and so did Henry Aaron. He'd see that thing coming in there and he'd just close his eyes and look up at the sky. And, in a sense, that's exactly why I threw it. To make him think. To distract him. I didn't feel I had all the weapons I needed against left-handed batters, so I used the spitter mostly on them. But against a great right-handed batter like Aaron, I always figured it never hurt to wet one early and then let them look for moisture the rest of the game.

Pitching, after all, is partly the art of deception, of outguessing the batter who's trying to guess along with you. If you can play mind games with hitters, then you've got a little edge psychologically. Remember, anything for an edge. Clay Bryant, who used to coach third for the Dodgers, had this little scheme of keeping the infield ball in his back pocket when we were up. Then, at the end of the half-inning, when the umpires weren't looking, he'd leave the infield ball at the mound for us instead of the shiny, new game ball. That would allow the Dodger pitcher maybe two, three pitches with this scuffed-up old thing until the batter or umpire realized what was going on. Then, the green ball would be thrown out of the game and a nice white ball would be put in play and you went back to your business of pitching. We did that only when one of the other team's good hitters was leading off the next inning. You didn't want to waste a green ball on a guy batting .190.

My introduction to the spitball came when I was in the minor leagues with Montreal. We were playing the Havana Sugar Kings in Cuba and they had a pitcher, Emilio Cueche, who was loading 'em up left and right. My teammates were getting upset, and they convinced me to try fighting fire with fire. Or, rather, water with water. I knew nothing about spitballs at the time, but I got a crash course from some of the guys who'd been around, like my catcher,

Johnny Bucha. I wasn't very scientific about it then, and I'm still not, but I found if I kept my fingers off the seams and put a little saliva on the ball, the bottom would drop out just when the ball got to the plate.

It was like a new toy, a very nice new toy. I wasn't too sophisticated about trotting out my new toy that day in Havana, either. I just went to my mouth and let fly. I was in one tough situation with men on base when their big catcher, Pete Montalvo, came to bat. Havana's manager, Reggie Otero, saw me load one up and he was screaming like hell from the dugout for Montalvo to step out. But Montalvo never heard him, and I struck him out. Reggie was madder than a hornet. It was okay for *his* pitcher to wet 'em, but not okay for me to do the same. For years, Reggie and I had a few chuckles about that day in Havana. Till the day he died, he never let me forget how I'd taken the law into my own hands against his Sugar Kings.

Through the years, I called on my spitter at times to get out of jams. I wasn't the only one, believe me. Gaylord Perry wrote a book on it. Bob Shaw and my fellow Dodger, Phil Regan, had fingers pointed at them, too. You'll have to ask them. But my good buddy, Gene Mauch, singled me out. He said I threw the best spitter in the National League because I threw it the hardest. Thanks, Gene.

I was accused of applying all sorts of foreign substances to the ball, from KY jelly to Vaseline. Bill Rigney, the manager of the Giants for a while, swore I had some gook on the inside of my belt. All I was doing, though, was drying off my thumb after going to my mouth to get some saliva. I wet the index and middle fingers and then spread the moisture around with my thumb. Some guys could throw the spitter with their thumb wet, but I couldn't. I couldn't grab onto the ball properly. So, I found that I had to dry off the thumb. While Rigney thought I was reaching for stuff, I actually was dumping some fuel, but that's okay. Deception. Make them think. That's what I always said. Make them think.

The only other thing I ever used was slippery elm, and you had to mix it with gum because it tasted so terrible. At the end of a game, or the next day, your mouth felt like you'd been in the Gobi Desert. It felt like cotton. I never had stuff in my hair or on my neck or face, despite what some managers and umpires suspected. Spit was a lot more convenient, and you'd be amazed at

195

how uncomplicated the process was. When I wanted to throw a spitter, I would just look at my catcher and call it myself, usually by doing something with my lips, like moistening them in broad daylight. Real cloak-and-dagger stuff, huh? Then I'd stick my fingers in my mouth, dry off my thumb, and let it go. Remember, as I said before, if you're going to war, you better bring all your weapons.

The rules in those days, of course, were a little more relaxed than they are now. You could go to your mouth right on the mound. Now, you have to step off if you want to blow on your hand, or whatever. That makes for a lot of unnecessary movement, not that I think many of these umpires now would know what the hell to look for. Maybe a couple of real veterans like Doug Harvey or John Kibler, but that's all. The game's been so sanitized that pitchers can't throw what the umpires couldn't find if they knew what they were looking for.

The ridiculous part of all this is that the spitball, though it's been outlawed since 1920, is no danger to the game. If you know how to throw it, it's no harder to control than a split-fingered fastball. In fact, if I were a pitcher now who wanted to add the spitter to my repertoire, that's exactly what I'd do. I'd grab hold of my ballclub's public relations person and tell him to spread the word around that I'd been working on a split-fingered fastball during the winter. Then, I could go out and throw fifty spitters a game and nobody would know the difference. The spitter would have much the same action as a split-fingered fastball, and it would be easier on the arm, too. I could get out of a lot of jams and everybody would think I was terrific, working on a new pitch during the off-season when I could have been playing golf or fishing.

Unfortunately, by the time that spring training of 1969 rolled around, I needed more than spitballs to get me out of trouble. I could talk about them with Ted Williams in Vero Beach, but I was hurting. I had pitched during my career with broken ribs and shin splints and shingles and even a broken bone in my finger in the minors, but my right shoulder was really bothering me. After pitching for so many years, I knew how my arm responded, or was supposed to respond, to different situations. And there was a pain, an ouchiness, in that right shoulder at the start of 1969 that meant trouble, and I knew it. I didn't say anything. I kept my mind open, hoping for improvement, but it wasn't to be.

196

As it turned out, I'd suffered a torn rotator cuff. Dr. Robert Kerlan told me that after an examination during the summer. I didn't know what he meant by a torn rotator cuff. That wasn't a common term then. I don't remember pitchers being aware of it, and I don't know that doctors had much knowledge of it. Now, of course, every pitcher lives in mortal fear of a rotator-cuff injury because that's the toughest injury of all to come back from.

Dr. Kerlan, a world-famous physician, told me that he could try surgery. But he also said that it wouldn't be foolproof. He could cut, and I could still wake up any morning and try to shave and not be able to lift my arm. I didn't like the percentages, and I didn't like the way the season was going. Not one bit. I was on the disabled list twice, and I knew that I wasn't really helping the ballclub. We had an outside chance to finish first, and if I hung around, Walt Alston was going to be tempted to pitch me every time my turn came up. Just like he'd always done, just like I'd always done. But I couldn't do it. I can handle pain, but this pain was unbelievable. It was like somebody was sticking an ice pick in my shoulder. I could maybe get my arm back, but when I brought it forward to near my release point, the pain was brutal.

I tried pills, of course. Oh, did I try medication. Every doctor I went to, including Dr. Kerlan, thought he was the only guy I was seeing. But in truth, I must have had five different doctors giving me five different things to relieve the pain. I was so drugged up at times that I couldn't see the scoreboard from the mound. I was a walking drugstore. I had to cover one eye, like a drunk driver does when he wants to see the road. Roberto Clemente hit a line drive back through the box that could have killed me. I never saw it. I still haven't seen it. I was that fuzzy, that blurred. But I heard it. Did I ever hear it. And I felt it, too. After I'd escaped being hit, I felt a little sensation on the left side of my neck, like I had a mosquito sitting there, waiting to bite it. I brushed the area with my hand and looked down and my hand was dripping with blood. Clemente's line drive had taken the skin right off the edge of my ear. How's that for a gentle reminder that you've about had it?

"That's it," I said to myself. And it was. I could have been hit right in the coconut. Bob Will had done that to me once in Wrigley Field. In the ninth inning of a 0–0 ballgame, he'd cranked a ball right off my forehead. Norm Larker caught the ball between first base and the mound for the first out, but then Ernie Banks came

197

up. I tried to get him to fish for a curveball away, but the pitch hung up, and Banks hit it out to beat me 1–0. At least I saw that, though. Afterward, I went to Northwestern Hospital, and as Dizzy Dean used to say, X-rays of my head showed nothing.

But I didn't need any X-rays of my shoulder in the summer of '69 to convince me that I'd had enough. My teammates must have sensed it, too, because they gave me a going-away present in San Diego. My last victory was over the Padres on July 28 by a score of 19–0. All those runs I was begging for all those years, I got that game. That was my forty-ninth and last shutout, but don't be too impressed. I was by no means overpowering, and with 19 runs to play with, I didn't exactly have to strike out every batter. My arm felt so-so. I was going downhill without any brakes and I knew it, but at 19–0, I survived.

I knew it wasn't going to last. It was just a matter of time before it was going to blow up. I wasn't as depressed as I was annoyed. I'd never really had any arm problems, but nothing worked—pills, heat, rest, disabled list. I even tried dropping my arm down even lower than usual and throwing like Dan Quisenberry. That's the easiest way to throw, but it was a little late in my career to be changing mechanics. As I look back, I think I was probably so disgusted that I was doing so poorly that I just said, the hell with it. My earned run average for the season at that point was well over 4 a game, and that wasn't for me.

I had one more examination with Dr. Frank Jobe, who is as good as they come. He prescribed complete rest. But I couldn't wind up the rubber band anymore. I had no snap to my throws and I could hardly sleep at night. I discussed the situation with Walter O'Malley and my wife Ginger. Then I met with Walter O'Malley again. Walt Alston was understanding. Sandy Koufax was long gone, having retired after the 1966 World Series because of an arthritic elbow. I think Walt would have been at peace giving me the rest of the year off and not seeing me until spring training. But I had made up my mind, and Walt wasn't the type to talk you out of something like that. I could have maybe gotten another year on a contract and increased my pension by a bundle. Somebody figured out that if I'd have stayed one more season, thrown one pitch in 1970, the pension, set up as it is now, would have kicked in an extra $750,000 at age sixty-five. But I didn't want to make a fool of myself.

So we had a press conference at the Stadium Club over the right-field corner of Dodger Stadium on Monday, August 11, 1969.

"Yesterday, when I went upstairs to meet Walter O'Malley," I said, "I sat in the stands to watch a few innings of the game and I heard a sound that I had not heard since I was a boy.

"In all the years that I pitched, it was as if I'd become immune to the sound of bat hitting ball and ball hitting mitt.

"It had always been a magnetic click for me and I saw my whole childhood again. I knew then that all my dreams had come true."

I meant what I said, too. From the bottom of my heart. The place was packed with reporters and microphones and one of the questions was, What was my greatest thrill in baseball? I know it sounds corny now, and it probably sounded just as corny then, but my greatest thrill was just putting on that Dodger uniform for the first time. There was a magic to that jersey when I was a kid, and I still feel that magic now when I look out from the broadcast booth and see Dodger Blue.

If you had told me in 1968, while I was throwing all those shutout innings, that I'd have been forced to retire a year later, I would have lost my house and my lot and everything else I owned on that bet. I was only thirty-three, and I surely thought I'd be able to pitch for a couple more years. But there's an old saying about pitchers having so many pitches in their arm and when you use that number up, it's over. I sort of believed that. There's no way to trace the wheres and whens of an injury like mine. Was it the wear-and-tear of the scoreless streak? Nah, no way. I was young enough to keep going, but age means nothing if you can't get it done, and the hitters were the first to let me know. They always are.

I can't say that the injury prevented me from attaining any goals because I never really had any. I never set out to win so many games or strike out so many batters or anything like that. I guess if I had an objective, it was to play as long as possible and to make as much money as possible. I'd had a comfortable childhood, but it wasn't like Dad and Mom were rich. They were great parents who did everything they could, and when I started to make what was considered big money, I got more pleasure out of doing things for them. I enjoyed giving to them more than I enjoyed accumulating possessions for myself and my family.

When I did quit, some opinions were voiced about whether it was really final. Maury Wills, the Dodger shortstop, predicted that I would have second thoughts, that I'd miss it so much, I'd change my mind over the winter. Then there was Al Campanis, who had taken over Buzzie Bavasi's job when Buzzie left to run the Padres. Campanis never said it to my face, and I never saw it in print, but some friends told me that Al was saying behind my back that he thought I could have continued to pitch. I don't know why he felt that way if he did. God knows, I loved playing professional baseball. I wouldn't trade one minute of my sixteen years as a player for anything. But my arm was gone, and I didn't want to be taking up space as a four-inning pitcher. There are three things that are inevitable—death, taxes, and the retirement of professional athletes, and I would only have hurt myself and the Dodgers if I'd have prolonged the agony. I never did talk to Al Campanis about what he said. I didn't think it was worth the time and effort. If there's one thing I stood for as a pitcher for the Dodgers, it was my ability and willingness to take the ball every fourth day and pitch.

I wound up with a 5–4 record in 1969 with a 4.45 earned run average in only 63 innings. Time to go. That was the first year since 1957 that I hadn't pitched at least 200 innings. In four straight years, from 1962 through 1965, I topped 300 innings per season. I'm still second on the all-time Dodger list to Don Sutton in career victories with 209, starts (465), strikeouts (2,486), innings pitched (3,432), and shutouts. I was lucky enough to be on Dodger teams that won five pennants and three World Series. (And, by the way, five times I led the National League in hit batsmen. I liked my own record of 18 in 1959 so much that I broke it two years later with 20.)

But the upside of all those hit batsmen was that it was economical. Once Alston came out to the mound and instructed me to walk Donn Clendenon of the Pirates. I wound up hitting him instead.

"I thought I told you to put him on base intentionally," Walt said later.

"I did," I told him, "but why waste four pitches when one will do?"

At the end of the 1969 season, the Dodgers held a day for me at Dodger Stadium. The Dodgers were playing the Giants, of all people, our fiercest rivals. And the Giants gave me a bottle of Vitalis and a tube of Vaseline. Kelly got a puppy dog and I got more gifts than I deserved—a car, a ring with "53" in diamonds, and several plaques. Governor Ronald Reagan of California had a few nice words, and so did Vin Scully, who said, "Big D, you stood as tall in defeat as you did in victory. You were a man for all seasons. You were the spirit of the Dodgers." Nice. Very nice.

I sucked it up and said my piece:

"I can only say, thank you—thank you baseball, thank you Dodgers, and thank you Walter Alston, who never changed, who stayed with me through good and bad.

"I want to say thank you, too, to my wife, who put the pieces back together when they so often fell apart. I want to say thank you to my parents, who sacrificed so that I could have the opportunity to play.

"I want to say thank you to the fans and the news media, and last but certainly not least, I say thank you, God, for giving me the strength and the arm."

I had been retired for a few weeks, so I was already getting used to the other side of life. Instead of being a night person, as I'd been all those years as a ballplayer, I found myself going to bed by nine-thirty or so at night and waking up early. I was living like a normal human being, and it was fun. I tried to make as clean a break as possible from baseball by not even listening to Dodger games on the radio. The rest of that year, I dived right into the horse business by running some thoroughbreds at Del Mar, near San Diego. I went to the track every day, not to bet, but to work. And I went to one old-timers' game that the Angels held. I was busy and I wasn't looking back. That was good for me.

Naturally, whenever you retire, you are vulnerable to regrets. One of the biggest mistakes an athlete can make is kidding himself and staying that one extra year. But you also can make the mistake of quitting too soon, and I felt a twinge of that the next spring when I was in Florida with the Montreal Expos as their part-time broadcaster and minor league pitching instructor.

One day in West Palm Beach, I was out on the field. Gene Mauch, the Expos' manager, was there and so were Don Zimmer and Jerry Zimmerman, two of his coaches. Mauch had the pitchers around second base in sort of a meeting. Zim and Zimmerman were at home plate, waiting for the drills to get going. I got a little itch to throw the baseball, so I grabbed a glove, went to the mound,

201

and starting tossing some pitches to Zimmerman. Pretty soon, Zim stepped in and pretended he was the hitter.

I threw and threw and threw and damn, if I wasn't hitting spots like I was a kid all over again.

"Give me one outside," Zim would say, and I'd throw the ball right there.

"Give me one down and in," Zim would say, and I'd throw the ball right where I wanted to.

I was in a Montreal uniform, feeling just super and concentrating so hard on what I was doing that I didn't notice what had happened behind me. I must have been throwing for five minutes, as well as I could throw, and Mauch had brought in all his pitchers from second base to watch me. They didn't say anything and neither did I. And then I turned around and did a double take.

"What are you doing?" I asked Gene.

"I just wanted to show these kids what it's like when a pitcher gets into his rhythm," Mauch said.

That was very flattering to an old washed-up pitcher like me. I had thrown at maybe half- to three-quarter speed, and was considered worth watching by Mauch and his pitchers.

"Why don't you show these fellas how you grip your fastball?" Mauch said.

Well, it was at that point when I realized that my decision to quit was the right one. I stuck my right arm out to display the proper grip, and not only did my shoulder start aching like hell, but my hand was shaking like a leaf. It was like I had some form of palsy. It was so bad that I had to use my left arm to steady my right wrist to keep it still. I knew more than ever that my run was over. I was done. Stick a fork in me.

Fifteen years after I'd retired—on August 12, 1984—I was standing at the podium before the Baseball Hall of Fame in Cooperstown, New York. Thank God my parents, Scotty and Verna, were still alive to see it. My daughter Kelly was there, too, and my sister Nancy and my future wife Ann. And as I looked out at the audience, trying to clear my throat and make my little speech, I saw a whole bunch of Dodger fans in the crowd—Brooklyn Dodger fans with that "B" on their caps.

I'd been cautioned that, no matter how hard I prepared for the day, it would be very emotional. And was it ever. But when I saw all those people there, and felt the warmth, I knew I had hit the nail on the head fifteen years earlier. All my dreams had indeed come true. I don't know what the heck I would have done if I hadn't been a professional ballplayer. I never really gave it a thought. I might have worked for the telephone company, like my dad.

But the way things turned out, and after all the great things that happened to me in baseball, I have to be very thankful that Roger Grabenstein never showed up to pitch that day when Dad sent me to the mound.

16

Life After Baseball

*D*uring the latter part of the 1987 season, my sixth
as a broadcaster with the Chicago White Sox, I
was in Minneapolis with the ballclub when I received a phone call in my hotel room. It was Jerry Reinsdorf,
chairman of the board of the White Sox. He was in Toronto at an
owners' meeting.

"Peter O'Malley has asked for permission to talk to you," he
said. "And I think you owe it to yourself to listen to what he has
to say."

I thanked Jerry, though I had no idea what was brewing. A
couple days later, Peter called. He told me that Jerry Doggett, who
had come with the Dodgers from Brooklyn and had been Vin
Scully's sidekick in the booth for years, was about to retire. The
Dodgers were looking for a replacement. Peter asked to meet with
me when I was next on the West Coast with the White Sox, which
was the third week in September.

The White Sox had a Wednesday night game in Anaheim
against the Angels, and I had a meeting that morning in Los
Angeles, so I arranged to see Peter in his Dodger Stadium office
at two P.M. I arrived about forty-five minutes early, which was nice,
because it gave me time to poke around the ballpark, always a
pleasure. When Peter was ready, we talked for about an hour-and-
a-half. That's like talking for three hours with anybody else, because you get a lot accomplished. Peter is like his dad in that
respect. If you begin to veer off the subject at all, Peter gets you

right back on the track. Mr. O'Malley, when he lit up that cigar and spread that Irish wit around, was a pretty outgoing person. Peter isn't quite that way, at least not yet. He's a little quieter, but he shares that one trait with his father. In conversation with either, you stay focused on the topic. Warm and businesslike, Peter never strays very far. No card tricks, no funny stuff. Just business.

"You're my number-one choice, far and away, to replace Jerry," Peter said. "And that's why I wanted to talk to you. I want to see if we can work something out for next year."

Well, I don't get too high or too low about anything in life, but I was excited at the prospect of returning to the Dodgers. In typical Dodger fashion, Peter had the team's general counsel draw up about two-and-a-half pages of guidelines—my duties, if I came aboard. Peter asked me to look them over. With rare exception—a slight change here and there—I had absolutely no problems with the proposal. I discussed the possibility of a few perks that I'd had in other jobs, like an automobile to drive. But the Dodgers were never big on fringe benefits like that, and Peter told me that he was the only one in the organization with a company car. End of issue.

I talked with my lawyers about the overall terms, and they talked with the Dodgers' attorneys, and when I got to Oakland on the next leg of that White Sox road trip, everything was pretty much in order. My wife Annie, who had been on pins and needles about the whole thing, had come up with our son Donnie to be with me for the weekend. I was off on Saturday—there was no TV back to Chicago because of the nationally televised "Game of the Week"—and that morning, I was just lying around the hotel room reading the newspaper when I got a call from the Dodgers. Peter and his legal expert, Sam Fernandez, were in Dodger Stadium and they let me know that they were going to send me a copy of the twenty-six-page contract over the FAX machine in the hotel office at the Oakland Hyatt. I talked to my people, Nick Lamprose and Jerry Roberts, in San Jose. Nick came up that afternoon to look it over with me at an early dinner, and the next morning, it was done. From Wednesday to Sunday at ten-thirty A.M., we had consummated the deal.

There had been a lot of speculation in the Los Angeles papers about Doggett's replacement, and Peter was a bit anxious. He didn't care for all the rumors, and he told me that he wanted to have an announcement as soon as possible. On Monday, I called

Chicago and couldn't reach Reinsdorf but I did get his partner, Eddie Einhorn. I owed them the first call, because both of those men were nothing but good to me in Chicago. They paid me more money than I'd ever made, and treated me absolutely super. I hadn't always agreed with some of their ownership moves, and I would have liked to give them a little more input, but I wasn't asked, and that was fine. I was hired as broadcaster for the Sox, and that's what I did.

Eddie thanked me for the speed of the negotiations, and for the courtesy of calling. He asked only that I hold off making any announcements until the end of the season. That was fine with me, but Peter wanted it out, and Eddie thought it over and said, okay. That afternoon, the Dodgers issued a release and Vinny—who had called me earlier to congratulate me personally—then called to do a pregame show before the Dodgers' broadcast that evening. The Sox were off that night, so I stayed home at our apartment in Lake Point Tower, and my telephone was jumping. And the common sentiment from friends and press people wanting interviews was this: it was right, it was absolutely natural for me to rejoin the Dodgers. I was practically born a Dodger; I was a Dodger again.

"They say you can't go home again," the White Sox's veteran catcher, Carlton Fisk, mentioned the next night at Comiskey Park. "But you are, and that's great."

I had made a lot of friends in Chicago, Annie and I loved the city, and the White Sox had played some good baseball at times—they won the American League West Division by a record 20 games in 1983. But not one person questioned the move, including Jerry Reinsdorf, who himself had grown up in Brooklyn and had experienced firsthand the Dodger aura. He realized from the first day Peter had asked permission to talk to me that it was a perfect fit.

I received a five-year contract from the Dodgers at an even better salary than the White Sox had paid me. I would work with Vin Scully, who was, in Brooklyn, a young legend-in-the-making when I came up to the Dodgers in 1956. Our threesome also included Ross Porter, another fine veteran sportscaster in Los Angeles who'd been working with Vin and Jerry Doggett for many years. There's no doubt who's number one—Vinny. But he's so busy doing baseball and golf for NBC that there's plenty of work to go around.

We've gotten along very well, which is essential. I'm sure that booth can be like a prison if you've got clashing egos or personalities, because during the long season, you wind up seeing more of your fellow broadcasters than you see your wife. I've been lucky that way. I've always had good relationships with announcers I've worked with. Ross, I suppose, could have been upset about me joining the broadcast team and being given equal billing. But he's never acted angry or hurt as far as I can see. Ross is a solid and well-respected broadcaster who's got a good job. There aren't many better places to go when you're a voice of the Los Angeles Dodgers.

I've been pleasantly surprised at how enjoyable it's been working with Vinny, and don't take that wrong for a minute. I'd always known him as the consummate professional, but because he was the broadcaster when I was playing for the Dodgers, I never knew what a terrific guy he is. Vinny keeps his distance with the athletes. He's cordial and friendly, but he believes it's not the broadcaster's function to become too close. Not until 1988, when I got to be in the booth with him, did I really get to know him socially. Let me tell you, this is one funny man with great lines and an outstanding knack for telling a good story. Lord knows, Vinny's seen it all. Perfect games, no-hitters, World Series, All-Star Games. And that's just baseball. Vinny is a professional broadcaster who could broadcast anything. And without cue cards.

In 1988, after the Dodgers surprised just about everybody by winning the National League pennant and World Series, the local TV channel in Los Angeles, KTTV, wanted us to do a half-hour special on the season. We didn't exactly wing it, but we didn't have a script, either. Well, the way Vinny pulled it all together and kept things moving as unofficial master of ceremonies was awesome. The great ones can do that.

Another aspect of Vinny's talents is his grasp of the game. Again, I wasn't surprised, because from all those years of listening to him, I knew that he had a real knowledge of baseball. But, being with him as often I have, has only added to my respect. Some play-by-play broadcasters have beautiful voices, but they don't see the inner game. Vinny does. He's done a lot in his career, and made a lot of money, and he deserves whatever fame and fortune come his way.

When I came his way in 1988, it marked the first time Vinny had worked with a former ballplayer on the Dodger broadcasts.

He's done it with the networks, of course, most recently with Tom Seaver. Before that, he was with Joe Garagiola. But he'd never had a "ex-jock" on the Dodger TV or radio teams until me, and I think he kind of likes it. I know I like working with him. Whenever we stop in the press room for a drink after a game, we have a lot of laughs. Vinny certainly carries himself well for a man who is so revered. Millions of people in Los Angeles learned baseball by listening to him, but he doesn't come across as bigger than the game. And for all the games he's done, he's up for every broadcast. I'm sure there are nights he'd rather be home than at the ball-park—we all get that way—but you'd never know it by listening to him or being around him.

Vinny always has preferred to work Dodger radio or TV games by himself. That is, if he's doing seven innings, he does them alone. There are no comments from Ross or me, no other voice on the air. Vinny's policy results from his belief that, if you're on by yourself, you're talking to the listeners or viewers. If you're on with somebody else, you wind up talking to your sidekick. Vinny feels he's there to talk to the listener, and you've got to respect that, even though everywhere else I've worked, there have been two or sometimes three broadcasters contributing at the same time. But Vinny's been so successful, how can you argue? I'm not about to.

Besides, as I said, there are plenty of innings to go around when you do something like 200 games—exhibition, regular season, postseason—from March through October. Vinny does about 100. He misses Saturdays when he's on the network, and some road games when we don't televise. On nights when he is on hand, at my suggestion, Ross and I take four or five days off during the season. That's another departure from customary broadcast arrangements in baseball, but I think it's a good one. Just get away from the ballpark for an entire day once in a while, spend it with your family, and come back the next day with your batteries recharged. When it's Ross's day off, I do what he normally does. And vice versa. I appreciate a breather, and I think Ross does, too.

In the years before I actually joined Vinny in the booth, he was more help to me than he'll ever realize. All I had to do was listen to him. It's like putting a burglar at a safe. The only time I didn't enjoy listening to Vinny was when I was still an active player, and the reason for that was simple. If I was listening to him do a Dodger game, it usually meant I was in the clubhouse after getting knocked out. Otherwise, he was a pleasure to tune in to.

The broadcast bug probably bit me before I even realized it. During my first year in Brooklyn, I often went down to the bullpen and did a mock play-by-play. A rookie didn't want to get caught doing that in the dugout, but the bullpen was okay. As a kid, my exposure to baseball broadcasting was limited. Besides the "Mutual Game of the Day" on radio, all we had in Southern California was Bob Kelly doing the Los Angeles Angels and Fred Haney on the Hollywood Stars. Then, later on, Buddy Blattner and Dizzy Dean teamed for the "Game of the Week" on NBC television. How much all of the above influenced my bullpen broadcasts, I don't know. I do remember a few veterans tiring of my babbling every so often and telling me either to shut up or go elsewhere.

When Pee Wee Reese retired as a player and went to NBC after a brief stint as Dodger coach, that struck me as a nice way to make a living after baseball. Pee Wee and I were close and I thought, If that's good enough for him, it's good enough for me. That really might have planted the seed. I began listening more closely to the broadcasters in each town—Bob Prince in Pittsburgh, Byrum Saam in Philadelphia, Harry Caray in St. Louis, Jack Brickhouse and Jack Quinlain in Chicago, Russ Hodges with the Giants in San Francisco. If I happened to be in the clubhouse, after being KO'd or after getting my work done for an upcoming start, my ears would perk up a bit. The radio was always on in the clubhouse.

After I retired in 1969, I went to Danny Thomas's golf tournament during the winter in Miami Beach. It hadn't hit me that I suddenly needed a job, because it was the natural time of year, the off-season, for me not to be working. After playing golf one afternoon, I went over to the Americana Hotel, where the major league meetings were being held. The first people I ran into were Gene Mauch and Gene Kirby. Mauch was managing the Montreal Expos. Kirby, who had worked on the NBC "Game of the Week," had become traveling secretary for the Expos. He was also in charge of their radio-TV arrangements. They asked me the natural question: What was I doing with myself? I said I had no idea. Gene suggested that I come to Montreal and do their TV games. The Expos had just joined the National League as an expansion team in 1969, and it sounded like a nice idea. Gene said he would talk to Charles Bronfman, the Expos' owner, and their general manager, John McHale. Mauch said he'd also use me in the spring.

That was the start of my broadcasting career. I helped Mauch with the major league pitchers during spring training, I was the minor league pitching instructor during the regular season, and I did the TV games. For all those jobs, I took a hell of a pay cut— from $115,000 as a player to $22,500 as a jack of all trades with the Expos. My broadcast duties weren't all that extensive. I worked basically on Wednesday nights in what was the Canadian version of the "Game of the Week." My partner was Hal Kelly, brother of the famous hockey broadcaster Dan, both of whom have passed away. I commuted from California to Montreal, or wherever the Expos were playing, and then I went home. In between, I bounced around the Expos' system, looking at their young pitchers.

That lasted one season. Before the next year, I told the Expos that I thought I wasn't being fair to them, their kid pitchers, or myself. I couldn't spend the proper time teaching and watching their prospects. They deserved a full-time tutor. The Expos agreed, and made me just their TV announcer. During that season, I also did a few games for the St. Louis Cardinals when their number-one man, Jack Buck, was away on network assignments. The Cardinals had a few of us from other teams coming in to make guest appearances.

That winter, Bob Short moved the Senators out of Washington to Arlington, Texas, where they became the Texas Rangers. They contacted me about being one of their two main broadcasters, and I took it. That meant doing more games and some play-by-play, too. I had done only color analysis on Expos' TV, but I had some feel for play-by-play from spring training. When time permitted, I watched the Expos play exhibitions and talked into a tape recorder. Then, Kirby would take me into his office and evaluate my "broadcast." That was a tremendous help to me, and I'll never forget Kirby for taking me under his wing when he didn't really have to. I also owe some thanks to a fellow named Bert Labarr, who worked in West Palm Beach, Florida, where the Expos and Atlanta Braves both trained. He did a live game every day on the local station, and I worked with him some, too. Between those two old pros—Kirby and Labarr—I learned to say "catch" instead of "ketch" and "get" instead of "git."

I took this vast fund of knowledge with me to Texas, where I was lucky enough to pair up with another real pro, Bill Mercer, who was not only a fine broadcaster but a professor of speech at North Texas State University. He had his hands full, too. One morning we were heading to an exhibition game, Bill driving while I was writing furiously in the shotgun seat. We had a bunch of interviews to tape, and I was doing my homework. At least, I thought I was.

"What the heck are you doing over there?" Bill asked.

"I'm writing down all these questions I want to ask these guys."

Bill asked to have a look. I gave him the piece of paper, he took one glance, and then threw it out the window.

"What the hell are you doing to me?" I said.

"Don, you don't need to use a script for interviews," Bill explained. "Good interviewers have ideas about what they want to talk about, but your subject will determine the course of your interview. For example, if you ask your guest what he's going to hit this year, and he says, 'two-twenty,' are you going to ask your next prepared question or are you going to ask him why he thinks he's going to hit only two-twenty? See what I mean?"

Bill was right, of course. In all the interviews I'd done as a player, I'd never once remembered the guy asking the questions with a list in front of him. I guess I wanted to be a pioneer of sorts.

Bill was very patient with me, and very constructive with his criticisms. And just when I thought I got my interviewing down, it was time for me to butcher other stuff. For what seemed to be weeks on end, we'd been reading this one promo about the New York Yankees coming to town for "Ball Night." Over and over. Here come the Yankees. Little League season right around the corner. See a game and get your Little Leaguer a souvenir. Over and over. Finally, I'd had enough.

"Bill," I said one day off-mike, "I sure am getting tired of this little drop-in advertisement of ours."

"Then ad-lib a little bit," he advised. "You've read it enough."

I obliged and was off to the races, imparting all sorts of information about that upcoming night against the Yankees.

"And don't forget," I said, "for all you little boys and girls who have no balls at home . . ."

Well, Bill just about fell out of his chair onto the floor and the engineer wasn't far behind him in hitting the deck. Bill was laughing so hard, he was almost choking. It was even money that he'd get back on the air, but being the seasoned veteran he was, Bill did manage to carry on. From then on, I took it easy on the ad-libs.

While I was in Texas that first season, Dick Enberg and I were having a sandwich in the press room when he asked me about my contractual obligations. I had only a one-year contract, and when he heard that, he asked me if I'd be interested in coming to California, to broadcast for the Angels. I was ecstatic about the possibility, and that materialized at the start of the 1973 season. I was lucky enough to be going to my native state, and lucky enough to be in the same booth with Dick and Dave Niehaus. If it sounds as though I'm a man who's been smiled on, I have. Dave, who has moved on to become the chief announcer for the Seattle Mariners, remains a good friend and I'll forever bow to Dick Enberg as one of the great influences on my career. He even brought me with him to do color on Los Angeles Rams' football for four years, and I got a real charge out of that.

I had played football and knew enough to get by, but what I learned most from Dick was the art of preparation. Anybody who thinks that all a broadcaster ever does is show up five minutes before gametime should spend some time around Dick. He is one of the hardest-working people I've ever met. Dick studies hard and he puts together pages and pages of notes and anecdotes, but he also has the ability to drop them in only when they're appropriate. He doesn't come on the air and read you everything he's got inside two innings. He paces himself and inserts items of information when appropriate. He might wind up using half of what he's got, or a third. If his notes don't apply, he might use none of them. I was with Dick for several years, and then he left for NBC, after which I became the number-one guy.

Dick was so smooth, and so good at carrying you through a difficult situation or at playing off your words. Plus, like Vinny, Dick knows the game. He was a baseball coach at San Fernando Valley State College when he was working on his doctor's degree, so there weren't any situations that caught Dick by surprise. He went right with the flow.

From 1978 through 1986, I worked for ABC on baseball and learned still more from another top professional, Keith Jackson. I also did a few other off-season events, and had a ball doing it. A couple years after I started with ABC, there was a change in ownership at the Angels' station, KMPC, and a new general manager wanted to start a whole new format—talk radio. The Dodgers had been on an all-talk station for many years, KABC, and it seemed that KMPC wanted to emulate the Dodgers. I got caught in a bit of a problem, because the new G.M. there didn't want me to do any network stuff. So, in 1981, I left the Angels and just did ABC assignments, which was different and more relaxing in that I didn't have to do a ballgame every day. I worked mostly on weekends. But by 1982, the White Sox had come to me with a heck of an offer. Harry Caray had gone over to the Cubs from the White Sox. So I met Reinsdorf and Einhorn one winter afternoon at the O'Hare Hilton outside Chicago, and I joined Kenny "Hawk" Harrelson—another great character—doing television for the White Sox. Harrelson, who came to Chicago after being a very popular voice of the Boston Red Sox, had me fighting tears one day when a guy swung at a pitch and broke his bat.

"Yeah, Don," Harrelson said right on the air, "these days, it's tough to find yourself a good piece of ash."

By being in the broadcasting business, I've gained tremendous admiration for the announcers who do it, night after night, year after year. A lot of players think it's a snap job, that you just turn in your uniform, then head upstairs and start saying, "Ball one, inside . . . strike one, right down the middle." It isn't easy at all. I've had Don Sutton ask me about broadcasting. Steve Garvey. Ron Fairly. A bunch of players. Sutton hooked on with the Atlanta Braves after he retired, Duke Snider took my spot in Montreal and worked there for many years. It's a nice way to make a living, yes, but it can be every bit as hard as playing. Broadcasting major league baseball can be tedious, if not because of the games, then because of the constant traveling. It's just like reliving your playing days.

As a former player, I didn't have that much trouble separating myself from the guys in uniform. I experienced some withdrawal pains at the start, but nothing serious. I knew, when conducting certain interviews, that I would know the answer to a question before I asked it. I suspected that a lot of my subjects realized as much, too. And I did have a little twinge of fear every so often that I'd ask a question and a player would turn around, look at me like I was crazy, and say, "What are you asking me that for? You know damn well what happened out there." But the listeners and viewers didn't want to hear about strategy from me, at least not during an interview with the star of the game. They wanted to hear about it from the star himself.

Being an outsider after all those years of being on the inside didn't worry me too much. As a Dodger, I'd been brought up with an appreciation for the role of the press and it was always part of the Dodger way to cooperate. That was just natural for me, and it came home to me when Steve Stone and I were doing a game together for ABC. We were discussing relationships between the media and the players, and he said, "You know, it's amazing, but I can't think of one Dodger player I've ever met who couldn't talk, who couldn't carry on a conversation. Even the kids they bring up fresh from the farm know how to handle an interview. You go into some clubhouses, and there are players who can't relate, or flat out won't."

Naturally, in the old days, the circumstances were different, more relaxed. There were fewer newspaper and radio and TV guys around a ballclub, and those who were seemed to be more easygoing than the new breed of journalists. When the Dodgers first moved to LA, we had a couple of writers, Bob Hunter and Frank Finch, who were great guys. They knew the ropes and they did their jobs well. But you were also able to have a drink with them after a game and tell them what was on your mind and you didn't have to worry that you'd see your name in headlines the next day. Every so often, Frank brought out that little pad of his at a bar and asked if he could write something you'd just told him. If you said no, then he'd put the pad right back in his pocket. Case closed. You didn't have to punctuate every sentence with "off the record."

There was a certain closeness you felt with guys like Hunter and Finch that isn't there today, I don't think. Maybe that's a reflection on the times, or maybe it's just a result of having so many more media representatives now. It's probably a little of both. It's also a result of newspapers looking for more controversy and, last but not least, it probably has something to do with the fact that some players are so wealthy now, they figure they don't need to talk to anybody, including their manager and a few of their teammates.

Players who I encounter now must figure I'm still part of the fraternity in a way. I have a job to do, but I'm not going to betray a trust. I have to work with these players every day, and I want them to work with me, and I certainly don't want to be referred to in terms that I've heard certain broadcasters discussed. I don't think that makes me a bad broadcaster or a weak human being or any of that stuff. Stu Nahan, a popular telecaster in Los Angeles, posed that issue on one of his shows as soon as I was named to the Dodger broadcasting job.

"What would you do," he asked me, "if you knew something about a Dodger player that the public didn't know?"

"Pertaining to what?" I responded. "The ballgame?"

"Well," he said, "suppose he had an argument with his wife that day."

"How does that affect the ballgame?"

"Well, it might affect his performance," he said.

"I'll be the judge of that," I answered.

And that's exactly how I feel about my role. I'll draw the line about reporting all I know, and if I get into trouble for not saying something, then I'll handle that when it happens. It hasn't happened yet. Nahan seemed to be reviving that old complaint about there being too many ex-jocks on the air now, that they don't really add a lot to a broadcast except name recognition. Once you get away from who they are and what they did, you aren't left with much, according to the critics. But I don't buy that theory. That's ancient history. Fans are too sophisticated now. They expect a former professional athlete to explain what actually happened, good or bad, and if they don't get what they want, they'll let you know in a hurry. An ex-jock who's just there sugar-coating isn't going to last. He's going to get buried.

I get as disgusted as anybody when the team I'm broadcasting with plays a lousy ballgame, and a listener who knows me well probably can tell from the inflection in my voice. But I'm from the school that says you broadcast right down the middle. Dick and Vinny are that way. If a guy makes an error, you say so and move on. What are you going to make of it? We're doing a ballgame, not a war. Are you going to take the guy out and shoot him? I'm not a homer, and I think there's a danger in being one. If you get so excited when your team wins, you have to get real down when your team loses. That violent swing in emotions will wear you out if it doesn't wear the listener out first. In Chicago, a city accustomed to announcers who do some cheerleading, I tried to be myself. I'm sure some White Sox fans wondered if I cared whether the team won or lost. I cared, but when you root, you've also got to whine. Harry Caray is a great broadcaster and a good friend, but I never felt any pressure working across town from him. Never thought about it. I'm myself and that's that. I don't see how you can copy another broadcaster's style. Al Michaels, who's outstanding, admits he copied Vinny. I might be crazy, but I see no similarity.

I mentioned earlier about the sophisticated listener's expectations of an ex-jock announcer. Well, that same listener or viewer knows when a professional broadcaster hasn't played the game and doesn't know enough to explain a situation. I've listened, and listened intently, to just about every broadcaster doing baseball nowadays, and most of them just don't know the intricacies of the game. Unless you've actually put on a jockstrap and gone down on that field and gotten yourself dirty, you're going to have one hell of a time identifying with a pitcher who's just walked in the winning run. Most professional broadcasters see the big things, but they just don't see the little things. An ex-jock has a trained eye to watch the nuances of what's happening out there. Some of us are better than others at seeing and relating. But I'm confident that I can see more in the booth, for instance, than a pitching coach. Part of the reason is that I've got a better seat. The worst place to watch a game is from the dugout.

I've felt the same way about most writers. I read some newspaper accounts of ballgames the day after and I wonder how a writer could have left out this or that from his story. It's almost like they were at a different game than I was. But I also realize that I have to catch myself and realize that I probably analyze a game in technical terms—probably too technical for the average listener or reader. I have to be careful not to broadcast like a manager, or even like a former pitcher. You can put your audience to sleep with too many details and too many hypothetical options. The best thing you can do is lay the groundwork, suggest the possibilities, and then let the game happen. Set the scene and then describe it. Don't talk unless you have to; don't manufacture things.

Vin Scully is great at letting the crowd tell the listeners what's happening. When Kirk Gibson hit that dramatic home run to win Game One of the 1988 World Series for the Dodgers over Oakland, Vinny just called it and then let the crowd roar. Terrific. Same with one of Gene Kirby's first bits of advice to me: "If you've got nothing to say, shut your mouth."

Howard, the One and Only

I mentioned earlier that I'd met Howard Cosell
during my rookie year with the Dodgers in
Brooklyn. In those days, he wasn't the Howard
Cosell we've all come to know in later years. He was just another
guy carrying around a big old tape recorder, talking to anybody
who would talk to him.

In time, of course, Howard became a larger-than-life figure on
radio and television and a controversial figure, too. Either you
loved Howard Cosell or hated him—there was no in-between—
and I'm proud and happy to say that I am among those who find
him to be a terrific guy and a good friend.

What the public doesn't know is the other side of Howard, the
side you don't see when he's on camera. He's a devoted family man
who totally adores his wife, Emmy, and with good reason. She's a
wonderful lady and maybe the only human being who can put
Howard in his place. I've been around them when she practically
tells him to shut up and sit down—in a humorous way, of course.
He obeys her like a puppy dog. That's quite a sight, I'll tell you.
Offstage, Howard's a doting father and husband—a completely
different person from the Howard Cosell you see onstage.

Unfortunately for Howard's image, all but a few of his friends
and coworkers only see the Cosell of "Monday Night Football."
That's how most people know him. They don't realize that here is
one of the funniest men you could ever meet and one of the
brightest. Also, Howard knows how to have a good time, and I

found it impossible not to have a good time whenever I was around him. And I was around him a lot when we were doing baseball games for ABC television.

I remember one evening when we were in Cincinnati. The game had been rained out, so we went back to the hotel and right to the bar to have a few drinks. There were four or five guys there from the same little town in Ohio—I can't think of its name. Naturally, they were thrilled that Howard had showed up at the same watering hole. They weren't about to let the opportunity slip by. They decided to goad him a little bit. It isn't every day that a guy gets to rub elbows with Howard Cosell, after all.

"So, there's the great Howard Cosell," one of them shouted from the other side of the bar. "I guarantee you, if we could ever get you down to our neck of the woods, we would knock you down to size."

"Is that right?" Howard answered, in that unique way of his, dripping sarcasm. "Where are you from?"

The guy mentioned the name of his hometown. Howard didn't miss a beat, didn't even blink.

"Oh, yeah," he said. "I've been there."

"Sure you've been there, Howard," said the guy, real sarcastically.

Again, Howard didn't flinch. He threw out the name of a street, maybe something like Birch Street or Beach Street. Well, now these guys were taken aback.

"Uh, Howard, how'd you know the name of that street?" one of them asked.

"Because I've been there," Howard explained. "That's not far from the high school where I spoke a few years ago. A very nice place, with very nice people. I especially enjoyed my visit to your city hall, which is not very far from the high school, as I recall."

And Howard went on and on about this little town. And the more he talked, the more these guys who had intended to give him a hard time, were absolutely eating out of his hand. It was incredible. Howard had them believing he knew every family in their town and every intersection, all as a result of that speaking engagement at the high school there. Naturally, I was flabbergasted. I was dying to talk to Howard about it, but I had to wait until these guys left, which they did, like they were on cloud nine.

"Howard," I said, "that was amazing. How the hell did you remember all that stuff about that little town? With all the traveling you do, you remembered all those details about that little town? How do you do it?"

"Twin D," he said straight-faced, "I've never been there in my life."

Well, we both just about hit the floor laughing. To this day, I have no idea how he managed to come up with the name of a street that worked, but he was so convincing that he had those guys completely fooled into thinking that he knew their hometown like the back of his hand. Amazing, but true. That's Howard Cosell.

Hilarious? Is he ever. Every January, just before the Bob Hope Classic in Palm Springs, Howard has a golf tournament of his own—a one-day shotgun charity event in his name featuring a bunch of big celebrities, plus a lot of the professional golfers in town to play in the Hope. He stands on the first tee with a microphone in his hand and introduces every player from every group as they come through. He has something to say about everyone, and it's all ad-libs. No cue cards, no nothing. It's unreal. The gallery lines up six deep at the first tee because those people know they're in for a four-hour show. Howard Cosell at his finest. And then they walk away just shaking their heads.

"How does he do it?" they ask.

Well, unless you've worked with Howard, it's hard to imagine. He's got a photographic memory, an unbelievable mind, and a hell of a sense of humor. Why Howard doesn't allow his personality to come through more, I also don't know. Maybe he thinks that antagonistic persona of his is a necessary part of his schtick. I've never quite figured it out, not that it's my business. The only time we ever really talked about it was after he strongly criticized a few of his coworkers at ABC—like Frank Gifford and Al Michaels—in one of his books. I couldn't understand Howard's motives and I told him so.

"Why did you have to do that?" I asked.

"Twin D," Howard answered, "I just felt that I had to get a few things off my chest. There were things about this business and the people in it that I had to say."

Case closed.

Howard had an ongoing feud with most of the sportswriters and radio-TV writers in the United States, or so it seemed. We

221

would be in a production meeting and some journalist's name would come up.

"I don't pay attention to that little twerp," Howard would say. "Who would ever believe what he wrote in that newspaper of his? He's as bad as that guy in Birmingham. Did you see what he wrote in his column the other day?"

"But Howard," somebody would answer, "I thought you said you don't read any of that crap in the newspapers."

"I don't," Howard would retort, "but somebody just happened to send me that clipping."

Naturally, that would be good for another laugh. You knew damn well that Howard Cosell was aware of every word being written about him. And not only did he read every word, he never forgot. Again, why he allowed himself to get all worked up over this kind of thing, I don't know. Maybe Howard thought he had to, to keep his edge.

I do know this. Until he backed off and decided to take it a lot easier a few years ago, Howard kept a schedule that few other people could maintain. He was forever busy with this program or that project. But it never was grueling enough to keep him from having a good time, if possible. During the Phillies–Astros playoff for the National League pennant in 1980—a terrific series—we were together and Howard was busy as a bee, as usual. But we still had our laughs, like during the off-night when we took him out for Mexican food. Howard didn't seem too keen on it, either before we got him to the restaurant or when we arrived. Howard wasn't too up on the virtues of Mexican dining, or so he had us believe that evening.

"What is all this crap?" Howard asked, looking at the menu and then at the dishes as the waiter brought them. "It all looks the same."

"Just shut up, Howard," said Keith Jackson. "We'll order your meal for you. Be a good boy, order a marguerita and you'll be fine."

"What do they put in a marguerita?" Howard asked. "If they don't make it with vodka, tell them to make mine with vodka."

Howard had a few drinks and he ate his supper and naturally, he was the life of the party. And, naturally, the next morning he let us all know that he wasn't feeling too good because of the Mexican food we had forced down his throat. He reported that he hadn't slept because of it. I don't know that he ever considered sleep all that necessary, not with his breakneck pace. I was in my room the evening after the fourth game of the same series. We had just come from having a few cocktails with Bowie Kuhn, then the commissioner of baseball, at his hotel. There was a knock at my door.

I opened it and there was Howard, whom I'd just left, standing there in his T-shirt, pants, with no toupee. He was laughing his ass off.

"What do you want?" I asked.

"I can't get into my room, Twin D," he said. "I jammed the goddamn key in the lock."

Had he ever. I went next door and worked on that thing for fifteen minutes before getting the key to release. Howard was very grateful. He invited me into his suite for a nightcap, one last vodka from room service. As we waited for the drinks to arrive, he stretched out on his couch, tired but obviously glad to have someone to talk to.

"Twin D," he began, staring at the ceiling, "my company's killing me. I gotta run here for this game, and there for that game. ABC is killing me. I've been invited to go to Dorado Beach with Gabe Paul, my good friend. Maybe I should. Maybe I should get away and relax."

"Why don't you?" I said.

"Because I've got too much to do, Twin D," he said. "This company is killing me."

"Let me tell you something, Howard. You're the one who's willing to do all this stuff. You can always say no if you want to. And let me tell you another thing. If you don't wake up tomorrow morning, if you die in your sleep, we're still going to go to the Astrodome tomorrow to televise the fifth game of this series."

"You *asshole!*" he roared, half-smiling. "I might have expected something like that from you. Twin D, I appreciate what you did for me and my lock, but you're still an *asshole!*"

And with that, I drank my vodka and left the room, laughing loudly.

"Get some sleep, Howard," I said.

"You *asshole!*" he yelled.

Another Howard story. A few years ago, Bob Uecker and I were in New York to tape a segment for the "Superstars" show on ABC. Howard got word that we were in town. He called and told us to meet him at this little cocktail lounge near the ABC offices for a drink. It was fairly empty when we all arrived, and we had a couple drinks, but pretty soon people started drifting in after work. It became pretty busy.

"C'mon," Howard said. "Let's go up to my place. We can have a couple drinks with Emmy over at the apartment. We'll take my limo over. You just have to promise me one thing. Do me one favor. Emmy and I are having someone over to dinner and we don't have enough food to serve you guys. So, after we have a couple drinks, I'd appreciate it very much if you two would take off so as not to make Emmy feel uncomfortable."

"No problem, Coach," said Uecker, who had that little twinkle in his eye.

We arrived at Howard's place, we gave Emmy a big kiss, and then we sat around and had a few cocktails. Finally, Howard's company arrived—just one fellow, another friend of his from ABC. I figured this was our cue to leave, but then I felt Uecker tapping on my knee. In other words, watch this.

"Howard," Uecker said, "Don and I just talked over our plans for the evening and we've decided that we'll stay for dinner after all."

Well, Howard turned white as a sheet.

"You *assholes!*" he screamed. "I told you there wasn't enough goddamn food in the apartment for you two *assholes!*"

Now Emmy joined in.

"Howard, what are you talking about?" she asked.

"Emmy, I told these two *assholes* that there wasn't enough food here to feed them."

"How dare you say that," Emmy said. "If they want to stay for dinner, we'll send out and have food brought in. Don and Bob, you stay right there and we'll have dinner, all of us together."

At that point, Uecker got up from his seat.

"No, Emmy," he said. "We appreciate your hospitality, but Howard doesn't want us here and Don and I don't want to be where we're not wanted."

And with that, Uecker and I got up and left the apartment with Howard yelling at our backs.

"You *assholes!*"

The best story of all might be from our last Monday night baseball game of the 1981 season—the season that was "split" due

224

to the players strike. There was a "first-half" division champion and a "second-half" champion and those two met at the end of the regular schedule to determine who would win the division.

Anyway, we were in Montreal, where the Expos were playing very well and the weather was as hot as the action. It was sticky and humid inside Olympic Stadium as we settled into our telecast booth, with Keith sitting on the left, Howard in the middle, and me on the right, as usual. The ballgame was going along routinely until about the third inning, when I heard something in my earphone from down below. Chet Forte, our director in the truck, was yelling at Howard to get on-mike.

Howard didn't acknowledge him until the end of the inning, when we cut away for a commercial. I was fiddling with my scorecard and I heard Howard talking through that cigar in his mouth to Forte.

"Chester," Howard said in his dry way, "why are you screaming at me like that?"

"Because we can't hear a damn thing you're saying over the air," Forte yelled. "It sounds like you're talking into a tunnel."

Well, at this point, I was done doing whatever busywork I had to do, so I looked over to see what all the commotion was about. Until the day I die, I will never forget the sight. Apparently, it was so hot in that stadium that the glue holding Howard's toupee to his head had melted, or become mushy, or whatever it is that happens to toupee glue. As a result, Howard's headset and his toupee had gotten stuck together like a helmet and had begun sliding across the top of his head. His hairpiece had skidded from its proper place across his forehead, down to where it was meeting his eyebrows. Naturally, the microphone attached to the headset had moved down, too, to well below Howard's chin. Which is why Forte couldn't understand what Howard was saying . . . along with millions of viewers. At the back of Howard's head, meanwhile, there was this divot sticking out like a decoration.

Well, it just so happened that when I glanced over to see what the trouble was, Keith did the same thing. Our eyes met, and it was a miracle of broadcasting that we ever made it through the ballgame that night. That's how hard we were laughing. Pretty soon, Howard started laughing because we were laughing, even though he didn't really know what we were laughing about. The only guy who wasn't laughing was Chet Forte, and if he had been able to see what Keith and I were seeing, Forte would have been on the floor, too.

"You got sixty seconds to straighten out whatever's wrong up there," he barked into our earphones.

I took it upon myself to fix Howard's problem. I merely reached toward his microphone attachment, which was just about level with his Adam's apple, and lifted it up, very carefully, very slowly. Sure enough, pretty soon we were able to see Howard's forehead again. His hairpiece helmet slid back into place, just like it had come loose. It was a perfect fit. Howard's mouth was even with the microphone once again.

"How's this, Chester?" Howard asked.

"Fine," said Forte. "That's much better."

Unfortunately, my fixing it once didn't quite get it done. A little while later, Howard dipped his head, and the damn helmet came slipping down again. Howard looked like a werewolf, Chet started screaming into our headphones, and I had to come to the rescue again.

"How's that, Chester?" Howard said.

"Fine," Forte said to us from the truck. "Only problem is we're on the air, Howard. People can hear you talking to me."

By this time, we were having a hard time keeping our minds on the game. We heard later that Roone Arledge, the big boss of ABC, had called Montreal from New York to complain that there was too much giggling in the booth. He couldn't have had any idea what was going on. It was so bad that I was afraid to look over at Keith, who had tears in his eyes. I knew that if my eyes met his again, we'd burst out laughing and lose it, right over the air. We made it through the telecast and don't ask me who won or what the final score was. I only know that night might have been the funniest in my life.

There was another time when we were in Boston for a Yankees–Red Sox game. A great rivalry, and the afternoon before the game, Howard called me over to his room at the hotel to shoot the bull. I went out on the patio to get some sun. It was a beautiful afternoon and as I lay there, Howard leaned on the railing and looked out over the city of Boston. He was in top form.

"There's the River Charles," he said from the balcony, in this dramatic voice. "And here we are in the cradle of American education. Harvard University, Boston College, MIT, Boston University. They have everything here in Boston, Massachusetts. Everything you could ask for, starting with the greatest educational institutions in this country of ours. The River Charles. Boston, Massachusetts."

Fine. So we went to the ballpark that night, and as usual, they opened the bleachers at Fenway Park early, to let the college kids in. Howard and I were walking around the batting cage, gathering material and mingling a little bit, when we noticed Reggie Jackson in right field for the Yankees. As he shagged fly balls out there, the fans in the bleachers were yelling.

"What are they chanting, Twin D?" Howard asked.

I listened for a minute.

"You don't want to know, Howard," I said.

"What do you mean I don't want to know?" said Howard. "Of course I want to know. Why do you think I asked?"

"Well, what they're chanting is 'REG-GIE SUCKS . . . REG-GIE SUCKS,'" I reported. "Those scholars from all the nearby schools you were talking about this afternoon back at the hotel. That's what they're yelling at Reggie Jackson here in the education capital of the country."

"*Assholes!*" Howard said. "They're all disgraceful. They're all *assholes!*"

One of Howard's favorite tricks was to pit you against somebody else in a false set of circumstances, created by Howard himself. For instance, he might be talking to me about something when all of a sudden, say, Peter O'Malley would walk into the room. Cosell would seize the opportunity and go off on a tangent.

"Twin D," he'd say loud and clear, "I don't care what you say about Peter O'Malley, I think you're wrong. I think he's a better human being than you give him credit for."

Now, what are you to do in a situation like that except feel like ten cents? Howard loved it. The more uncomfortable he could make you, the better he liked it. One of a kind, Howard is. I only wish his detractors had a chance to see this man laugh and laugh at himself. I don't know that his critics fully appreciated what Howard could do. I mean, there was many a night when we'd be done with a ballgame and he'd have to tape a radio show or do a segment for "Good Morning, America" the next day. With absolutely no preparation, he'd stand up there and do it perfectly in one take—no mistakes, no cue cards, no nothing. And good stuff, too. It was uncanny.

If Howard left ABC a bitter man, I'm sorry for it. Things were changing there. There was a period of uncertainty when ABC was taken over by Cap Cities. There were financial cutbacks. I could have lived off the money ABC spent on limousine bills in one year. If you needed a helicopter or a Lear jet to get from one game to another, you usually got it. They did things first class at ABC. But with the new management came a new philosophy, and maybe that bothered Howard. I don't know. He certainly had no reason to feel empty or frustrated about his career because, my god, he did everything there was to do. He had absolutely nothing to prove.

Howard, of course, always was pretty fiesty. And it was a good thing we were still traveling to and from ballparks in those nice heavy limos during the 1979 World Series between the Pittsburgh Pirates and Baltimore Orioles. Howard became a focal point then, too. After the sixth game in Baltimore, won by Pittsburgh to tie the Series at 3–3, Howard left Memorial Stadium in a limo—but not before fans rocked it, tore the rear-view mirrors off it, and generally created a little havoc. Keith and I were in the second limo.

When we all gathered a while later at our hotel, the Cross Keys Inn, Howard was pretty shaken. We were having a drink at the bar when he spotted Bowie Kuhn and his wife Louisa. Howard went over, ranting and raving about the lack of security. Bowie listened patiently and made sure Howard had a couple more drinks and finally, Howard settled down. Then he returned to our table, where I couldn't resist agitating him all over again.

"Well," Howard said, "I finally got that squared away with Bowie. There'll be no repeat of that violent stuff tomorrow night."

"Gee," I said. "I wouldn't be too sure about that. If the Orioles win, those fans are going to think those limos are toys. If the Orioles lose the World Series, then they're really going to be pissed. Either way, it's trouble."

Howard thought about that for a minute.

"Twin D, you're right. Jesus Christ, you're right!"

No sooner had he calmed down than he was all upset again. He jumped up and went back to Bowie's table, where the commissioner just smiled. The next night, the Pirates won but Howard made it safely to his limo at a secret location. I didn't see any reason for the controversy in the first place. Baltimore fans listening to Howard thought he'd been too nice to Pittsburgh. Pittsburgh fans thought he'd been leaning toward the Orioles. Same old story. To me, that's an indication you're doing a good job of reporting. Nobody can ever knock Howard's work to me.

But he was destined to stir the kettle. That was Howard and that's why he was one of the few broadcasters ever seen with a couple of body guards. It looked pretty ominous, but those guards used to have a ball being around him. Howard was the biggest star in the industry for a lot of years. Davey Marr, ABC's golf analyst, told me about this place in Houston where they'd put up an old black-and-white TV set on Monday nights during the football season. The idea was for fans to throw a shoe through the screen and hit Howard. That's what I call *big*.

If Howard tended to overreact to criticism of him, I also think writers tended to overreact in criticizing him. You can overlook certain things in this business. God knows, when we're out covering a ballgame, it's not like we're covering World War II. But the adversarial relationship between Howard and certain members of the press was so intense that there wasn't much room for good feelings. Howard had an ongoing feud with the late Dick Young, the veteran New York columnist, and Jack Craig, the TV-radio columnist in Boston. I saw Howard really cut into Craig one day in that Fenway Park press room and I just walked away. I wanted no part of it. There had to be a better way to coexist, but if Howard never took the time to be more patient with his critics, they rarely made the effort to see the other side of Howard.

Howard Cosell made "Monday Night Football" the institution it still is in the United States. No question about it. Monday nights became a traditional party night around the country because of those games on ABC, and he was the prime guy. Wherever the game was, that's where the party was at its height, and I'm sure Howard probably enjoyed that a lot. I mean, the guy's an entertainer and a damn good one. But this rap that Howard treated baseball as an afterthought or that he didn't like the game at all is false. I know because I did the games with him. He enjoyed the sport and he knew it.

Howard always was pretty sharp at getting the news, too. Telling it like it is, as he said. I'll never forget how he got a scoop of sorts back in 1984, a scoop that was a big moment in my life. I was playing in that golf tournament of his—the "Cosell," just before the "Hope." That morning, I had spoken to Jack Lang, the secretary-treasurer of the Baseball Writers Association of America. He was in New York, where the Hall of Fame voting would be revealed the same day.

"Where are you going to be in the afternoon?" Jack asked me.

"I'll be here in Rancho Mirage, playing in Cosell's little outing," I told him.

"Can you get to a phone somehow?"

"I'll call you whenever I get to the clubhouse," I said.

As it turned out, my first hole at the Morningside Club that day was number ten, which meant I was making the turn after number eighteen. I ducked inside and called Jack.

"Congratulations," Lang said. "You've just been voted into the Hall of Fame. When can you get back to New York for a press conference?"

Well, you could have hit me in the head with a hammer. I went out to the first tee and saw Dad. I told him about the phone call I'd just made and he was thrilled. Then I got ready to play the first hole, but first Howard had to do his thing, introducing all the members in our group.

Howard made it through all the other players in our foursome, and then he got to me.

He mentioned that I was a tall, lanky righthander who'd pitched for the Dodgers, first in Brooklyn, then in Los Angeles.

He mentioned that first major league victory of mine in Philadelphia.

He mentioned my strikeouts and shutouts and wins and losses and all those stats.

And then Howard paused.

"I want you people here today to be among the first to know," Howard said. "Don Drysdale has just been elected to Baseball's Hall of Fame."

Well, I almost dropped. I thought I might whiff the ball off the tee. By some miracle, I hit one of my best drives of the day. My eyes were a little misty at that point. A lot had happened to me in just a few minutes' time, and there was Howard Cosell right in the middle of things. How he got the news so fast, I'll never know. He's a genius, Howard is. And I'm happy and proud to say he's my friend. I only wish that more people would have the chance to know him as I know him.

18

The Game I Love, But . . .

When I was broadcasting for the White Sox, I brought some pitching strings with me to their spring training headquarters in Sarasota, Florida. Those were the same pitching strings the Dodgers used when I came up, and still use. I thought I might try the power of suggestion, but I didn't get a very warm response.

"We've got pretty much a veteran staff here," I was told by a coach who shall remain anonymous. "I don't think our guys would go for something like pitching strings at this stage in their careers. We don't want to do anything that will mess them up."

Well, the White Sox by no means had a veteran staff at the time, and by no means did all their pitchers have the kind of control you need to be consistent winners. Mess them up? Have you checked lately where the White Sox are in the American League standings? I haven't seen them winning any pennants. I haven't seen their pitchers exactly mowing down the opposition.

But that episode reinforced in my mind how insecure coaches are in the major leagues these days, which is just one of the many eye-openers I've had during all these years of being around ball-clubs and ballplayers. I've formed a lot of impressions about the game, not all of them good. And I've seen and heard a lot of things, some of them scary.

The last thing I want to do as a broadcaster is interfere with anybody else's business. I'm not one to spend a lot of time in the clubhouses or hang around the players. But if a pitcher comes to

231

me and asks my advice on something, I'll be glad to let him pick my brain, at least what's left of it. Problem is, there are some coaches and managers who are so paranoid that the minute they see you talking with one of their pitchers—it might be about golf or a good restaurant you went to the night before—damned if they don't break out into a cold sweat. Many a time with the White Sox, I was just tempted to go up to one of those coaches and tell them the honest truth. I don't want their jobs for one good reason. I couldn't afford the pay cut.

I know from being taught the right way, and from being a pitcher, that control can be taught. A qualified instructor can watch a pitcher's mechanics and work with that pitcher and teach control. But in many cases, it isn't taught because too often, major league coaches are either unqualified or afraid of trying something new. They might see their pitcher throw ball after ball or walk man after man, but they'll do nothing about it. It's mind-boggling, but it's true.

I'm glad I'm where I am, for more reasons than one. If I were pitching now instead of broadcasting, I might have a difficult time adjusting to how polite baseball has become. My personality is such that I'd have to pitch inside, and if people didn't like it, they'd have to stop me. I'd challenge the umpires and the league presidents the same way I'd challenge the batters. If I brought along a few other guys, like Bob Gibson and Sandy Koufax and Sam Jones and Larry Jackson, we'd be in the definite minority. We'd be the outcasts, the dinosaurs. We wouldn't be part of the fraternity. I'd probably lead the league in warnings and fines. I don't think any of these pitchers now think the way I used to—that two of the other team's guys should go down for one of our guys. I don't know how many of these modern-day pitchers are even told about keeping hitters on their toes, and I don't know that they would have the fortitude to brush batters back even if they were told.

It's amazing, really. I don't like the designated hitter rule used in the American League, and never have. Never mind that the game was meant to be played with nine guys on a side. Never mind that it's helped ruin entire pitching staffs, like Oakland's under manager Billy Martin a few years ago—Mike Norris, Rick Langford, Steve McCatty. Where are they all now? They were young. What happened to them? I know this: if I'd pitched in the DH era, I'd have flamed out in a hurry. I'd have stayed in too many games too long, not wanting to come out. I'm losing 9–4? Hell, I'll hang in there on the chance that I can win 10–9, even if it is killing my arm.

But, on top of all the other bad things it's done, the DH has occasionally encouraged false bravado on the part of some American League pitchers. I thought that the minute the DH was instituted, and nothing's changed my mind. Pitchers who know they won't have to bat develop a little extra courage, a bigger heart and backbone than they really have. And yet you still see pitchers who get knocked around inning after inning in the American League. They're allowed to stay in there, and they don't do anything about the other team just digging in and swinging from the heels. Some of it is sickening, ludicrous. It's like a brother-in-law league—a grown person taking beatings out there on the mound because he's afraid to throw a brushback or even afraid to throw a strike.

That's right. Afraid to throw a strike. You can see in some pitchers today a definite timidity as soon as they wind up and draw it back. They're afraid to let the ball go. If you've got any kind of eye for the game, you can spot these guys a mile away. They can't go out and challenge a batter. And the reason is, a lot of these pitchers who are in the big leagues now know they don't belong there. At the Morningside Club in Rancho Mirage, where I play a lot of golf, Lee Trevino plays a lot of golf, too. Well, I have no more business challenging him to eighteen holes than some of these so-called major league pitchers today have to being where they are. Some of these guys wear beards to make them look intimidating, but they don't look so tough when they have to deliver the ball. Their abilities and attitudes don't back up their beards.

Where are these players going to learn? Probably not by asking or listening because there's a general lack of conversation now. With the old Dodgers, I picked up a lot of pointers about pitching by listening to hitters talk. And hitters used to tell us they learned a lot by listening to us pitchers gab. But nowadays, after games, you walk into some clubhouses and it's like somebody yelled *"Fire!"* Everybody rushes off. That's one problem.

The other problem is, Where do you go if you are a player who wants to learn? I don't think there are enough major league people teaching in the major leagues anymore. I don't know where they all went, but there aren't enough around. Now, I know somebody's

233

going to say, How can Sparky Anderson be such a great manager because he wasn't a great player? Or, How could Walt Alston have been such a great manager when he played only one game in the major leagues? My answer would be that they were great students at a great school who went on to become great teachers. The great school was the Dodger school. Tommy Lasorda wasn't a great pitcher. But he learned the game in the Dodger system and had the drive and desire to make it as a coach, then as a manager. He also had the knowledge. Tommy's a little better in the dugout than a lot of people think, you know.

Branch Rickey used to say spring training with the Dodgers was more like a factory than a camp, and in a way he was right. It was more fun, I'm sure, than working on the assembly line, but there was a purpose to every hour of every day. They even taught you the correct way to wear a uniform. On rainy days, we had written tests in the auditorium on rules and game situations. If you told players nowadays that they had to do that, there'd be a rebellion.

I fault the owners for that. They let the game get away. They put themselves in a terrible position by giving in to the players' demand for arbitration. I'm not talking free agency now. Hell, I was ready to challenge the illegality of the reserve clause long before it was overturned. This is America. The draft is illegal, too, in all sports. What right do owners have to tell a kid from Philadelphia that he has to play in Oakland? That's like telling a kid when he gets out of college that he has to go to work for the Ford Motor Company when he wants to work at AT&T. Would that stand up in a court of law? Would you tell a judge today that he's got to be a clerk tomorrow? How professional sports escape operating by the laws of the land, I don't know.

But arbitration is a different animal. It's a no-win situation. You have players going from $200,000 a year to $1 million. That's a hell of a jump. But when a precedent has been set by previous arbitration rulings, what's an arbitrator to do? He sees that a pitcher did "X" one year, and so that pitcher is awarded the same money as the last pitcher who did "X." All the arbitrator does is fit each player into a category, a hole. And that, more than anything, has made the salary structure go out of whack. If I'm an owner wanting to pay you $600,000, and you're asking $1 million, I've got to offer you $800,000 just in the hope of winning the arbitration case. And even if the owner wins, he loses, because he's paying $200,000 more than he wanted to pay in the beginning.

That's how these utility players who bat .230 make fortunes. The late Bill Veeck said it wasn't the high price of stardom that annoyed him but the high price of mediocrity. The owners made a terrible choice when they said they'd accept arbitration. Ask today's owners, and they'd give the players almost anything if they could rid the game of arbitration. Anything. But the players have it, and they'd be crazy to give it back. And they're not going to, no matter how the owners threaten them with lockouts or claims that they're going broke.

The one thing owners have done lately is get away from long-term contracts. Instead of signing a player for five years, you sign him for two, or one. That's really the best way to fight back, given the present system. And I see nothing wrong with that. I don't begrudge the players getting all these dollars, because nobody's putting a gun to the owners' heads. But a saner way to handle salaries is to pay on what a player did the year before, and not on what he tells you he's going to do three years from now. Pay on performances, not on promises. I had good seasons, and I got some nice raises at the time. But I also had bad seasons, and I took pay cuts. In fact, I had a two-year contract with Buzzie Bavasi when such a thing was almost unheard of. And I didn't like it. I don't think I got lazy, but I did find my mind wandering. We're all human, and if you're sure about next year's money this year, it's like opening presents two days before Christmas. Something just doesn't seem right. That was the first and last multiyear contract I had with the Dodgers as a player.

While salaries have exploded, the quality of the game has gone down. Agents are part of the reason. Some of the things they do make you want to vomit. Some of the crap is unbelievable. You have to wonder, when two players on different teams have the same agent, who are these players really loyal to? The agent or their teams? I can just see an agent calling one of his players and saying to him, Why did you give Joe Blow, another of my clients, such a hard time the other day during the game? I mean, that's a fine state of affairs if you destroy the competitive edge to that extent.

I have very little sympathy for the owners, though. The corporate mentality in the game today is certainly not going to enhance it, but that mentality's everywhere. So are three-piece suits, taking spots that baseball people used to have. It's remarkable. They created this monster, and yet when George Steinbrenner or Gene Autry goes out and tries to buy a pennant, the other owners get mad. Meanwhile, all Steinbrenner and Autry are doing is playing by the rules.

I don't dislike corporate ownership per se, because getting new money and new blood into the sport is healthy. But you have to chuckle at some of the things you see. To a lot of these corporations, the ballclub is just another account, another department. In some cases, it's just another tax deduction. It's a bottom-line business where a lot of gray suits are brought in and then, within two years, these guys suddenly know everything about baseball. They're telling the baseball people who've been in the game all their lives what it's all about. These corporate guys wouldn't be able to go to a high-school game and tell you the difference between a prospect and a suspect, and yet they're taking over the baseball end of the business. I don't understand why these barons of the bottom line don't let the baseball people handle the baseball. Wouldn't that be the most efficient way to run the operation? By having experts work in their area of expertise? You can bring any accountant in off the street and have him check the bottom line. But if you're a corporate guy, stay the hell away from the baseball end of baseball.

I've thought of getting into ownership on occasion and still do, and I wouldn't care what the hell the other owners wanted me to do. I would just do whatever it takes to win. There's a big nostalgia kick in the United States these days. Maybe that would be the way to go. Do everything the way they used to do it thirty years ago. Take all the weight machines out of the clubhouses, and instead of all these psychologists and nutritionists filling players' heads with ideas and telling them to eat fruit and nuts, let the players have a steak and a few beers and talk baseball with their teammates. If a team tried that, that team might just win it all for old times' sake, who knows? I suspect one thing. If the players stopped pumping iron, there would be fewer injuries. Whitey Herzog of the St. Louis Cardinals says these players are so lean now, they sneeze and they break a rib. These players might look good at the beach, but you wonder if their bodies are suited for the day-in, day-out game of baseball.

Expansion? God help us. They've got twenty-six franchises today, and they're talking about adding more, and I don't know where they're going to find the players. There isn't an organization in baseball today that has enough pitching. The Minnesota Twins won the World Series in 1987 with two starting pitchers—Frank Viola and Bert Blyleven. Unbelievable, but it happened. You could take all the players in the major leagues now, put them on sixteen ballclubs, and have pretty good baseball. But twenty-six teams, going on maybe thirty? No way. The quality isn't near what it used to be, and if baseball scouts don't tell you that, it's only because they're afraid they'll see it in print and lose their jobs. You take the roster of most major league teams, and the eighteenth- to twenty-fourth players can be real borderline cases. But compared with the sixteen-team setup, you've created 240 jobs for 240 players who might not belong. What do you expect?

With supposedly bigger and better athletes coming into professional sports, why is this so? Again, I go back to instruction. That's a real wasteland. We talk about the scarcity of playing talent in baseball, but there's an even more serious scarcity of nonplaying talent. Owners won't pay for top-notch instruction, so they're not getting it. Players who are supposed to be learning the game on the lower levels aren't, and then they're getting force-fed and rushed to the majors when they aren't ready and doing on-the-job training there. It's a chain reaction, and a sorry one at that. Players who should be making their mistakes in the bushes are making them in the big cities, before 40,000 fans.

The veteran managers now will tell you that they're having to tell players in the big leagues things that should have been learned when the players were five years younger. That isn't the fault of the players. That's the fault of major league baseball. As a result, the quality of the minor leagues suffer, too, and the colleges don't necessarily fill the void, either, because not all the coaches there know what they're doing. They certainly aren't all training players in what it takes to be major leaguers. First of all, a lot of the college coaches don't know what it takes. Secondly, college coaches are there to win, or they aren't there very long.

A successful sports organization is a little like the army. You have to have layers of good people below the top to make it work. A franchise is only as good as its scouts and its instructors. If I were running a ballclub, I'd hire the best baseball people possible and pay them—pay them enough so that they don't work for me for two years and then realize they have to go out and sell insurance to make a living wage. There's this huge financial pie out there, and baseball is only giving a sliver of it to these very important people—the instructors and scouts. I don't understand the shoddy treatment of these people, any more than I understand how a ballclub can install a former catcher as pitching instructor. Talk about putting a square peg in a round hole. What's next? A pitcher as a hitting instructor?

Another question people always ask me—and a question I ask myself—is why don't today's players seem to be having any fun? Why don't they enjoy themselves the way we did? I surely can't answer that, other than to say it's true. A lot of these guys go to the ballpark like it's a job. Maybe that's a reflection of a change in society itself. They say the more money you make, the more you worry about keeping it, or making more. I know from being around ballclubs that the camaraderie isn't there. You don't see fifteen guys going out for a beer anymore. You see twenty-four guys living in twenty-four different single rooms on the road, and in some instances, taking twenty-four different cabs to the stadium. A guy gets into a slump, and he's got no one to talk to.

Maybe the salary structure has something to do with that. It breeds independence. A guy who's making the minimum doesn't feel he belongs with a veteran making $1 million, and the veteran doesn't feel compelled to take a rookie under his wing. Maybe if you've got a baseball-related problem now, you go to your agent instead of a coach or a teammate. The clubhouse has become more of an office than a second home. The general manager who took over the White Sox, Larry Himes, banned beer in the clubhouse a couple years ago. I don't know if this bright idea came from him or above. And he wasn't alone. That's another new trend, the sterilized clubhouse. It used to be the place where guys came early and stayed late. No more. The close atmosphere isn't there.

Of course, that all affects the competitive edge. If a player has a five-year guaranteed contract for $1 million a year, I wonder how much it really hurts him if he goes 0-for-4 during a game or makes a bad error. I don't doubt that today's players want to win. That's instilled in an athlete, no matter what the era. But I do wonder how much they hate to lose, and how much they're willing to sacrifice. There isn't the emphasis on doing well now, because you know the money is going to be there. You also can look around and see who else is in the clubhouse, or in the minor leagues, and you know that your job isn't in jeopardy. That was one thing that kept us going years ago, the mortal fear that if you screwed up or if you got hurt, somebody else just as good was going to be in your place the next day. And maybe the day after, too. Maybe forever. There isn't that pressure now. Some teams practically have to get an act of Congress to send a player down to the minor leagues, and if that happens, depending on his contract, he might get paid major league dollars, anyway. That tends to take the sting out of a demotion. Don't get me wrong. We had some softies in my day, too. We had guys who didn't run out ground balls on occasion. But we also had guys who would see that and jump on the guy's back, spikes first. And if the guy who loafed didn't change his ways, he was gone.

As for the Major League Players Association, at times I wouldn't give you eight cents for what they represent or the people in it. Sour grapes? No. I would stand to make a lot more pension money if the union went further back, and took better care of players who quit before 1970. That's the cutoff now. But I don't need the money. I've been lucky. I'm doing well. A lot of other guys aren't, though, and I wonder how these players can forget the players who started the whole damn thing back in 1946. They were the founders, and a lot of them who are still around are struggling.

I'll give you an example. When you talk about the only World Series championship ever in Brooklyn, in 1955, what comes to mind? Of course, "The Catch"—the catch that Sandy Amoros made for the Dodgers in left field at Yankee Stadium against Yogi Berra. It came on Berra's slicing line drive, and it was the most spectacular play of the seventh game that Johnny Podres won for Brooklyn, 2–0. Well, Sandy's down in Miami now and not long ago, he had to have his leg amputated. But Chico Fernandez had to call up and beg for help for him, because Sandy didn't want to do it. Too much pride. He didn't want to bother anybody. Is that right? I know of a lot of circumstances like that, former players who can dearly use an extra $200 a month.

Joe Garagiola has been very active with a group called the Baseball Alumni Team, or BAT. There's another group, the Professional Baseball Players of America. These people have tried to help former players who need it, but they've basically generated their own support. Same for the Equitable Old-Timers Series that has staged games in various sites. I think that's great, but I also think the Players Association could do more. I don't know whether these guys are greedy or what, but I do know that they've got short memories. From everything I've heard, the union today has more money lying around than it knows what to do with. What are they holding on to it for? A fund for the next strike? Why do they just throw these old-timers crumbs? Can't they spare a little more? It's the former players who need the pension money, not the current players. If the current players need a pension after the money they're making now, they had better run a thorough check on their agents or investment counselors.

As long as I'm talking fantasy here, I'd like to see artificial turf eliminated. I see some things happening on the carpet that just don't belong in the game. It's not baseball. I'd also like to see realignment of the two leagues on a geographical basis. The base-ball business is good now. Very good. But management and labor are talking another strike or lockout in spring 1990, and I don't know how long the fans are going to keep coming to the ballpark in droves. If fan support falls off, or if the economy slows down, that might be baseball's trump card, to stir up natural rivalries. That thinking is probably too logical, and the National League might be first to oppose the idea because it has the better cities, better races, and better balance.

The drug problem is another thing that I never saw in my day. I don't think our guys knew what the hell cocaine was, and if anybody was smoking marijuana, I certainly wasn't aware of it. The former commissioner, Peter Ueberroth, came out and said that baseball was drug-free after that famous trial in Pittsburgh a few years ago. I'm not so sure the commissioner was right about that. But the best way to make baseball truly free of drugs is to ban the players who get caught using drugs. Just get rid of them. No second chances. No third chances. When you keep giving a user or abuser another chance, all you're doing is hurting the game's credibility.

Sooner or later, baseball has to realize that we do live in a glass house. You can debate the merits of whether players should be role models, but the fact is that people are watching us. There is an awful lot of crap that players have to put up with, a lot of invasions of privacy. But when you put on that uniform, you have

240

to understand that there are certain things you can do, and certain things you can't do. Drugs are out. Whether the commissioner says so or not, drugs are illegal. You do drugs and you're breaking the law. I don't know how much simpler it can be than that. It's not the law that provided any loopholes. It's baseball. Look at Steve Howe, the former Dodger relief pitcher. I feel sorry for him. He had a chance to make $1 million a year and he just kept screwing it up.

Maybe the problem with athletes today is that they have too much free time. It was a great life when I played, but it's got to be even greater now. They don't have to play as long or as hard to achieve financial security for a lifetime. They've got agents handling all their financial and personal affairs. They get more meal money than they need on the road. They've got more opportunities than ever to earn extra money with appearances, commercials, and endorsements. All the athletes have to do now is stay in shape and be ready to play. They don't have to worry about off-season employment to make ends meet, because they only need the job they've got. Go to a gym three times a week and keep your noses clean. And some of them can't even handle that.

What's really aggravating to me—and I am a fan, remember—is that management and labor should be able to reach some sort of compromise, but they can't. Both sides know that there's plenty of money out there to satisfy everybody, but it's still a tug-of-war. For too many years, the owners had it all their way. It was completely out of whack. Then the pendulum swung, and now it's gone crazy to the players' benefit. You would think that the owners and the union could sit down and work out an agreement that they could both live with for ten years at a time. Yet, how many labor problems did baseball experience during the 1980s? Too many. And it looks as if the 1990s will start out the same way. That may sound like I'm wishing on a star, but is it all that unreasonable?

To hear all the threats, the war of 1990 might be the bloodiest yet. The latest Basic Agreement was to expire on December 31, 1989, and the vibes were all bad. And if it happens, if players stay away or they get locked out, I wouldn't be surprised to see owners bring up all their minor leaguers and stage the games anyway. That's what the National Football League did during its strike a couple years ago, and who knows? If baseball fans are that starved for the game, that hungry for entertainment, they might pay to see these replacement players and not be able to tell the difference. There's even talk of another "major league" in the works. When the Washington Redskins won their last Super Bowl, they did it with a few guys on the roster who came in while the regulars were walking the picket lines. Anything can happen, and if I'm a baseball owner with a stadium lease and with bills to pay, I might just promote the minor leaguers and put a major league label on it.

I'm talking like I'm pro management now, but really, what the hell more can the players get? How much more selfish can they get? When is enough enough? Where's the reason? Where's the leadership? I don't believe for a moment that these players need one dime more than they're getting. Likewise, I don't believe for a minute that the owners are broke, or losing money, or anything close to it. I suspect that there's some creative bookkeeping going on. If all these owners are hurting so badly, first of all they've got to be some kind of stupid. Secondly, if that's true, then why don't they get out? Why don't they sell their ballclubs if they can't turn a profit? And if you believe that all these horror stories are true, try to buy a ballclub sometime. Just try.

19

Another Title for Dodger Blue

*A*fter I managed to pitch 58⅔ consecutive scoreless innings in 1968, some baseball people suggested that it was one of those records that
would last a long time. Well, as I've said often, I'm not much of
a nut on statistics, so when it lasted "only" twenty years, that was
fine by me. Twenty years is long enough, and besides, Orel Hershiser's terrific streak was a big part of the Dodgers winning another world championship in 1988—my "rookie" year in the Los
Angeles broadcast booth.

Again, I ask: how lucky can a guy like me get? My first season
back home with the Dodgers, and they came from nowhere to win
the World Series.

I never thought my record was untouchable, particularly the
way the game is now. Let's face it, the product has been somewhat
diluted throughout the years. You see players with a bat in their
hands now who couldn't have made it past the Double A level
before expansion, and if that sounds like a knock on Hershiser's
accomplishment, it isn't. He's a terrific pitcher, an outstanding
person, and he had what you have to have to do what he did—great
stuff, good support, and a little bit of luck. That's what I had in
1968, that's what he had in 1988.

If you had asked me who would break my record, I'd have said
probably a power pitcher, like Roger Clemens of Boston. But
Orel's feat was no fluke, and from where I was sitting, I could see
it building. He started the string by blanking the Montreal Expos

243

in the last four innings of his 4–2 victory on August 30. Then he pitched five consecutive shutouts—beating Atlanta, 3–0, Cincinnati, 5–0, the Braves again, 1–0, Houston, 1–0, and San Francisco, 3–0. Then, in his last start of the regular season, Orel pitched ten scoreless innings at San Diego September 28 before leaving the game. That made it fifty-nine innings in a row without yielding a run.

Oddly enough, a controversial ruling against the Giants figured in his record, just as it did mine. I had the Dick Dietz incident, where he was told to stay at the plate after failing to make an honest effort to avoid a pitched ball. The decision that helped Hershiser also came in the fifth shutout of his streak, also in a game that wound up 3–0 in his favor. Déjà vu.

Jose Uribe was on second base and Brett Butler was the runner at first with 1 out in the third inning. Ernest Riles, the San Francisco batter, hit what looked like a potential double-play grounder, but Riles beat out shortstop Alfredo Griffin's relay to first base. Uribe came home, apparently with the run breaking the shutout streak. But umpire Paul Runge ruled that Butler had run out of the baseline and interfered with Griffin in trying to break up the double play. That meant Riles was out on an inning-ending double play. Uribe's run, of course, didn't count. The string was alive and well.

Actually, that was the last real opportunity opponents had to score a run against Hershiser. He was that good. Oh, he had situations with runners in scoring position, but he was on such a roll that you never felt he was being threatened. He was in a perfect frame of mind, he got into a groove with his pitches, and everything fell into place. That sounds easy, but Orel has the type of personality to deal with it. He can keep that rubber band wound up for a while. Other pitchers can't. Orel is the right kind of guy and he was in the right places at the right times.

Naturally, as the streak grew, more and more writers and broadcasters came to me for opinions on what Orel was doing and how he was dealing with the pressure. I was happy to talk, but I didn't talk very much to Orel himself during that period. I did the normal pre- and postgame shows on radio that the job called for, but otherwise, I didn't want to jinx him. I was a little superstitious, so when I did interview him, I tried to be very much matter-of-fact. I didn't want to inject my record into conversations, because people don't give a damn about what I did twenty years ago. People are interested in what's happening now. They aren't interested in ancient history. Off the field, away from the ballpark, I didn't seek Orel out, and he didn't seek me out. If you know anything about Orel Hershiser, you realize he doesn't need any fatherly advice.

To show you what a genuinely good person he is, Orel was quoted as saying in San Diego after he reached his fifty-eighth scoreless inning that he was content to have it end there. That was his last appearance of the regular season, and he was at peace having me retain at least the all-time scoreless streak for one season. Tommy Lasorda, the manager, and Ron Perranoski, the pitching coach, told Orel that that wasn't such a good idea, and I totally agree. If I'd been running the ballclub and had heard that he was willing to take a bow so that Don Drysdale could still claim the record, I'd have kicked Orel in the ass and told him to get back out there on the mound. Go as far as you can go with this thing, and the hell with the record books. My scoreless streak probably had a lot to do with me getting in the Hall of Fame, and I appreciate it. But the momentos from my streak were gathering dust. Time marches on. Don't stop now.

I heard a few people suggest during the 1988 season that it was no coincidence that Orel Hershiser had his greatest year just after I appeared. It was as though I had some influence on Orel's pitching strategy, that I taught him how to be mean or how to throw a spitball. Well, I wish it were that easy. I had absolutely no effect on Hershiser, and to think that I did is a slight on Orel's talents. During the entire season, and well before the streak, there might have been a question or two that he asked about this or that. And during the streak, we dissected those games pretty thoroughly in our little radio gab sessions. But to equate my arrival on the Dodger scene with Orel Hershiser's magnificent year is folly. He is a great kid, loose and confident but not cocky, and I was just along for the ride.

When Orel actually broke my record in San Diego, Vin Scully was doing the play-by-play upstairs and I was down at field level, talking back and forth with Vin and waiting for Orel to come to the dugout. I was rooting like hell for him, and when he got there, I gave him a big hug and congratulated him. I realized what an accomplishment it was, and I also like the way Orel handled himself during the whole thing. In at least one respect, he had a lot more pressure to deal with than I did in my streak—pressure that came from the sheer number of writers and broadcasters who followed his every move. In 1968, players didn't have to face all those microphones before or after games. But Orel never lost his poise.

Like Orel himself, the ballclub seemed destined for good things. The more you expected the 1988 Dodgers to fold, the more they fooled you. Don't forget, the previous two seasons, the Dodgers had finished with identical records of 73 wins and 89 losses. A lot of franchises would dismiss that as a slump or the inevitable downside of rebuilding, but not the Dodgers. They didn't get to be the best organization in professional sports by tolerating mediocrity, even for a couple of seasons.

Still, when spring training started, I didn't think the Dodgers had a contending ballclub. If you looked at the team on paper, it just wasn't that impressive, position-by-position. During the off-season, the Dodgers had acquired Kirk Gibson, from the Detroit Tigers. He had been declared a free agent from the Detroit Tigers after baseball owners were found guilty of collusion in their dealings with available players. The owners bid low on free agents, if at all. Gibson made headlines right away. Jesse Orosco, a relief pitcher for the Dodgers, put some eye-black in the sweatband of Gibson's cap before an exhibition game. It was a harmless prank, but when Gibson put his hat on, he just came apart. It didn't fit into his game plan or his sense of humor, and he just took off. He left the ballpark. Gibson was in effect saying, "If that's the way this team operates, then maybe the Dodgers made a mistake signing me."

I guess I'm old-fashioned, but I never thought it was that big a deal. I was in the minority, though, because Gibson's reaction was credited with changing the entire attitude of the Dodgers. This was a guy who was all-business, a winner, or so he was portrayed in the press. Well, Kirk Gibson is definitely a throwback, and I said years before when I was broadcasting in the American League that here was one guy I'd pay to see play. But can one incident like that rearrange an entire team's chemistry and priorities? My answer to that would be, if you need one such incident to wake up a ballclub, that ballclub must be in pretty sad shape to begin with. If I were another player and I had to read that I needed Kirk Gibson walking off the field in spring training to open my eyes, I'd be a little embarrassed about my attitude. Especially after going 73–89 for two years in a row. That doesn't reflect very well on the entire organization, does it?

I know this, and this might be the old-school side of me speaking: thirty years ago, Gibson wouldn't have stood out like a sore thumb. He'd have been just another intense guy busting his tail, trying to find himself a place in the lineup. Jackie Robinson wouldn't have needed a Kirk Gibson to get him motivated in spring training. None of those old Dodgers would have. But that's the way it was. You had a dozen or more Kirk Gibsons years ago. Now, if you have one who gets his uniform dirty, he stands out as a spiritual leader. Which is fine, because that's what sells in today's market. Kirk Gibson would have fit in with a lot of the players when I started. But he wouldn't have been unique or alone. Not by any stretch of the imagination.

If Gibson's actions in Vero Beach served as a rallying cry, it served its purpose well. I hadn't seen all the National League clubs, because I'd been in the American League for years, but if you listened to baseball people talk, it was only a matter of time before Houston or San Francisco or Cincinnati caught and passed the Dodgers. Nobody did, of course, and that says a lot for stars like Gibson and Hershiser, but also for guys like Tim Crews and Brian Holton, who came out of the Dodger bullpen and pitched a lot of important middle innings. The Dodgers really did get a lot of help from a lot of people, which is the only way to win in the long run.

If there was a turning point in the season, I'd say it had to be right after the All-Star break, when the Dodgers walked into Wrigley Field and swept a five-game series. I don't care who you're playing, it's not easy to win five straight from anybody. The Dodgers were 2½ games up at the All-Star break—having been in first place since May 26—but when they left Chicago, they were ahead by 7 games. The lead dwindled to 1½ in mid-August, when that doubt surfaced again, but the Dodgers never did fall apart.

And they did it pretty much without Fernando Valenzuela, who's never been the same pitcher since his great years during the early to middle eighties. Why? Here's where you have to wonder about some of these newspaper reporters who cover a ballclub day-in and day-out. When asked about Valenzuela, Tommy said, Fernando's arm has been hurting. How long? For a couple of years, Tommy said. When did you first notice it? At the beginning of last year, Tommy said. Now, to me, the obvious question to Lasorda would be, If he was hurt, then why the hell did you keep pitching him? I never heard that question asked.

I don't pretend to have all the answers, but it would seem that all those innings he pitched took their toll on his arm. Not only the innings he pitched with the Dodgers, but all the innings you don't know about that he pitched back home in Mexico—before and after he became Dodger property. If you're going to have a guy like Fernando throw as many pitches as he threw in games with the Dodgers, sooner or later you've got to be concerned. You just can't throw 150 or 175 pitches every fourth or fifth day without suffering some consequences. You hear the stories about how Fernando is a great competitor, that he doesn't want to come out of ballgames. Well, that sounds nice. But here's a guy who represents a hell of an investment, a $2-million-a-year arm. And, to boot, a left arm that throws a lot of screwballs, a tougher pitch than most to throw. The human arm wasn't meant to throw a baseball in the first place, let alone screwballs, which require an unnatural motion on top of an unnatural motion.

What did Kirk Gibson mean to the Dodgers? Well, he won the Most Valuable Player award in the National League, and he'd have had my vote if I'd had one. Darryl Strawberry and Kevin McReynolds of the Mets had better numbers, but Gibson represented the classic case of what a player means to a team. There's always been a gray area about what "most valuable player" means exactly. In 1987, Andre Dawson had a fabulous season for the Cubs, but they finished in last place. With what Gibson did for the Dodgers on the field—and considering how he evidently affected them off the field—how could anyone not think of him as the most valuable player in the league? If he helped restore some pride in the Dodger tradition—a tradition that might have been lost in the previous two years—then he was the MVP hands down.

Of course, Lasorda deserved a lot of credit for what happened in 1988, too. Tommy is a great one for getting his players jacked up. There was a point during the World Series when he heard that Bob Costas, who was working the telecasts for NBC, had said on the air that the Dodgers were the worst-looking team that had been in the fall classic for some time. Lasorda pounced on that and held a pregame meeting about it, and by the time he was done shouting and screaming, his players didn't know whether they were the 1988

Dodgers or the 1927 Yankees. Again, I'm not much of one for those rah-rah sessions, but Tommy can sense the pulse of his ballclub and play off seemingly insignificant things like what a network telecaster says about your team. I played for one guy in the major leagues, Walt Alston, who was the exact opposite of Lasorda. The only time Alston raised his voice was when he was ready to pinch somebody's head off. I don't think I would have reacted well to "win one for the Gipper" speeches. I think I'd have probably turned a deaf ear. But Tommy makes it work, and God bless him for it.

Besides, Lasorda got the Dodgers back to the top in 1988 by doing more than talking. He had to. He had the knack of getting guys in and out of the lineup at just the right times. His tactics were interesting to watch, because he didn't always go by the book. He rolled the dice on occasion, and more often than not, he came up smelling like a rose. There's some luck in that, sure. But there's also a lot of skill involved. You have to know your personnel. Tommy's good at what he does, and he's not afraid to delegate authority. He's got a good staff, and Perranoski is excellent at handling pitchers.

Tommy had to contend with a lot of injuries, particularly during the postseason. If you took one look at the lineup he put out there during the World Series at Oakland, you'd have sworn that the gamblers had gotten to him. But it worked, and they won, and Tommy faced another new set of circumstances with the 1989 season. I always figured that Steve Sax, the second baseman, was the Dodger catalyst. When he didn't get on base, the Dodgers had trouble scoring. I was very surprised when they let him get away to the New York Yankees during the off-season, but, then, there are a lot of things I don't understand. After Sax left in a dispute over money—and after the Dodgers imposed a strange deadline for settling his contract—management did go out and get Eddie Murray from the Baltimore Orioles and Willie Randolph from the Yankees to replace Sax.

Toward the end of the 1988 season, during a road trip in Cincinnati, Tommy and I were talking about the "what-ifs" of the postseason. He asked me, if the Dodgers got by the New York Mets in the playoffs, who would I rather see them play in the World Series—Oakland or Boston? I told him, Oakland. I had seen a lot of both those teams in previous seasons while I was broadcasting for the White Sox, and I felt that the Athletics could be pitched to. The Red Sox had more young and aggressive hitters, and I felt that Oakland's big guns—Jose Canseco and Mark McGwire—could be handled. Both of them are power hitters with big swings; both of them like to get their arms extended. By riding the ball in on them, jamming them, I thought the Dodger staff could do well against Oakland.

Naturally, it's easy to say that and not so easy to execute. Furthermore, the Dodgers had to get by the Mets before worrying about Boston or Oakland, and that wasn't so easy, either. Then came the first playoff game against the Mets, and you figured the Dodgers had run out of miracles. They led New York 2–0 after eight innings behind Hershiser, only to have the Mets stage one of their typical eleventh-hour rallies with 3 runs in the ninth for a 3–2 victory. You had to think that was it. The Cinderella story was beginning to unravel before your eyes.

The Dodgers won Game Two, then lost Game Three when the Mets got 5 runs in the eighth inning. In Game Four, the Mets were leading 4–2 in the ninth at Shea Stadium with their best pitcher on the mound, Dwight Gooden. You had to like their chances of taking a 3–1 lead in the best-of-seven series. But here came the Dodgers again. John Shelby drew a walk from Gooden, and then Mike Scioscia hit Gooden's first pitch over the right-field wall for a game-tying home run. Then in the twelfth inning, Gibson hit a dramatic solo home run to give the Dodgers a 5–4 victory to tie the series at two games each.

That game turned the entire series around. I don't know how Gooden feels about it. He's a great pitcher. But the last thing you do in the situation he was in is give a hitter a ball he can hit out of the park, particularly a guy like Scioscia, who had hit only 3 home runs during the entire regular season. I've got to believe that that gopher ball will stay with Dwight Gooden for quite a while, because the Dodgers really became aroused after Mike did his thing. And all of this came a day after the Dodgers suffered another traumatic experience in Game Three. That was the game when their ace reliever, Jay Howell, was ejected because umpires discovered that he had pine tar in his glove. Not only was he thrown out of the game, but he was suspended for two games by Bart Giamatti, the league president. I don't doubt for a minute that Howell had pine tar in his glove, and I don't doubt that pine tar helped him put some action on the ball if he used it. But suspending him for two days—originally Giamatti docked him for three days, then changed his mind—was a little strong. Are we going to let the players play, or will we not be satisfied until we completely sterilize the game of baseball? We had some tough, great umpires when I played, but they never thought of themselves as bigger than the game itself. They never deluded themselves into thinking that fans paid to watch them umpire. I'm all for respecting the authority of umpires. But the players are the game. Not the umpires. I'll leave it at that.

The Dodgers went on to win Game Five in New York, and Game Seven at Dodger Stadium behind Hershiser's 6–0 gem, and that meant the pennant. They'd have broken every gambling house in Las Vegas, especially after losing the playoff opener, but one thing that was consistent about the 1988 Dodgers. Pitching. They had outstanding pitching, and that kept them afloat from the first day of the season. Their pitchers got the job done, and sometimes they did it by taking up other roles. You saw Hershiser come in to get the save in that fourth game against the Mets. That showed you something about the Dodgers and about Hershiser. A lot of people were flabbergasted, but he did what he had to do to help the ballclub. To see your ace in the bullpen warming up has to be a big lift to the rest of the guys, but at that point in the season, that's the way it should be. You don't see enough of that in the current era, but Orel isn't your ordinary guy, any more than Gibson is. They don't have to call their agents or contact the Players Association for approval to enter a game when they're hurt or when it's not their turn to pitch.

Once the Dodgers made it into the World Series, I firmly believe that there was no doubt in their minds that they were going to win. They didn't know how, they just knew they would. Canseco hit a grand-slam home run in the second inning of the World Series opener, and they took a 4–2 lead as everybody expected. The A's were overwhelming favorites to win. But I was delighted for the Dodgers when Tony LaRussa, the Oakland manager, lifted Dave Stewart and brought in Dennis Eckersley in the ninth inning. As a starting pitcher, Stewart worried me more than anybody on the Oakland staff. I thought he was capable of having a big Series, and when LaRussa took him out, basically for no reason, I was happy for the Dodgers. Stewart had a 4–3 lead in the ninth, and he was just as capable of finishing that game as Eckersley was, even though Eckersley had had a tremendous regular season and was coming off four straight saves in Oakland's sweep of the Red Sox for the American League pennant.

Unless you were sleeping under a rock, you know what happened. With 2 out, pinch-hitter Mike Davis walked for the Dodgers. Then Gibson came out of the trainers' room, hobbling on a bad leg, and he ripped a 2-run pinch-hit home run into the right-field bleachers for a 5-4 Dodger victory. Vinny was broadcasting for the network during the Series, of course, so I was doing the ninth inning on local radio in Los Angeles and, believe me, it was exciting. Somebody sent me a tape of my broadcast, and I got goosebumps all over again listening to it. Not because I gave it such a great call, but because it was such a dramatic moment. They'll be talking about that one swing for the next fifty years. That wound up being Gibson's only at-bat of the World Series, but it was a huge contribution. One swing from your best player, and that was enough. And, again on the subject of Gibson, you know if he didn't play, he couldn't play. He had to be hurt. He had to be really hurting.

Hershiser won Game Two at Dodger Stadium with another masterpiece, 6-0 with 8 strikeouts and a three-hitter. That gave the Dodgers a 2-0 lead and, finally, I was convinced that this thing was for real. There was no turning back now. The Dodgers were going to be World Champions. Orel was still on an incredible roll, and he was going to have at least two more starts if needed—in Game Five and in Game Seven.

The A's won Game Three in Oakland, 2-1, on McGwire's home run in the ninth, but the Dodgers took the next two games by 4-3 and 5-2, the latter another complete game from Hershiser. The Dodgers did it with pitching, of course, but with contributions from guys like Mickey Hatcher and Davis, too. Canseco wound up with that 1 home run in 19 at-bats for an average of .053 while McGwire's homer was his only hit in 17 at-bats for an .059 average. Hershiser, who had 3 hits in the second game, wound up with more hits than Oakland's "Bash Brothers" combined! Oakland's mighty team batted just .177 for five games.

That was vintage Dodgers, in more ways than one. They need terrific scouting reports, which is what they got from Mel Didier and Jerry Stephenson and Steve Boros, who had been a manager in Oakland before LaRussa. The Dodgers always were famous for doing their homework. The Dodgers also have been known for superior execution, which was very much in evidence during the playoffs and World Series. You can have the best and most-detailed scouting reports in the world, but if you don't implement them, you might as well throw them in the fireplace. The other typical Dodger aspect of their unlikely championship was pitching. You always hear that pitching is seventy-five percent of the game or eighty percent, and the Dodgers have always believed it. During the 1988 season, who knows? You could make a case and say that pitching was ninety percent of the Dodgers' success.

Were they the best team? I don't know and it doesn't really matter, does it? Stack up the Dodgers position-by-position against New York, and clearly the Mets were better. Same with Oakland. But that's not the Dodgers' problem. They had to listen to the talk all year that the bottom was going to fall out, and it never did. I was as guilty as anybody, if not on the air, then in private discussions. I waited for the Astros to make a move, but they came up short. San Francisco's pitching staff was shot, and something was wrong in Cincinnati. With all that talent, the Reds should have been better. They're a real mystery to me. I kept telling my wife Annie that we'd be able to do this and that as soon as the regular season was over, because I didn't think the Dodgers were going to hang on. But they proved me wrong, and I'm glad of it.

Another bonus to me was returning to the National League. I'd almost forgotten what it was like, but there is a huge difference from the American League, and one reason is the designated hitter. As I've said, I'm not a big advocate of it. It's a little hokey, a little too contrived for me. Baseball was played for 100 years with nine guys on a side, and I see no reason to mess with success. Don't fix what's not broken.

There's also the aspect of strategy. There really isn't as much in the American League, where teams tend to wait more for the three-run homer. But it's been that way for a while. One of the best modern-day managers, Earl Weaver of Baltimore, was a proponent of the "big-bang" theory. I guess that stands to reason if you've got another hitter, usually a power hitter, in your lineup instead of a pitcher. But that takes a lot away from the game. In the National League, you have more managers making things happen with hit-and-run plays, stolen bases, sacrifices. The National

League games are played at a quicker, more intense pace. The designated hitter can make managers and players sit back and wait for things to happen. In the American League, they seem to lose sight of some of baseball's nuances, those extra little aspects of the inner game that make baseball the greatest sport for spectators. After all, what's more fun for a fan besides watching a game than trying to first-guess, and then second-guess, the manager? That's one beauty of baseball that no other game can offer.

In the National League, the pitching is harder. Pitchers don't try to trick you as much as in the American League. The National League still believes that the best pitch in the game is the fastball, and I second that. The National League is more aggressive. You'll see more runners trying to knock down infielders, attempting to break up double plays. You'll see more pitchers challenging hitters. Part of the reason for these differences is that the American League has two more teams. Obviously, that means that there are more players over there holding down jobs—forty-eight players in the American League who wouldn't have jobs in the National League. You see that and you have to wonder how major league baseball can even conceive of expanding again in the near future, but you know it's going to happen. And as long as the public bites, that's no crime.

I'm dealing from the perspective of a guy who used to play when there were only sixteen teams, and I realize that. I can state my case, but for me to impose my values on today's public isn't realistic. If you put the major league label on a team or a game, and the public buys tickets to be entertained, there's absolutely nothing wrong with that. If you don't know anything about a Cadillac, then you'll settle for a Chevrolet. Doesn't mean you can't take the family to the ballpark and have a great day. And that certainly doesn't mean I go to the ballpark in 1988 and wish for 1958. No way. Life goes on.

For me, broadcasting for the World Series champions in my first year back was the icing on the cake, not that I really needed any. I'd been away doing the White Sox games for a while, and enjoyed it, but the first time I walked into Dodger Stadium, it was like I'd returned to where I belonged after a brief commercial break. Annie and I rented a townhouse at the La Canada Country Club, and it was only about fifteen minutes from the ballpark. For home games, Annie could drive in with Donnie and sit to watch a few innings, then take off. If I wasn't on the air at the time, I came down to their seats and spent some time with them. It was perfect. Now, Annie and I are living in a new home we've built in Pasadena, right near the Rose Bowl. Again, we're not far from Dodger Stadium. And Donnie is starting to develop an interest in baseball. You should see him swing the bat.

I don't know what the Dodgers or Orel Hershiser can do to top 1988, but I consider myself fortunate to have seen what I saw. They were great, and because of Orel, I got more publicity than I ever bargained for, not all of it my kind.

The morning after Hershiser broke my record against the Padres, I was back home in Los Angeles after driving up from San Diego. I was in bed, in fact, when the telephone rang. It was some reporter calling from New York to pick my brain. Good luck.

"Well," he said, "it looks like your record is gone. Orel did it last night."

"That's right," I agreed, "he did a great job."

"At least you still have half the record. Hershiser only broke half of your record."

"Half?" I said. "What are you talking about?"

"Hershiser broke your record for most scoreless innings in a row, but you still have the record for most consecutive shutouts. You had six in a row in nineteen sixty-eight. He only had five in a row."

"Oh?" I said. "Is that so? Well, that's nice. Uh, can I go back to sleep now?"

Like I said, I never was much for numbers. Especially at that hour of the morning.

20

Happier Than Ever

*A*s I write this, I can honestly say that I've never been happier in my life. I'm broadcasting for the best organization in baseball, the Los Angeles Dodgers, I feel so healthy that I can't believe I've reached my old uniform number, fifty-three, and part of the reason for that is I've got a great family—wife Annie, daughter Kelly, and sons Donnie and Darren.

Annie is the former Ann Meyers, who has quite a sports background herself. A great all-around athlete, and particularly a great basketball player, Annie became the first woman to carry the United States flag in international competition at the 1978 Pan American Games in Puerto Rico. That same year, she won the Broderick Cup as the nation's best female athlete. She was a four-time All-American at UCLA and was the first woman ever drafted and given a tryout by a team in the National Basketball Association. She went to camp with the Indiana Pacers in 1979.

I could go on and on about her athletic prowess. I've struggled all my life with golf, and yet, the first time Annie ever touched a club, she was able to hit the ball straight and long. Now, it's gotten to the point where I have to cheat to beat her. And remember, I've been playing the game for more than thirty years. Or at least, playing at it.

I first met Annie in the winter of 1979, when I was down in the Bahamas to broadcast the "Superstars" competition for ABC television, along with Bob Uecker. She was with the New Jersey

Gems of the Women's Basketball League then, and had come into the wardrobe room to be fitted for her uniforms for all the events. She was with her mom, who's from Milwaukee, so she and Uecker had plenty in common. That's where Bob broadcasts baseball, for the Brewers. I had heard and read about Annie, but she didn't know who I was. In fact, she thought I was Don Meredith, the Dallas Cowboys quarterback.

Annie finished fourth in her first try at the "Superstars." I don't think she really knew what it was all about until she got there. When she realized what kind of money they were throwing around, though, she decided to come back. And she did. And she won it the next three years. By that time, she had learned that I was Don Drysdale, not Don Meredith. And I had learned that Annie was a terrific person who's a lot of fun to be around. We really enjoyed each other's company, whenever we had the opportunity.

By this point, my first marriage was going under. I had married the former Ginger Dubberly in September 1958, right after the baseball season. She was a model from Pasadena whom I'd met at the ballpark. She'd come out to do a newspaper spread featuring the Dodgers, and I started dating her. At the time, I was still living at home with my folks in the Valley. Ginger and I fell in love, we had our daughter Kelly the year after we were married, and everything went along well for a long spell. Ginger was a wonderful mother to Kelly, Ginger had good business sense, Ginger was a terrific person in many ways.

What happened to our relationship? I guess the best way to explain it is that you can fall in love with somebody and you can fall out of love with somebody. If the latter happens, you can try to keep things together or you can cut it off and continue your lives separately. We'd gotten to the point where there was almost constant bickering about this and that, and I just couldn't handle it anymore. I fell out of love with Ginger, and I detested all the arguing. It's that's simple, really. I have never been able to deal with petty stuff in my life. I'd rather just walk away from a bad situation, and that's in essence what I did with Ginger.

We started our marriage in an apartment in Van Nuys, then bought our first home, also in Van Nuys. Kelly was just a toddler then. Ginger then ran into some people who owned a big home in Hidden Hills but were unable to keep it for financial reasons. We went to a real-estate agent and in effect traded homes with these people. Our new place had some acreage, which was great, because Ginger was fond of jumping horses. All that space also allowed us to build an apartmentlike addition onto the house for my parents. In time, Ginger and I got into the thoroughbred business. We ran horses at Santa Anita and Hollywood Park. At one point, we had seven or eight on the track and some young ones at our place in Hidden Hills.

They call thoroughbred racing the "sport of kings," and I can see why. It's not a cheap endeavor. As someone once told me, whether horses run fast or not, they all eat the same. (I suppose you could say the same thing about ballplayers. Whether they hit .180 or .380, they're all going to use up that meal money. Don't fall in love with a horse any more than you should fall in love with a ballplayer, because they're destined to disappoint you.) Anyway, we never developed delusions of grandeur. You don't run a $7,000 claimer in a $20,000 claiming race any more than you would bring up a minor leaguer to pitch in the World Series if he isn't ready. We tried to enter our horses in races where they had a chance to win, and it turned out very well for us. Our home in Hidden Hills became a working ranch, and we wound up making a little bit of money. Everything went pretty well.

Kelly has matured into an outstanding person, and I've got to thank Ginger for a lot of that. I'm probably closer to Kelly now than I was when I was a player, because as a player, you're on the road so much. You're fighting and striving to be a success during the summer, and then during the winter, you worked, too. I didn't start making big money (for those days) until I'd been with the Dodgers awhile, and besides, it was just my nature and upbringing to want to work. As a kid, when I got that $13.50 a month for delivering the *Valley Times,* it was like getting $13 million.

I had various odd jobs in Southern California before I got to the point where my family could live comfortably off my baseball salary. I want to say that my last winter job was with Meadow Gold Dairies in Pasadena, in the early sixties. The general manager there was a fellow named Bill Hutchinson, a Canadian who became a self-made millionaire. A great guy. Bill somehow got to know Harry Truman, and it wasn't unusual for him to pick up the phone at a moment's notice and call the former President at his home in Independence, Missouri.

Eventually, Ginger and I separated. We had a home in Rancho

Mirage, at the Springs Club near Palm Springs, but we spent a lot of time during the winter in Hawaii. I'd stopped in Hawaii many years ago, on that trip with the Brooklyn Dodgers to Japan, and I'd decided to do whatever I could to spend more time there. I wound up investing in real estate and restaurants there, again with good success. We had a couple of condominiums in Maui, and a couple of condos and the restaurant on the big island—"Don Drysdale's Club 53." I had been in on a couple of restaurants in California, first in Van Nuys and then in Santa Ana, and our setup in Hawaii was something I hoped Ginger and I could do together.

We made some good investments, Ginger and I did, but the marriage was fading. I don't know whether she believed that I would ever leave, but I did. I bought a place at The Morningside Club in Rancho Mirage during the winter of 1982, then headed off that next spring to start my new job as broadcaster with the Chicago White Sox.

When I came to Chicago in 1983, I was pretty much on my own. Starting over, in a way. The owners of the White Sox, Jerry Reinsdorf and Eddie Einhorn, treated me as well as I could have been treated. I haven't always agreed with their philosophy of running a ballclub, but I could never say a bad word about the way they treated me. I made some good friends in Chicago, and generally had a nice time. Plus, I started seeing more and more of Annie, who is just a terrific person with so many good sides. I'm still finding out things about her, like how religious she is. Annie is a faithful Catholic, forever going to church, which I think is great.

I'm Methodist—part German, part Scotch—and I do believe in a superior being. It's just that, like Bill Veeck used to say, I'm a little fuzzy about the details. I remember discussing this with Frank Sinatra one time. Frank does things for people and the community that you'll never hear about. He's a good person. A better than good person. But he's not a regular churchgoer, nor am I. I used to go to church a lot as a kid. Heck, I won a Bible once in Sunday school in a contest. After we won the 1963 World Series, though, some people from the Methodist church came over and asked me to donate some money to help buy an organ. They'd read that I'd earned $12,300 as my World Series share.

Well, it wasn't really $12,300, after taxes and all the deductions for tickets bought. They were going to put my name on a brass plate beside the organ as one of the contributors. My name was going to be right next to Dorothy Chandler's. Only, Dorothy Chandler and Don Drysdale were two very different people. The Chandler family owned the *Los Angeles Times* and had a street named after them. Chandler Boulevard, in Van Nuys. Now, they have a Dorothy Chandler Pavilion in Los Angeles. I don't have any streets or pavilions named after me in Southern California. When the people from Van Nuys Methodist Church visited me that day, I said thanks and I'll be in touch. I never did contact them, and I guess that whole episode made me a little suspicious. It kind of soured me, I suppose, although Kelly was baptized at that very same Methodist Church of Van Nuys.

Annie and I were married on November 1, 1986, at the Morningside Club. Ed Johnsen, who runs the club, opened it a week early so that we could have the wedding there. At the time, Annie was thirty and I was forty-nine. That was something we talked about, the age difference between us, but it doesn't mean all that much. The more time we spent together, the more we enjoyed each other's company. We never had an argument about anything, which was a nice change for me. It was like a new lease on life, because there was certainly a time after I separated from Ginger that I didn't know whether I'd ever be married again, or ever want to be. I certainly didn't want to work my butt off to wind up giving half of it away again, and to have to argue about everything beforehand. No way. I would just as soon have stayed single. Ginger and I were married twenty-four years and we had good times. I've read many stories about people in the public eye who have had marriages break up amicably. I wish ours could have ended like that, instead of in the lousy, rotten way it did. I'm antiaggravation, even if it means being alone or lonely on occasion. I really don't go looking for trouble or enjoy it one bit.

That might amaze some people who don't really know me and who think that I'm confrontational, because of the way I pitched. Well, I think I've established that I'm a different person off the field than I used to be on the field. Way back when I pitched in Brooklyn, a fellow for the *New York Post* named Sid Friedlander wrote an article describing me as Dr. Jekyll–Mr. Hyde. That pretty well hits the nail on the head, I suppose. I hope that Ginger can find a life after Don Drysdale, because I have found a life after her.

Being around Annie removed my fears of having a replay of my first marriage. I was a little concerned about the disparity in our ages at first, but not for long. Annie has never met Ginger, but Annie knew about my marriage and what she didn't know, I told her. There was nothing to hide, and I can honestly say that I wasn't surprised to find myself considering Annie as a second wife. I really cared for her, so that age business wasn't really relevant. It isn't my nature to get depressed over things. Angry, yes. But I'm not one to sit in my hotel room for two days or drown my sorrows in a bar by myself or take long, soulful drives out into the country. That's not me. I'm one to move on, and if my baseball personality allowed me to be mentally tough, then fine. Maybe that helped. I guess I looked upon the experience with Ginger as a hanging curveball. I screwed up, but I didn't want to dwell on it. I know that sounds blunt or unfeeling, but everybody has their own way of getting through a crisis. Mine is not to stew or to seek the help of a shrink.

One thing about Annie that makes me so happy is how much everybody else likes her, too. She's not only fun for me to be around. She obviously relates to most everybody with that great personality of hers. And now that we've got Donnie, Jr.—who has the same birthday as me, July 23—and Darren—August 23, born two years and one month later—everything is that much better. Annie has been a great mother. And Annie gets along just super with Kelly. And Kelly has a ball with Donnie, Jr. and Darren. I'm doing things I never thought I'd be doing at my age, like building a new home near Pasadena and picking out flooring for it. After all these years and after living in all the different places I've lived, I'm still doing some interior decorating. I'm picking out plumbing fixtures and kitchen fixtures and having a heck of a good time doing it.

Also, quite obviously, I never had any thoughts of being a father again. We had Donnie when I was still working in Chicago with the White Sox, and it was a tremendous feeling. When he was born, I was celebrating my fifty-first birthday. Quite a birthday present. A lot of people that age are doing other things, and a lot of people have kidded me about fathering a child so late in life. Well, I'd strongly advise it. As a matter of fact two is just fine with us. I know having Donnie around made me feel younger, so much so that Annie and I decided to have another child. If I'm going to be sixty when Donnie's nine and Darren' seven, so what? I don't feel my age now, and I don't see any reason for that to change if I can remain healthy. And if something should happen to me, Annie will have two companions, Donnie, Jr. and Darren. Junior Gilliam always used to say, "What's it matter what your birth certificate says if you can still play the game?" My sentiments exactly. Our friends say that, considering our genes, Donnie and Darren have to be a super athletes. I don't know. If so, great. If not, so what? I'm just happy to have the little guys around. Not that they're all that little. And I can tell you this. They already know what baseball is all about. Whenever Annie takes Donnie to Dodger Stadium, his eyes light up. He's aware that he's in the midst of something pretty special. Darren's still adjusting.

Kelly, meanwhile, is doing very well. She's working for the Don Drysdale Foundation, which I established a couple years ago. We have a Hall of Fame golf tournament every year in January near Palm Springs, and it's gone nicely. We invite athletes who have qualified for halls of fame in all sports, and then each one plays in a group of business executives who pay for the privilege to rub elbows with Joe DiMaggio or Tom Fears or Yogi Berra or Boom Boom Geoffrion or John Havlicek. It's turned out to be quite a tournament, if I do say so myself. The openings for amateurs sell out in a hurry—we don't even have to publicize the thing—and they have a wonderful week playing with all these athletes they grew up watching and admiring. Your typical business executive nowadays is in the age bracket where he identifies more with Hall of Famers than the younger players, so this is quite a kick.

Kelly works for the Foundation, which funnels monies from the tournament to desert charities. Our tournament is a three-day event at three different clubs in the area, and we ask each club to specify a charity to which one-third of the funds will go. Last year, for instance, we sent money to the Alzheimer's Unit at the Eisenhower Medical Center in Palm Springs. We also provided money to buy one van each for the boys' and girls' clubs of the Coachella Valley to transport underprivileged children. The Drysdale Foundation is a nonprofit organization, and we're very happy with it.

Kelly also does some free-lance television work. She worked on the ABC production crew for the Winter Olympics at Sarajevo, Yugoslavia, in 1984 and the 1988 Summer Olympics at Los Angeles. She's done some booth directing in baseball and hockey and

NCAA football. I'm very proud of her. She's also contributed to my happiness.

The more I'm around athletes from my era and the current generation, the more I realize how fortunate I've been. I had a very rewarding career with the Dodgers, and then stepped into another profession that I enjoy tremendously—broadcasting. That keeps me in touch with the game, keeps me around people who I enjoy. I had a marriage that went well for a while, then turned sour, and along came Annie. It's really been one lucky turn after another for me. I was perfectly happy working for the White Sox and had every intention of staying with them. But then Peter O'Malley of the Dodgers asked permission to talk to me. Returning home was another break.

Why me? Why do I deserve all this good fortune? I don't know. I go to these old-timers' camps and realize that I can't move around like I used to. I can't throw and I can't hit like I once did. But I still don't feel old. I'm able to go on a diet every so often and shed a few pounds without a lot of trouble. I've always been a meat-and-potatoes guy. I look at some of these books now and read what they say about food and I wonder how I made it this far, because you're only supposed to eat all this natural stuff. I think I'll keep doing what I'm doing.

I've seen some former athletes who are my age and somewhat bitter. I can't say that I am, about anything. I've been blessed with a positive attitude about keeping busy, an attitude I probably got from my folks. Dad will joke that I was so comfortable with work that I could lie down right beside it and not blink. But I think in his heart he knows I've never been afraid to apply myself to whatever task was at hand. I think I've also been blessed by being a people person. It's when I get cooped up in a hotel room that I get a little nervous and start dialing up friends. I make a point of not hanging around the current players, because I don't think they have any desire to see an old guy like me shadowing them. If they ask my advice on something, fine, but I'm not about to impose myself. I'll go out on the team bus with the Dodgers most of the time during road trips, but otherwise, I don't see the players very often. I'll see my fellow broadcasters, like Vin or Ross, and maybe a writer or two, but it's a different breed of cat now. There isn't that togetherness you used to see with a club on a road trip.

I don't know what the next step for me might be, if there is one. A year or so ago, I was part of a group that purchased the Visalia club in the California State League. Visalia is between Bakersfield and Fresno; the California State League is Class A. I bought it with a Japanese group called Japan Sports System. I was contacted a couple years ago to run an instructional camp for the Tokyo Giants in Palm Springs. It went well. Then I went over to Japan for a week for a baseball summit including various baseball people from the United States. We gave clinics and that sort of thing and during that time, the Japan Sports System project came about. I was named president of the group in the United States and with some of their money and some of mine, we bought the Visalia Oaks team. It's a Minnesota farm club.

I told the people from the Visalia club and the Twins that I believe I've spent most of my baseball years with the best organization in the major leagues, the Dodgers. And I'd like to inject a little of that into the Visalia franchise. I'd like to try to win. I'd like to do things first class, the right way, the Dodger way. Where will this all lead? I have no idea. I signed a five-year contract to broadcast for the Dodgers and I have every intention of honoring that. I think I could certainly drive up to Visalia on occasion to see how things are going. It's not that big a deal to make a trip there on a day when I'm not broadcasting. We've tried upgrading some things for the Visalia club already, such as outfitting them with new traveling bags and improving their dressing room facilities. If you've ever been in a minor league stadium, you know that sometimes you're lucky to have a nail to hang your clothes on. Try to take a shower, and the water only comes out of three holes, the rest are clogged up. So we rebuilt the entire clubhouse. It seems like such a small thing, but they were tickled pink with it. Not only the people in Visalia, but the parent club in Minnesota was excited, too. And the kids who play there appreciate it. When they have a decent duffel bag to carry their stuff around in rather than some ragged thing, it makes a difference. It gives them a little better feeling about what they're doing and who they're working for. Pride. It gives them a little more pride, even on the Class A level.

Even as a broadcaster, I think sometimes like a general manager or a manager. I ask myself, What can be done here to make it better? Or, Why isn't this working? I don't think you can spend all the time I've spent in baseball without being more analytical than the average fan, and I'm forever seeing an "inner game," a game beyond the obvious one that you see out on the field or on television. I'm sure I'm not alone in that way. Any former player or manager has to feel the same about what he sees.

In the past, I've been approached about heading up a group to buy a ballclub. Seattle, for one. There have been others. But the way baseball is structured now, local ownership seems preferable. If money comes in to purchase a franchise, the ideal is for it to come from local people. And I can certainly understand that philosophy. I can't say that I will feel unfulfilled if I never participate in owning a major league franchise. Still, it's natural to want to do something like that. Every so often you get the bug to be a manager, or a general manager. But broadcasting is a very good life—a very, very good life—without the pressures of having to worry about whether your team wins or loses. I mean, I don't like it when the Dodgers lose, but I can still go home at night and sleep. Plus, in broadcasting, there is that great plus of having the off-season pretty much to yourself. It isn't like being a year-round executive. There's a lot to be said for that, particularly after you've been traveling for thirty-five years the way I have. In the middle of the winter, if I'm broadcasting for the Dodgers, I can wake up in the morning and play with Donnie and Darren or play golf with Annie. I don't have to worry about baseball until spring training.

Baseball has been my life, though, and the one drawback about broadcasting—if you can really call it a drawback—is that it doesn't get your competitive juices going. You really can't apply your talents to a situation and make it better because that's not your job. It's not your job to have a hand in the decision making of a ballclub. On a very small scale, we've taken a step to upgrade the Visalia club beyond new locker rooms and traveling bags. A high-school team had been working out on the same field, sometimes even keeping our club off it. I didn't like telling the high-school team to go to another field when the Visalia team was in town, but I had to. Our team needed to have the field when it wanted it, and our team needed to have it in the best possible shape. A top prospect for the Minnesota Twins has to have the best possible conditions to improve his skills. If a kid gets hit in the eye with a baseball because the field is torn up, is that right? I don't think so. There are other ways to go. There are other places for the high-school team to practice when the Visalia team is in town. I hope the high school understood. If the high school didn't, well,

266

I'm sorry. One of my first decisions as president of JSS-USA was unpopular. That's baseball.

I'd enjoy a more active role if it weren't for the road trips— thirty-five years of traveling is a lot of room service, a lot of getting on and off airplanes. It's glamorous to a point, but how many people want to do it for one or two years and how many can do it for thirty-five? But don't get me wrong. I'm not complaining, not for a minute. I've been so lucky, and if you ask why I've done as well as I have, I'd say maybe it's because people respect me a little bit. I've had a succession of good jobs, and maybe it's because I have a certain degree of expertise. I don't enjoy patting myself on the back, but when people ask your advice on baseball matters, it does make you feel good about what you've done and what you represent.

I don't pretend to understand everything about this new generation of baseball executive, but I'm not one, so that's not my department. Maybe that's partly why I've survived. I don't kiss a lot of behinds, I don't play politics, but I also don't intervene unless I'm asked. I've been on the inside and I've been on the outside, and I think I can identify with both.

I'll never understand why management and labor don't get along better. For either side to even contemplate the thought of another strike with all the money available is unthinkable to me. I played baseball in an era when the game was illegal, if you really want to be honest. It was illegal because the players have gone to court since and found that the reserve clause was unlawful. Just like the NFL draft would be found illegal, I believe, if it was ever challenged in the court.

But what matters most is that baseball is still the greatest game of all and, thank God, I've been able to be a part of it. That trip I took back to Brooklyn brought it all back to me, those wonderful years with the Bums and the Dodgers. Yet for all the memories of Brooklyn and Los Angeles and the guys I played with and learned from—Duke, Gil, Pee Wee, Jackie, Sal, Sandy, and the rest—I've never been luckier than I am now. I've never been happier.

Index

274